Growing Up
–in– Scotland

Growing Up
_in_ Scotland

An Anthology

EDITED BY ROBBIE & NORA KYDD

Polygon

Edinburgh University Press
22 George Square, Edinburgh

Typeset in 10 on 12.5 point Bulmer
by Hewer Text Composition Services, and
printed and bound in Great Britain

A CIP record for this book is available from the British Library

ISBN 0 7486 6233 2

The Publisher acknowledges subsidy from

THE SCOTTISH ARTS COUNCIL

towards the publication of this volume.

for Angela, Sandy and Elspeth
who grew up in Scotland

CONTENTS

INTRODUCTION

We hope that our readers will share some of the pleasure we have had in researching this book. It was not always easy for us to stop reading some autobiographies and novels at the end of the childhood sections. It was not easy either to reject for reasons of space much material which was revealing, touching, fascinating or amusing.

At the beginning of each of our sections readers will find a list of books from which we have taken our extracts, along with the names of the authors. This is to help those who want this information before starting to read. However, we have not identified the authors of our extracts within the sections in the hope that other readers will want to read them several at a time in sequence, focusing first of all on how they comment on, illuminate, or thumb their noses at each other, rather than on who wrote them. In the Index of Sources at the back we print fuller information about the publications and their authors, along with a few notes.

Inevitably, someone will want to detect in our choices a pattern (such as a theory of Child Development) or an agenda (such as a retrospective campaign against corporal punishment). We have not *consciously* tried to illustrate a particular theory, or conduct a campaign, but if before our respective retirements we had been schoolteachers or policemen or tycoons instead of social workers our selection from the vast amount of material available would surely have been different.

Some of our chapter headings relate only approximately to their contents. For example, the reader will find a passage by George MacDonald in the chapter on 'Schooldays' which ends with a description of a little boy's feelings for his father. To any reader who wonders why we have chapters headed 'Grannies' and 'Fathers and Father-Figures', but not one headed 'Mothers', we should explain that we have found mothers to be omnipresent though sometimes, admittedly, taken for granted, as in real life. In fact, well over half our extracts contain references, explicit or implicit, to mothers.

The dates (sometimes approximate) at the top of the extracts are those of the happenings described rather than of their composition.

We have printed copyright material unaltered except where we have cut sentences or paragraphs for reasons of space. In all extracts our cuts within paragraphs are indicated by . . ., and cuts of one or more whole paragraphs by a line space between paragraphs. In some out-of-copyright passages we have broken up long paragraphs into shorter ones to suit present-day tastes.

Our thanks are due to all the authors and copyright-owners listed in the Index of Sources and Acknowledgements; to Elaine Bär-Arthur of Zürich, for compiling the bibliography which was our starting-point; and to Irene and Edward Thomas of Kirkcaldy, Tom and Jean Crawford of Aberdeen, Gail Young of Newcastle and Judy Moir of Edinburgh for useful suggestions, photocopies and the loan of books.

Robbie and Nora Kydd
Edinburgh 1997

ACKNOWLEDGEMENTS

Grateful acknowledgement is made to the following sources for permission to reproduce material. Every effort has been made to trace copyright holders, but if any have been inadvertently overlooked, the publisher will be pleased to make the necessary arrangement at the first opportunity.

Addison Wesley Longman for extracts from Donald Cameron, *The Field of Sighing*, Longman 1966.

Routledge for the extract from Amy Stewart Fraser, *The Hills of Home*, Routledge and Kegan Paul 1973.

HarperCollins Publishers Ltd for extracts from Tom Steel, *The Life and Death of St Kilda*, Fontana/Collins 1975.

Mrs R. Martin for the extract from Smeddum by Lewis Grassic Gibbon (James Leslie Mitchell).

Random House UK Ltd for extracts from Edwin Muir, *An Autobiography*, Hogarth Press 1954.

Extracts from Christopher Rush, *A Twelvemonth and a Day* reproduced with the kind permission of Canongate Books Ltd, 14 High Street, Edinburgh EH1 1TE.

Extract from Alasdair Gray, *Lanark* reproduced with the kind permission of Canongate Books Ltd, 14 High Street, Edinburgh EH1 1TE.

Extract from James Bridie, *One Way of Living* reproduced by permission of The Agency (London) Ltd, © James Bridie 1939. First published by Constable 1939. All rights reserved and enquiries to The Agency (London) Ltd, 24 Pottery Lane, London W11 4LZ. Fax 0171 727 9037.

André Deutsch Ltd for extracts from Sir Denis Forman, *Son of Adam*, 1990.

Gavin Maxwell Enterprises Ltd. for the extract from Gavin Maxwell, *The House of Elrig*.

Mainstream Publishing for extracts from James Mackay, *Vagabond of Verse*, 1995.

Acknowledgements

Extracts from Jessie Kesson, *The White Bird Passes*, © Jessie Kesson 1958, published by B & W Publishing, Edinburgh 1996.

Random House UK Ltd for the extract from John R. Allan, *Farmers Boy*, Methuen 1935.

Random House UK Ltd for extracts from David Thomson, *Nairn in Darkness and Light*, Hutchinson 1987.

Meg Henderson for extracts from *Finding Peggy*, Corgi/Transworld 1994.

Extracts from Molly Weir, *Shoes Were for Sunday*, Hutchinson 1970 by kind permission of Random House and David Higham Associates.

The Saltire Society for the extract from Robert Garioch, *Complete Poetical Works*, Macdonald Publishers 1983.

Extracts from Catherine Carswell, *Lying Awake* reproduced with the kind permission of Canongate Books Ltd, 14 High Street, Edinburgh EH1 1TE.

Random House UK Ltd for the extract from Neil M. Gunn, *Highland River*, Arrow paperback 1960.

Extract from Muriel Spark, *The Life of Miss Jean Brodie*, Penguin, 1965 by kind permission of David Higham Associates.

John S. Gray for extracts from Dorothy K. Haynes, *Haste Ye Back*, Jarrold 1973.

Bloodaxe Books for lines from Jackie Kay, *The Adoption Papers*, 1991.

John Murray (Publishers) Ltd for extracts from Christian Miller, *A Childhood in Scotland*, 1981.

Mainstream Publishing for extracts from Anne Lorne Gillies, *Song of Myself*, 1991.

Dr Nora Hunter for Margaret Hamilton, 'Lament for a Lost Dinner Ticket'.

Voluntary Service Aberdeen for extracts from *A Patchwork of Memories*.

Larousse for extracts from Betsy Whyte, *The Yellow on the Broom*, Chambers 1979.

Extract from Robin Jenkins, *Fergus Lamont* reproduced with the kind permission of Canongate Books Ltd, 14 High Street, Edinburgh EH1 1TE.

Extract from Robert McLellan, *Linmill: Short Stories in Scots* reproduced with the kind permission of Canongate Books Ltd, 14 High Street, Edinburgh EH1 1TE.

Extract from Julia Mary Grant, *St Leonards School: 1877–1927* by permission of St Leonards School.

Material from Catherine Carswell, *The Life of Robert Burns*, published by Canongate, is included by kind permission of John Carswell and Canongate Books Ltd, 14 High Street, Edinburgh EH1 1TE.

The Estate of the Late Jane Duncan and A. M. Heath & Co. Ltd for the extract from Jane Duncan, *My Friends the Miss Boyds*, Macmillan 1959. © Jane Duncan 1959.

Roderick Wilkinson for extracts from his autobiography *Memories of Maryhill*.

Macmillan General Books for the extract from Hugh Collins, *Autobiography of a Murderer*, Macmillan 1997. © Hugh Collins 1997.

Extract from Allan Campbell McLean, *The Year of the Stranger*, © The Estate of the Late Allan Campbell McLean.

Sussex University Press and David Higham Associates for extracts from David Daiches, *Two Worlds*. Extracts taken from Canongate Classic edition, 1997.

Acknowledgements

Little Brown for the extract from Finlay J. Macdonald, *The Corncrake and the Lysander*, Macdonald 1985. © Finlay J. Macdonald 1985.

Mainstream Publishing for the extract from William McIlvanney, *Docherty*, 1983.

Extract from Ralph Glasser, *Growing up in the Gorbals*, Chatto 1986 by kind permission of Random House and David Higham Associates.

Jack McLean for 'Real, real gone', first published in the *Scotsman*, 15 August 1997.

Sheil Land Associates for the extract from Evelyn Cowan, *Spring Remembered*. © Evelyn Cowan 1974.

Random House UK Ltd for the extract from Helen B. Cruickshank, *Up the Noran Water*, Methuen.

EARLY DAYS

❧

taken from

. . . Mrs Gallon, the exciseman's wife, was overtaken with her pains, of all places in the world, in the kirk, on a Sabbath afternoon. They came on her suddenly, and she gave a skirle that took the breath with terror from the minister, as he was enlarging with great bir on the ninth clause of the seventh head of his discourse. Every body stood up. The whole congregation rose upon the seats, and in every face was pale consternation. At last the minister said, that on account of the visible working of Providence in the midst of us, yea in the very kirk itself, the congregation should skail: whereupon skail they did; so that in a short time I [the howdie, or midwife] had completed my work, in which I was assisted by some decent ladies staying to lend me their Christian assistance; which they did, by standing in a circle round the table seat where the ploy was going on, with their backs to the crying mother, holding out their gowns in a minaway fashion, as the maids of honour are said to do, when the queen is bringing forth a prince in public.

The bairn being born, it was not taken out of the kirk till the minister himself was brought back, and baptized it with a scriptural name; for it was every body's opinion that surely in time it would be a brave minister, and become a great and shining light in the Lord's vineyard to us all. But it is often the will and pleasure of Providence to hamper in the fulfilment the carnal wishes of corrupt human nature. Matthew Gallon had not in after life the seed of a godly element in his whole carcase; quite the contrary, for he turned out the most rank ringing enemy that was ever in our country-side; and when he came to years of discretion, which in a sense he never did, he fled the country as a soldier, and for some splore with the Session, though he was born in the kirk; – another plain fact that shows how little reason there is in some cases to believe that births and prognostications have no natural connexion.

2.   West Highlands 1926

The journal lived in the kitchen above the meal-ark, and hung by its
string from a bacon hook . . . The entry made on the day I was born
resembled thousands which had been written before and the thousands written afterward. Only the last part differed. 'Hard south wind
slackening before dinner,' it ran, 'then veering round Craigclamhan
and freshened to promise of a night gale. Ordered tar and paraffin.
Paid Duncan for a dog-fox shot on the burn side of Craighar. Three
pairs of sandpipers on lochan and starwart [sic] by the Earl's Park.
Two fine cock crabs from Postie. Wee boy came before second
milking, eight days overdue. R is in fine feckle.'

. . . R was my mother, Rhona, who had no need of any clock other
than the changing time of nature.

3.   Deeside *c.* 1900

Inevitably as I write I am aware of a misty something which is partly
daydreams and partly the dawn of an actual recollection. From out of
the bright mist emerges a day which, had I known it, conferred on a
four-year-old the responsible role of Elder Sister. That morning my
mother bustled from room to room, trimming lamps, making beds,
preparing sundry jugs and basins in readiness for the new arrival,
while I traipsed after her, wondering why she was in such a hurry. My
father had gone on foot to Ballater to fetch the doctor, returning later
with him and the nurse in the doctor's gig, but nobody thought of
telling me what was afoot. Later that day, sitting on my father's knee in
the room adjoining the best bedroom and hearing strange noises
through the wall, I recall patting his cheek and saying, 'Give Mama a
sweetie and tell her not to cry'.

I shall never forget the stir caused by having a baby in the house; the
trays of covered jugs, the scent of scalded milk, the feeding bottles with
glass screws, long glass tubes inside, even longer rubber tubing outside
from which dangled a rubber teat. The teat was inserted through a bone
washer designed, one supposes, to prevent the baby getting more than
the teat in her mouth and strangling herself with tubing. How the whole
contraption was sterilized was a miracle. I have no recollection of lines of

nappies but I saw plenty of baby garments . . . long day-gowns, nainsook petticoats, flannel barricoats, fine lawn vests and flannel squares which covered the napkin of turkish towelling. Nightgowns were shorter and plainer, but the barrie and flannel square were still worn at night. Everything was handsewn and embroidered, even the flannels. A head-shawl was worn indoors, and for the briefest airing a bonnet tied on with a net veil for protection from the wind or sun. The baby was then swathed in a knitted shawl, and for good measure my mother would wrap a fringed plaid round herself and the baby, making a cosy sling, gipsy fashion, in which to cradle the child, and would pace the avenue with her till she fell asleep.

The fashion was for the day-gowns and long robes to have low necks and short puffed sleeves, and my mother added knitted sleeves and little jackets to keep the baby cosy.

At three months the baby was 'shortened', long gowns being discarded; the day outfit then consisted of a pinafore over a short dress (which nevertheless reached the feet), two petticoats (one being of flannel), a flannel pilch over the nappie, and knitted bootees. When the baby began to 'feel its feet' she was promoted to knitted socks and soft shoes. Nightwear remained unchanged.

nainsook: muslin; *barricoat* = *barrie*: a baby's flannel coat (Concise Scots Dictionary)

4.   West Highlands 1930s

The news that I [Donald] was to have a brother or sister came to me not from my mother on one of those afternoons together, but from children in the school playground. They despised me for not already knowing such a thing and laughed when I denied it. Rhona [my mother] confirmed the children's remarks and after a while came for shorter and shorter distances to meet me from school. The girls in the playground jeered and said my mother was so big and heavy that there would surely be twins and, they said cruelly, that would mean Rhona would stop loving me for she would be too busy. I worried about this, though without really believing that Rhona would ever stop loving me. She did stop, however, for her new son was stillborn and she herself died giving birth.

5

Of the death itself hardly anything comes to me out of the past except the following day when the doctor came. I was hiding in the barn, my place of escape when anything unpleasant was happening in the house. Nobody could ever find me among the rows of fleeces and sacks hung up to dry.

On that awful afternoon, Mirren flung the back door open and fled across the yard and up the steps of the bothie where Alec the shepherd slept.

'They've cut her throat,' she cried over and over in a demented way, a gruesome chorus which the township children were pleased to take up afterwards.

I bolted from the barn into the house, expecting to see some mad man rushing about, brandishing my father's cut-throat razor. All that had happened was the doctor, in accordance with my mother's wishes, had severed her jugular vein. She had a fear of being buried while still alive, a fear not uncommon in our part of the world.

Rhona's coffin was put on the Forestry Commission's lorry and smothered with flowers from the local gardens. I had never seen so many men before in my life. Long files of them came from mountain farms around to follow the slow-moving lorry with its bright, sad load of flowers. I could not really believe that my mother lay underneath them.

We made the oystercatchers angry by stopping on the shore to build a funeral cairn. Neither the thousands of flowers nor the red peony petals which my father told me to drop into the yawning hole impressed me so much as Alec's masterpiece. In his role as the Blarosnich shepherd, he had dug the grave. The top sods were neatly rolled round a pole in one long unbroken carpet. After the service, while the others hurried away to take the traditional whisky and cheese by the gate, Alec unrolled this grass carpet so that the ugly scar was healed immediately. I loitered behind to watch him. My mother would have approved of this neat workmanship. And somehow this made her burial more acceptable.

5.   St Kilda 1886

A son was born to Neil Mackinnon's wife a little after midnight on 14 December 1886. The child was big and looked sturdy. No one, however, on St Kilda was surprised when, unchristened, the baby died within a fortnight.

'Last night at 10.30,' wrote George Murray, the schoolmaster, in his diary on 27 December, 'after six days of intense suffering the child departed this life. Every one expressed great wonder how it lived so long after being seized with illness, as they generally succumb at the end of a week after they are born. This one was thirteen days except one and a half hours. It had a frequent cry since it was born; but the first sign of its being dangerously ill was at the end of a week, when it ceased to suck the breast, but still sucked the bottle. The following day, *thuit na gialan* (the jaws fell), when all hope of its recovery was given up. From that time till its death it occasionally took a little milk in a spoon or out of the bottle. The last two days a little wine in water was given once or twice. It very often yawned and sometimes looked hard at you. It was pitiful to see the poor little thing in the pangs of death. May God prepare us all for the same end.'

Within twenty-four hours, the child was buried in the little cemetery. Murray followed the funeral procession. 'In the grave which was opened,' he wrote, 'I saw the coffins of its two little brothers that died the same way. The one coffin was still quite whole, there being only about sixteen months since it was interred; the other was in pieces. I sympathise with the parents in their bereavement.'

That which strangled children was . . . 'the sickness of eight days' of the St Kildan, known to medical science as Tetanus Infantum . . . The staggering fact that emerges from the records, however, is that of all the deaths that occurred on Hirta during that period [1855–76] all but one male death and a few female deaths were the result of tetanus infantum.

According to the St Kildans nothing could be done. 'If it is God's will that babies should die,' they told Emily Macleod when she suggested that a trained nurse might help to avoid so many deaths, 'nothing you can do will save them.' Robert Connel, who visited St Kilda in 1885 as a special correspondent for the *Glasgow Herald*, discovered on his return to Glasgow that the simple-minded minister of Hirta was not alone in his view of the situation. He met up with 'a great gun of the Free Church, who was not ashamed to say that this lock-jaw was a wise device of the Almighty for keeping the population within the resources of the island'.

6.   Angus *c.* 1900

She'd had nine of a family in her time, Mistress Menzies, and brought
the nine of them up forbye – some near by the scruff of the neck, you
would say. They were sniftering and weakly, two-three of the bairns,
sniftering in their cradles to get into their coffins; but she'd shake them
into life, and dose them with salts and feed them up until they couldn't
but live. And she'd plonk one down – finishing the wiping of the
creature's neb or the unco dosing of an ill bit stomach or the binding of
a broken head – with a look on her face as much as to say *Die on me
now and see what you'll get!*

7.   Orkney *c.* 1890

My first definite memory is of being baptized. Why I was not baptized
in Deerness, where there were two churches, I have never been able to
find out; but the ceremony was postponed for some reason until I was
three years old. I was dressed for the occasion in a scarlet suit with
petticoats instead of breeches, for boys were not given boys' clothes
then until they were five. The suit was made of some fine but slightly
rough material like serge; the sun must have been shining that day, for
the cloth seemed to glow from within with its own light; it was fastened
with large glittering gold buttons. I think it must have been the first
time that I saw the colours of gold and scarlet, for it is this suit that
makes me remember that day, and it still burns in my memory more
brightly than anything I have ever seen since. In the afternoon my
father and mother led me by the hand to the school, where Mr Pirie,
the minister of Rousay, had come to baptize me. Some people had
gathered. I was lifted up by my father, face upward; I saw Mr Pirie's
kind face with its thin beard inclined diagonally over me (for he had a
glass eye and looked at everything from the side), then I felt cold water
and began to cry. As if the baptismal water had been a deluge, all the
rest of the day is damp and drowned, the burning scarlet and the gold
sunk in darkness.

8.   Fife 1920s

At my baptism there was ice in the font. Alec Fergusson, the old
beadle, had placed the water there the night before, so that when the
Reverend Kinnear went to perform the sacrament he was prevented by
a frozen silver shield which his fingers could not penetrate. But his arm
was strong to smite, as all the Sunday schoolers knew, and his fist great
as his faith. He brought his huge clenched knuckles down into the
stone font with force enough, my mother said, to kill a whale. The
shield splintered but yielded no water. There was none to be had in
the church either at that time, and Mr Kinnear stood breaking the
third commandment between his teeth and muttering his determination to break others. So the old beadle ran down the outer steps of the
church, to where a bursting sea was spraying the tombstones of my
ancestors. He brought back a glimmer of cold brine in a brass
collection plate. That was how it happened that the waters of the
firth, which had been wetting the bones of my forefathers for
uncountable tides, were used that morning to baptize me – in the
name of the Eternal Father (strong to save) and of his Son and of the
Holy Ghost.

9.   Cromarty *c.* 1805

I was born, the first child of this marriage, on the 10th day of October
1802, in the low, long house built by my great-grandfather the
buccaneer. My memory awoke early. I have recollections which date
several months ere the completion of my third year; but, like those of
the golden age of the world, they are chiefly of a mythologic character.
I remember, for instance, getting out unobserved one day to my
father's little garden, and seeing there a minute duckling covered with
soft yellow hair, growing out of the soil by its feet, and beside it a plant
that bore as its flowers a crop of little mussel shells of a deep red
colour. I know not what prodigy of the vegetable kingdom produced
the little duckling; but the plant with the shells must, I think, have
been a scarlet runner, and the shells themselves the papilionaceous
blossoms.

I have a distinct recollection, too – but it belongs to a later period, –
of seeing my ancestor, old John Feddes the buccaneer, though he must

have been dead at the time considerably more than half a century. I had learned to take an interest in his story, as preserved and told in the antique dwelling which he had built more than a hundred years before. To forget a love disappointment, he had set out early in life for the Spanish Main, where, after giving and receiving some hard blows, he succeeded in filling a little bag with dollars and doubloons; and then coming home, he found his old sweetheart a widow, and so much inclined to listen to reason, that she ultimately became his wife.

There were some little circumstances in his history which must have laid hold of my imagination; for I used over and over to demand its repetition; and one of my first attempts at a work of art was to scrabble his initials with my fingers, in red paint, on the house door. One day, when playing all alone at the stair foot – for the inmates of the house had gone out – something extraordinary had caught my eye on the landing-place above; and looking up, there stood John Feddes – for I somehow instinctively divined that it was none other than he – in the form of a large, tall, very old man, attired in a light blue greatcoat. He seemed to be steadfastly regarding me with apparent complacency; but I was sadly frightened; and for years after, when passing through the dingy, ill-lighted room out of which I had inferred he had come, I used to feel not at all sure that I might not tilt against old John in the dark.

I retain vivid recollections of the joy which used to light up the household on my father's arrival; and I remember that I learned to distinguish for myself his sloop when in the offing, by the two slim stripes of white which ran along her sides, and her two square topsails.

I have my golden memories, too, of splendid toys that he used to bring home with him, – among the rest, of a magnificent four-wheeled wagon of painted tin, drawn by four wooden horses and a string; and of getting it into a quiet corner, immediately on its being delivered over to me, and there breaking up every wheel and horse, and the vehicle itself, into their original bits, until not two of the pieces were left sticking together.

Further, I still remember my disappointment at not finding something curious within at least the horses and wheels; and as unquestionably the main enjoyment derivable from such things is to be had in the breaking of them, I sometimes wonder that our ingenious toymen do not fall upon the way of at once extending their trade, and adding to its philosophy, by putting some of their more brilliant things where nature puts the nut-kernel, – inside.

. . . The reign of the first nurse was very short, she being accidentally discovered in a public-house, while her tender charge, done up in a parcel, lay tucked out of sight on a shelf behind the bar. The second nurse proved no better; but the third, Alison Cunningham, familiarly called Cummy, proved an estimable woman, who soon won the confidence of the family.

Cummy's piety was her strongest recommendation, but her convictions and consequent teachings, believing as she did in a literal hell along with the other tenets of her church, were rather strong meat for the mental digestion of an imaginative, nervous child. My husband has told me of the terrors of the night, when he dared not go to sleep lest he should wake amid the flames of eternal torment, and how he would be taken from his bed in the morning unrefreshed, feverish, and ill, but rejoicing that he had gained at least a respite from what he believed to be his just doom; Cummy, kindly soul, never dreaming of the dire effect of her religious training. The nursery, in the custom of the time, was kept almost hermetically closed, so that not a breath of air could penetrate from the outside; if little Smoutie, as he was called, waked from his dreams with cries of fright, the watchful Cummy was ready to make him a fresh drink of coffee, which she considered a particularly soothing beverage. According to her lights she was faithful and conscientious, and the child regarded her with the deepest affection.

Judged by the standards of to-day, the methods of the medical profession were inconceivably harsh and ignorant, and it seems a miracle that my husband should have survived their treatment and grown to manhood. When the little Louis was stricken with gastric fever he was dosed with powerful drugs; no one thought of looking into the sanitary condition of the premises, which were afterwards found to have been for years in a most dangerous state. And when the child, weakened by an attack of pneumonia, took cold after cold, antimonial wine was administered continually for a period extending into months; 'enough,' said Dr George Balfour, 'to ruin his constitution for life.' No wonder that after a little time at play he became so feverishly excited that his toys must be removed and his playmates sent away.

11.   Glasgow mid-twentieth century

It was a cream-coloured wall patterned with brownish-pink roses. A beam of early morning summer sunlight shone on it and on me. I was sitting in bed with the wall on one side and two chairs on the other. It seemed a very big bed, though it was an ordinary single one, and the two chairs had been placed to stop my falling out. My legs were covered by a quilt on which lay a tobacco pipe with a broken stem, a small slipper and a book with bright cloth pages. I was perfectly happy and singing a song on one note: *oolooloolooloo*. When tired of that I sang *dadadadada* for I had discovered the difference between *loo* and *da* and was interested in it. Later still, having tired of singing, I took the slipper and thumped the wall until my mother came. Each morning she lay in bed with a thin solemn young man on the other side of the roses. Her warmth reached me through the wall so I was never cold or lonely. I don't suppose my mother was unnaturally tall but she seemed twice the size of anyone else, and brown-haired, and regally slender above the hips. Below the hips she changed a lot, being often pregnant. I remember seeing her upper body rising behind the curve of her stomach like a giantess half-hidden by the horizon of a calm sea. I remember sitting on that curve with the back of my head between her breasts, knowing her face was somewhere above and feeling very sure of myself. I can't remember her features at all. Light or darkness came from them according to her mood, and I am certain this was more than the fantasy of a small child. I remember her sitting very still in a room of chattering strangers and steadily reducing them to whispers by the sullen silent fury she radiated. Her good moods were equally radiant and made the dullest company feel gallant and glamorous. She was never happy or depressed, she was glorious or sombre, and very attractive to modest dependable men. The men I called father were all of that kind. Apart from loving her they had no peculiarities. She must have attracted them like an extravagant vice for she was a poor housekeeper; on coming to live with a man she tried to prepare meals and keep things tidy, but the effort soon waned. I think the first house I remember was the happiest because it had only two small rooms and my first father was not fastidious. I believe he was a garage mechanic, for there was a car engine beside my bed and some huge tyres under the recess bed in the kitchen. As I grew older my mother was less ready to come when I thumped the wall, so I learned to crawl or stagger to the bed next door and be pulled in. She would lie reading newspapers and smoking cigarettes while my father made a hill under the blankets with his knees and suddenly flattened it when I had climbed on top. Later he would rise and bring us a breakfast of tea and fried bread and eggs.

The house was in a tenement with a narrow, busy street in front and a cracked asphalt yard at the back. Behind the yard was the embankment of a canal, and on sunny days my mother dragged me up this by straps fastened to a harness round my chest and we made a nest in the long grass beside the mossy towpath. The canal was choked with rushes and leafy weeds; nobody passed by but an old man with a greyhound or boys who should have been at school. I played with the tobacco pipe and my slipper, pretending I was my mother and the pipe me and the slipper my bed, or pretending the slipper was a car with the pipe driving. She read or daydreamed as she did at home, and I know now that her power came from those dreams, for where else could an almost silent woman without abilities learn the glamour of an enslaved princess, the authority of an exiled queen. The place where we lay was level with our kitchen window, and when my father returned from work he would prepare a meal and call us in to eat it. He seemed a contented man, and I am sure the quarrels were not his fault. One night I was wakened by noise from the dark wall at my ear, my mother's voice beating like high waves over protesting mutters. The noise stopped and she entered the room and hugged me hungrily. This happened several times, filling the nights with anticipation and delight and leaving me stupefied all day, for her thundering kisses exploded like fireworks in my ears and for long spells annihilated thought entirely. So I hardly noticed when she dressed me, and packed a suitcase, and took me away from that house.

12.

A NURSERY RHYME

'If your child shuns his knife and fork at meal times and treats his baby spoon with contempt, preferring to use his hands, don't worry. . . .

Early Days

He likes to play with his potatoes, and to mould and feel things. It leads to intellectual development.'

A child psychologist,
quoted in *The Bulletin*, 31 March 1951

Clap, clap handies,
  My bonny man
Ye sall hae tatties
  Het frae the pan.
*I'*ll put them *in* the dish:
  *Ye'*ll tak them *oot*;
Syne dad them on the tablecloth
  And row then rounaboot.

Tak yer wee handies,
  My bonnie pet;
Dab them in your parritch
  To see if they're het.
When they're weel slaistert,
  Gie them a bit dicht
On your faither's new breeks –
  That'll put them richt.

Take your wee handies,
  My bonny lamb;
Draw them through the butter,
  And dook them in the jam.
When ye're sticky to the wrists
  And dinna want nae mair,
Juist wipe them on the wa'paper
  As ye gang up the stair.

Hey, bonnie bairnie,
  Wow, but it's fun
To splairge a' your fingers
  In a muckle cream bun.
When they're a' weel clartit,
  Gie them a bit sook;
Syne gang and turn the pages
  O' the Telephone Book.

Use your wee handies,
And ye'll be a man
As wise as ony that hae been
Sin' first the warld began.
Aye splash and plouter
And never use your spune,
And ye'll be as gleg as Solomon
Afore your day is done.

13.   East Kilbride *c.* 1900

I dreamed that I woke in a state of drowsy content. I looked at the bars of the Venetian blinds shadowed on the wall. I looked at the crack in the ceiling – and it was going from left to right instead of from right to left! I was in the wrong world. I struggled out of my dream like a drowning swimmer . . .

Sometimes the dream went further – that was in the early days – and I was cheated into deeper waters of unreality. I was awake. I was in bed. It was my own room. But there was something wrong. I must get into the light and speak to my father and mother. They would calm my uneasiness and protect me from – whatever it was. I got up. I went into the corridor. It was bright with gas-light but very quiet. I called out. My father and mother came out into the corridor and confidence flowed back into me to be stopped with a jerk. These people who looked like my father and mother were not my father and mother at all. They were strangers. They were malignant strangers. They made fierce hideous triumphant faces at me. The passage gradually filled with simulacra of my brother, my uncles, my aunts, my nurse . . .

In some form or other this dream repeated itself again and again and it was necessary to find some antidote. I ran true to anthropology and invented two formulae. The first was pictorial, the second verbal. Before I went to sleep, I shut my eyes tight and saw a number of red devils in blue jackets dancing round a cauldron surrounded by leaping flames. From time to time I use this formula still. It is wonderfully effective . . .

* * *

15

The second exorcism was a couplet, and I am sorry, for more than one reason, to tell you that I have forgotten it. It was an invocation to birds, beasts, flowers and Jesus. It came to me in a dream and I spent a waking day learning it desperately by heart. If I felt uneasiness and strangeness coming over me when I was asleep I had only to repeat that couplet and I woke, quiet and comforted.

The alternative method of waking – that of shouting myself up through two or three layers of waking consciousness left me sweating, exhausted and afraid to go to sleep again.

The invocation was a sovereign remedy against the incubus, the succubus, brownies and bogles, lang-leggity beasties and things that went bump in the dark. You will perceive that I had within me the elements of natural religion.

14.   1980s

Me [Fiona] and Beastie have the sharpestest ears in the house and we listen very very hard for My Daddy opening the front gate. At last we hear him and we're out of the room and behind the front door before Mummy and Morag notice anything.

When he opens the door I shriek 'Daddy! Daddy!' and drop Beastie on the floor and fling myself at him. My Daddy swings me up and kisses me with his soft lips, but his moustache and his bristly chin tickle me and I have to squeal. With My Daddy, I like squealing. He gives me a 'beardie' and I squeal again. He settles me on his hip and I see that Mummy-frog has arrived and is looking at him.

Mummy-frog and My Daddy-horse are always talking to each other with their eyes. Most of the time I know perfectly well what they are saying. Just now Mummy-frog is telling My Daddy that I have been very naughty while he was at his work. In fact, she is saying that I have been *wicked*. I look at My Daddy's eyes and he is telling Mummy-frog that he doesn't care if I've been wicked, I'm still his Princess. He gives me a little squeeze and I can feel all the horsy muscles in his arm, but I don't squeal because Mummy-frog is cross.

I put my arm round My Daddy's neck and rest my head on his shoulder. This makes Mummy even crosser. I can see her saying, 'I'm fed up with minding children, especially that little bitch! Pick up Morag Mouse too, she's been *good*!'

Messy Morag is hanging on to My Daddy's leg, of course, and wailing 'Da-da! Da-da!' She is always doing that. He bends down to pick her up and settles her on his other hip. I manage to kick her three times, though. I'd have kicked her *twelve* times if My Daddy wasn't so clever at stopping me. I can count up to twelve but Morag can't even count up to two.

Mummy is now telling My Daddy something else. Her eyes are very bright and she is putting out the tip of her tongue a little. Before I can look to see what My Daddy is saying back to her there is a funny little sound at the front door. It could be Mrs Linkletter's geriatric doggie scratching. He does that sometimes. Mummy pushes past us and opens the door. My friend from down the street, Andy the Stick Insect, is standing there. He has nothing on but his vest. I can see his thingie. He is looking down at the doorstep and he is shivery and blue all over. He must have run away again. He would be much happier at my play-group, living in a jar and eating leaves.

15.   Dumfriesshire 1920s

. . . Round the top storey of the house, just below the level of the windows, there ran a lead gutter perhaps eighteen inches wide. Bored to distraction by enforced rest ['one hour flat on the back, books allowed but no talking'], I piled up furniture high enough to reach the window fastening. I unfastened it, opened the window and crawled out along the lead guttering. There was no motivation for this foolhardy act, only the conviction that to do something was better than doing nothing. Some forty feet below my sister Sheila was passing by: she looked up, saw me, and was duly appalled. With characteristic presence of mind she shouted 'I've got a special sweet for you in the nursery. If you go back in I will give it to you.' I then discovered a thing that many ledge-crawlers must have found out before me – you cannot turn around. I therefore backed towards the window – a good ten feet away – and as I did so was aware that the room inside was filling up. When I got within reach I felt my father's strong hand seize my waistband and whisk me back inside. There I saw sisters, brothers, nurses and my father all reacting to shock by laughing, crying, kissing me. It was terrific, and although subsequently lectured and told how near death I had been, there was no punishment. But Davy Sloan had rabbit wire nailed across the apertures of the two windows within the hour.

Subsequently when visitors came to tea I heard these two examples of bad behaviour recounted with relish, and I began to realise that bad rated more attention than good. Shortly after this time, too, I saw on our Kodak projector, along with Charlie Chaplin two-reelers, a short called *Pecks Bad Boy in Church*. In this instance the bad boy lets ants loose in church so that they crawled up the legs of all his elderly relations, and higher. It was an interesting idea, but I had no ants. The general conclusion, however, did not escape me, namely that the bad boy is a sort of hero to those who dare not be so bad as he. I thought there might be a career in it and from that time on was to cultivate my bad boy persona with some success. It gave me a cachet with the grown ups and enhanced my status in the nursery. The little ones were fed on the belief that I was so bad I might do anything and hence they treated me with circumspection and were all the quicker to fall in with my wishes in the matter of giving up favourite toys and the like. Even my seniors treated me with caution, as they treated the nursery dog that occasionally snapped. The one that never snapped had a much harder life.

16.   1767

OF BEHAVIOUR TO THE FAMILY

1. If you have Sisters or Brothers, it is your Duty to love them: They will love you for it, and it will be pleasing to your Parents, and a Pleasure to yourselves.
2. Be ready to give them any Thing they like, and they will give you what you desire.
3. If you think they are cross to you, be silent and gentle; and if that does not make them kind, complain to your Father, Mother, or Relations.
4. Never revenge yourself, for that is wicked; your relations will always take your Part, when you behave with Quietness.
5. Never Quarrel with your Brothers and Sisters.

THE MESSAGE

Little brother I got a message for you
not from Santa no
it's from Da.
Listen will you.

See before you got born
see Da still had a job to do.
We got bacon and eggs for breakfast.
Ma used to afford to get a hair-do.

Then she goes and gets pregnant again
and even although it was by accident
Da says we could maybe still afford it.
He meant you.

It turns out we can't.

The other thing is
this room before you came along
only had the one bed in it.
Mine.

See there isn't really room for the two.
So what with one thing and another
and since you were the last to arrive
Da says you've got to go little brother.

Here is your bag it's packed ready
with your beanos pyjamas and a few
biscuits for when you get hungry
I'm sure you'll be better off wherever

you end up so good luck and
goodbye.

I was brought up very tenderly. Consequently I began at an early age to be indisposed, and people pitied me as a very delicate child. My mother was extremely kind, but she was too anxious when I had some small ailment. If I did not feel well, I was treated with excessive attention. I was not made to go to school, which I detested. She gave me sweetmeats and all sorts of pretty things to amuse me. When my health was restored, my slavery would begin again. I knew it, and I preferred being weak and ill to being strong and healthy. What a perverted notion! Nature must receive a terrible shock before it submits to such a change. In a state of Nature, a child should feel miserable in illness and joyful in health. It is for that reason that he is encouraged to struggle with his illnesses. I encouraged them; and instead of jumping and running about, I lolled in an armchair. I was discontented and capricious. It is surprising that I did not often say that I was ill when I was actually well. But my worthy father had impressed upon me a respect for the truth which has always remained firm in my mind. Accordingly I never lied, but I hung my head down towards the floor until I got a headache, and then I complained that I was ill.

BEING GOOD

The system of punishment I was brought up with was relatively benign and straightforward. I was punished (i) for disobedience, (ii) for *what* I did wrong – that is, both for disobedience, which is wrong in itself, and for what, in being disobedient, I had done which I should not have done, because it was wrong in itself to do that, whether I had been told not to or not. I was told not to do things only because it was wrong for me to do them.

I was taught not to pick my nose; not to slouch in a chair; not to put a finger in my ear; not to keep my mouth open; not to hum and haw; not to make a noise when eating; not to drink out of a saucer, let alone to slop anything on it in the first place; to lift a teacup up to my lips, not my lips down to it, with two fingers; to blow my nose properly;

how to brush my teeth, comb my hair, tie my shoelaces, do my tie, always to have my socks pulled; how to shit properly and wipe my arse properly; not to turn up my eyes; how to speak properly; when and to whom to speak, with proper diction – for instance not 'sing-song' or some of the at least half-dozen forbidden accents, and a considerable amount of vulgar vocabulary.

From the age of seven I was expected to get myself up in the morning, do my teeth, wash my hands, arms, face, neck, gargle, pee and do No. 1, wash, wipe and dry my hands and all parts, put on my clothes correctly, brush my hair, sit down for breakfast on time, eat it not reading a book, check myself in the mirror, put on cap and, if necessary, galoshes, scarf, coat, gloves, and with a kiss and a 'cheerio' be off to school with fare there and back, a clean handkerchief, a pen, a pencil, a ruler, a rubber, a geometry set, a pocket knife, and my books in my bag on my back.

I would be back at four-thirty unless it was an afternoon at the playing field, when it would be later. Then out for a music lesson or out to play. Back by six for tea when my father would have come home, practise before it was too late for the neighbours, maybe a bit of radio, 'The Brains Trust' (C. E. M. Joad, Julian Huxley, the anonymous Scottish doctor whom I later discovered to have been Edward Glover, the pychoanalyst), 'Henry Hall's Guest Night', Charlie Kunz and Chopin; and then homework, and then bath, bed, prayers and sleep, or the fire, bed, prayers and sleep, negotiating through a reverse process from the morning of undressing, bathing, peeing, doing No. 1, washing my hands and then to bed, lights out, no reading, no talking.

For most of the time (except for one or two incidents which I shall describe), apart from when there were minor frictions, provided I looked all right, smelt all right and sounded all right, as long as my thoughts were good and my heart was pure, I was as free as a bird.

If I had done my practice and my homework and if it was not my bedtime I was perfectly entitled to sit musing in front of the fire. Neither my mother nor my father would see any reason to interrupt me without some special reason. We lived a quiet life. There were hardly ever any special reasons. The same with practising, homework, reading. I was never unfairly interrupted.

I would lie in bed in any position I wanted. Provided I kept quiet, I did not have to be asleep.

As long as you do this (and that's not asking too much considering what we have done and are doing and will still have to do for you) and don't do that (and there is a good reason for our telling you everything we tell you not to do), you need feel no guilt or shame for anything you think, feel, imagine or do, provided it is not bad.

You *know*, we don't have to tell you, when you are doing wrong. You *know* if you are telling a lie. You *know* (you are not depraved) what is a clean thought and a dirty thought. You *know* we don't have to tell you the difference between the truth and a lie and when you are telling the truth and when you are lying. And you *know*, we don't have to tell you, how to respect yourself (i.e. not masturbate), and how to respect the other sex. If you are in any doubt, remember that *God* sees it all, everything, all the time. Let your mind and your heart, your words and your deeds be, as they are anyway (that's the funny thing, isn't it?), an open book to God.

20.   Late nineteenth century

A GOOD BOY

I woke before the morning, I was happy all the day,
I never said an ugly word, but smiled and stuck to play.

And now at last the sun is going down behind the wood,
And I am very happy, for I know that I've been good.

My bed is waiting cool and fresh, with linen smooth and fair,
And I must off to sleepsin-by, and not forget my prayer.

I know that, till tomorrow I shall see the sun arise.
No ugly dreams shall fright my mind, no ugly sight my eyes.

But slumber hold me tightly till I waken in the dawn,
And hear the thrushes singing in the lilacs round the lawn.

21.   Glasgow *c.* 1920

My recollections of my early years at 'Gartnavel' are, without exception, extremely pleasant ones. Our house was part of the main building, and from the hall covered-in stairs led to 'The Tunnel' – an underground passage from which every part of the Institution could be reached, except a couple of detached villas in the sixty-six acre grounds.

From earliest childhood I was thus in close daily contact with the patients and was brought up – as were my brother and sister – to regard them as sick people to whom one must always be polite, friendly, and sympathetic, and of whom one must never, never, be afraid.

As we grew older, the patients who were well enough to be up and about became our familiar friends. We went all over the hospital without let or hindrance, visiting the workshops, the engine room, the laundry, the piggeries, the stables, the billiard room, the 'galleries', the garden, and the provision store, as the fancy took us, and chatting amiably with all and sundry. I had a particular affection for the dynamos and batteries which produced our electricity, and it was several years before I realised that the urbane magician who presided over them and would often produce fascinating spark effects with pieces of wire, was himself a patient.

I suppose that 'characters' were more common in those days – or perhaps it was that patients stayed longer because they didn't get 'cured' so quickly – but certainly I have glad and grateful recollections of many vivid and outstanding personalities, from whom I acquired a large stock of general knowledge as well as receiving a vast amount of first-class teaching on specific subjects. I owe my grounding in chess, billiards, golf, cricket and, above all, amateur theatricals, as well as many minor occupations and pastimes, to patients, one of whom was the finest all-round sportsman and the most versatile and cultured personality I have ever known.

Sunday, strange though it may seem, was an eagerly awaited day, because immediately after Divine Service, which the Chaplain con-ducted in those days in the large dining hall, we went 'round the wards' *en famille*. This meant a grand tour of the whole hospital, with no ward or department omitted. We looked upon this as a real treat, and great was our disappointment if it had to be forgone either due to our father's absence or as a punishment for some previous misdemeanour.

It was on one of these occasions that I received, for the first and only time, corporal punishment from my father. I must have been a very small boy at the time because I have but a dim recollection of being greeted with an affectionate though stentorian 'Good Morning' by a very stout lady of fearsome aspect in what I suppose would be popularly termed the 'refractory' ward. (That term, I may say, was never used in any one of the four mental hospitals in which I have lived and worked.) Rather bewildered by the noise and bustle, I failed to respond to this greeting, and when urged to do so by my parents, who had unfortunately overheard it, I abruptly declined. Persuasion and remonstrance proving vain, I was accommodated in a small side room to think the matter over, while the family returned home for Sunday dinner. On my father's return thereafter, I went the length of offering to say 'Good Night' as a compromise. This was refused, and after a further short period for reflection which proved fruitless, a good old-fashioned whipping was administered in the privacy of the side room, after which I made a pilgrimage round the entire ward saying 'Good Morning' to every patient in it. As the Sister in Charge rightly remarked, 'It was a lesson to us all!'

PRODIGIES

taken from

The boy [Kentigern] advanced, under the unction of good hope and holy disposition, in the discipline of learning as well as in the exercise of the sacred virtues. For there were bestowed upon him by the Father of Lights, from whom descendeth every good and perfect gift, a docile heart, a genius sharp at understanding, a memory tenacious in recollecting, and a tongue persuasive in bringing forth what he willed; a high, sweet, harmonious, and indefatigable voice for singing the Divine praises. All these gifts of grace were gilded by a worthy life, and therefore beyond all his companions he was precious and amiable in the eyes of the holy old man [St Servanus/St Serf], wherefore he was accustomed to call him in the language of his country, 'Munghu', which in Latin means 'Karissimus Amicus', and by this name even until the present time the common people are frequently used to call him, and to invoke him in their necessities.

The fellow-pupils of St Kentigern, seeing that he was loved beyond the rest by their master and spiritual father, hated him, and were unable either in public or private to say anything peaceable to him. Hence in many ways they intrigued against, abused, envied, and backbit him. But the Lord's boy ever had the eye of his heart fixed upon the Lord; and mourning more for them than for himself, cared little for all the unjust machinations of men.

Now a little bird, which, on account of the colour of his body, is called the redbreast, by the will of the Heavenly Father, without whose permission not even a sparrow falleth to the ground, was accustomed to receive its daily food from the hand of the servant of God, Servanus, and by such a custom being established it showed itself tame and domesticated unto him. Sometimes even it perched upon his head, or face, or shoulder, or bosom; sometimes it was with him when he read or prayed, and by the flapping of its wings, or by the sound of its inarticulate voice, or by some little gesture, it showed the love it had for him . . . And because that bird often approached and departed at the command and will of the man of God, it excited incredulity and hardness of heart in his disciples, and convicted them of disobedience.

Therefore on a certain day, when the saint entered his oratory to offer up to God the frankincense of prayer, the boys, availing themselves of the absence of the master, began to indulge themselves in play with the aforesaid little bird, and while they handled it among them, and sought to snatch it from each other, it got destroyed in their hands, and its head was torn from the body. On this play became sorrow, and they already in imagination saw the blows of the rods, which are wont to be the greatest torment of boys. Having taken counsel among themselves, they laid the blame on the boy Kentigern, who had kept himself entirely apart from the affair, and they showed him the dead bird, and threw it away from themselves before the old man arrived. But he took very ill the death of the bird, and threatened an extremely severe vengeance on its destroyer. The boys therefore rejoiced, thinking that they had escaped, and had turned on Kentigern the punishment due to them, and diminished the grace of friendship which Servanus had hitherto entertained for him.

When Kentigern, the pure child, learnt this, taking the bird in his hands, and putting the head upon the body, he signed it with the sign of the cross, and lifting up holy hands to the Lord, he said, 'Lord Jesus Christ, in Whose hands is the breath of every rational and irrational creature, give back to this bird the breath of life, that Thy blessed name may be glorified for ever.' These words spake the saint in prayer, and straightaway the bird revived, and not only with untrammeled flight rose in the air in safety, but also in its usual way it flew forth with joy to meet the holy old man as he returned from the church. On seeing this prodigy the heart of the old man rejoiced in the Lord, and his soul did magnify the Lord's boy in the Lord, and the Lord, Who alone doeth marvellous things, and was working in the boy.

2.   Edinburgh 1777

I last night supped at [a friend's]. He has the most extraordinary genius of a boy I ever saw. He was reading a poem to his mother when I went in. I made him read on; it was the description of a shipwreck. His passion rose with the storm. 'There's a mast gone,' says he. 'Crash it goes! They will all perish!' After his agitation he turns to me. 'That is too melancholy,' says he. 'I had better read you something more amusing.' I proposed a little chat and asked his opinion of Milton and other books he was reading, which he gave me wonderfully. One of his observations was, 'How strange it is that Adam, just new come into the world, should know everything – that must be the poet's fancy,' says he. But when he was told that he was created perfect by God, he instantly yielded. When taken to bed last night, he told his aunt he liked that lady. 'What lady?' says she. 'Why, Mrs C., For I think she is a virtuoso, like myself.' 'Dear [boy],' says Aunt Jenny, 'what is a virtuoso?' 'Don't you know? Why, it's one that wishes and will know everything.' Now, sir, you will think this is a very silly story. Pray, what age do you suppose that boy to be? Name it now, before I tell you. Why, twelve or fourteen. No such thing; he is not quite six years old. He has a lame leg, for which he was a year at Bath, and has acquired the perfect English accent, which he has not lost since he came, and he reads like a Garrick. You will allow this an uncommon exotic.

3.   East Lothian *c.* 1810

[JEANNIE – BY HER HUSBAND]

The school, I believe, was and is at the hither, western, end of the Nungate Bridge . . . A short furlong or so along paved streets, from her father's house. Thither daily at an early hour (perhaps eight A.M. in summer) might be seen my little Jeannie tripping nimbly and daintily along; her little satchel in hand; dressed by her mother (who had a great talent that way) in tasteful simplicity, – neat bit of pelisse ('light blue', sometimes) fastened with a black belt; dainty little cap, perhaps little *beaver*kin ('with flap turned up') and I think once at least with a modest 'little plume in it.' Fill that figure with *electric* intellect, ditto love, and a generous vivacity of all kinds; where in Nature will you find a prettier?

. . . In all things she strove to 'be a boy' in education; and yet by natural guidance never ceased to be the prettiest and gracefullest of little girls. Full of intelligence, of veracity, vivacity, and bright curiosity.

4.   East Lothian *c.* 1805–1811

[JEANNIE – BY A FRIEND]

On her road to school, when a very small child, she had to pass a gate where a horrid turkey-cock was generally standing. He always ran up to her, gobbling and looking very hideous and alarming. It frightened her at first a good deal; and she dreaded having to pass the place; but after a little time she hated the thought of living in fear. The next time she passed the gate several labourers and boys were near, who seemed to enjoy the thought of the turkey running at her. She gathered herself together and made up her mind. The turkey ran at her as usual, gobbling and swelling; she suddenly darted at him and seized him by the throat and swung him round! The men clapped their hands, and shouted 'Well done, little Jeannie!' and the Bubbly Jock never molested her again.

She was very anxious to learn lessons like a boy; and, when a very little thing, she asked her father to let her 'learn Latin like a boy.' Her mother did not wish her to learn so much; her father always tried to push her forwards; there was a division of opinion on the subject. Jeannie went to one of the town scholars in Haddington and made him teach her a noun of the first declension ('Penna, a pen,' I think it was). Armed with this, she watched her opportunity; instead of going to bed, she crept under the table, and was concealed by the cover. In a pause of conversation, a little voice was heard, '*Penna*, a pen; *pennae*, of a pen;' etc. and as there was a pause of surprise, she crept out, and went up to her father saying, 'I want to learn Latin; please let me be a boy.' Of course she had her own way in the matter.

Boys and girls went to the same school; they were in separate rooms, except for Arithmetic and Algebra. Jeannie was the best of the girls at Algebra. Of course she had many devoted slaves among the boys; one of them especially taught her, and helped her all he knew; but he was quite a poor boy, while Jeannie was one of the gentry of the place; but she felt no difficulty, and they were great friends.

One day in the boys' school-room, one of the boys said something to displease her. She lifted her hand, doubled it, and hit him hard; his nose began to bleed, and in the midst of the scuffle the master came in. He saw the traces of the fray, and said in an angry voice, 'You boys, you know, I have forbidden you to fight in school, and have promised that I would flog the next. Who has been fighting this time?' Nobody spoke; and the master grew angry, and threatened *tawse* all round unless the culprit were given up. Of course no boy would tell of a girl, so there was a pause; in the midst of it, Jeannie looked up and said, 'Please, I gave that black eye.' The master tried to look grave, and pursed up his mouth; but the boy was big, and Jeannie was little; so, instead of the *tawse* he burst out laughing and told her she was 'a little deevil,' and had no business there, and to go her ways back to the girls.

. . . She always would push everything to its extreme to find out if possible the ultimate consequence. One day her mother was ill, and a bag of ice had to be applied to her head. Jeannie wanted to know the sensation, and took an opportunity when no one saw her to get hold of the bag, and put it on her own head, and kept it on till she was found lying on the ground insensible.

She made great progress in Latin, and was in Virgil when nine years old. She always loved her doll; but when she got into Virgil she thought it shame to care for a doll. On her tenth birthday she built a funeral pile of lead pencils and sticks of cinnamon, and poured some sort of perfume over all, to represent a funeral pile. She then recited the speech of Dido, stabbed her doll and let out all the sawdust; after which she consumed her to ashes, and then burst into a passion of tears.

5.   Cromarty *c.* 1812

'At Wallace name what Scottish blood
But boils up in a spring-tide flood!
Oft have our fearless father strode
    By Wallace' side,
Still pressing onward, red wat shod,
    Or glorious died.' BURNS

I first became thoroughly a Scot some time in my tenth year; and the consciousness of country has remained tolerably strong within me ever since. My uncle James had procured for me from a neighbour the loan of Blind Harry's 'Wallace', as modernized by Hamilton; but after reading the first chapter, – a piece of dull genealogy, broken into very rude rhyme, – I tossed the volume aside as uninteresting; and only resumed it at the request of my uncle, who urged that, simply for *his* amusement and gratification, I should read some three or four chapters more. Accordingly, the three or four more chapters I did read; – I read 'how Wallace killed young Selbie the Constable's son;' 'how Wallace fished in Irvine Water;' and 'how Wallace killed the churl with his own staff in Ayr;' and then Uncle James told me, in the quiet way in which he used to make a joke tell, that the book seemed to be rather a rough sort of production, filled with accounts of quarrels and bloodshed, and that I might read no more of it unless I felt inclined.

But now I did feel inclined very strongly, and read on with increasing astonishment and delight. I was intoxicated with the fiery narratives of the blind minstrel, – with his fierce breathings of hot, intolerant patriotism, and his stories of astonishing prowess; and glorying in being a Scot, and the countryman of Wallace and the Graham, I longed for war with the Southron, that the wrongs and sufferings of these noble heroes might yet be avenged. All I had previously heard and read of the marvels of foreign parts, of the glories of modern battles, seemed tame and commonplace, compared with the incidents in the life of Wallace; and I never after vexed my mother by wishing myself big enough to be a sailor.

6.   Edinburgh 1810

[Lines from a seven-year-old's 'Journal']

> Three turkeys fair their last have breathed
> And now this world for ever leaved
> Their father and their mother too
> Will sigh and weep as well as you
> Mourning for their osprings fair
> Whom they did nurse with tender care
> Indeed the rats their bones have crunched
> To eternity are they launched

Their graceful form and pretty eyes
Their fellow pows did not despise
A direful death indeed they had
that would put any parent mad
But she was more than usual calm
She did not give a singel dam
She is as gentel as a lamb
Here ends this melancholy lay
Farewell poor turkeys I must say

7.   Galloway 1919

. . . Meanwhile [at five years old] I dictated the text to my sister, for none other than I could be trusted to unscramble the strange mysteries of these creatures' lives.

'*The Crested Bird.* This is a foreign bird you find his eggs in foreign lands they would be about as big as the biggest person's head if you compared the sizes. The bird in the picture is a cock bird he is called the Crested bird because of his great crest. The next picture is of the hen bird of this sort.

'*The Green Bird.* This bird lays 100 eggs in a year. They are brownish white. He has eggs of an eggish shape.

'*The Blue Headed Bird.* The nest of the blue Headed bird is made of moss and sticks and grass and bracken the eggs are white speckled with black. The hen bird of this sort is very suitable for her husband.

'*The Skiping Long Nose.* He lives in America like the Mustangs. He has babies almost as big as their mothers. The mothers are only as big as your head, and the babies only as big as that little bit of cardboard on the windowsill.

'*The Brown Legged Hinda.* Does eat chalks and knifes and blue eyes and grass his babies are brown and white.

'*The Ruvvled Bird.* You can see in the picture I was rather careless about for she was not in the mood for it. He has got blue eggs speckled with pink she is a very horrid bird.

'*The Blue Crested Bird.* This bird lays 12 eggs of white specled with black, it lays its eggs in various places though they are curious places too. She has red brown eyes the colour people admire.

'*The Nicest Bird.* She lays eggs bluish black, she lives in forests in Africa. She makes her nest strange to say in wild African's houses.
'Dear Mother
'from Gavin
'The End. Christmas 1919.'

8.   Ayrshire 1882

[A grace, composed and recited by a boy on his sixth birthday]

> God bless the cakes and bless the jam;
> Bless the cheese and the cold boiled ham;
> Bless the scones Aunt Jeannie makes,
> And save us all from bellyaches. Amen.

9.   2 Sulyarde Terrace, Torquay, Thursday [April 1866]

RESPECTED PATERNAL RELATIVE, – I write to make a request of the most moderate nature. Every year I have cost you an enormous – nay, elephantine – sum of money for drugs and physician's fees, and the most expensive time of the twelve months was March.

But this year the biting Oriental blasts, the howling tempests, and the general ailments of the human race have been successfuly braved by yours truly.

Does not this deserve remuneration? I appeal to your charity, I appeal to your generosity, I appeal to your justice, I appeal to your accounts, I appeal, in fine, to your purse.

My sense of generosity forbids the receipt of more – my sense of justice forbids the receipt of less – than half-a-crown. – Greeting from, Sir, your most affectionate and needy son,

[R.S. aged 15½]

GRANNIES

taken from

'I'm away to throw the hens some corn,' Grandmother said casually.
'I'll maybe have a look in bye the black pig too. Anybody like to
come?'

Janie jumped at the invitation. Inside the house Grandmother was
old and very wise, knowing the best cure for this ailment, and the
worst weather for that ailment. Knowing what Paul said to the
Corinthians. And what someone ought to say very soon to that
George Scobie for underpaying country folk and overcharging town
folk for their eggs. Outside the house was a different matter altogether.
No ailments existed round the garden, out by the steading or in the
wood. No one cared what Paul said to the Corinthians. According to
Grandmother when she got outside, Paul had once said something
quite different:

> *Paul said and Peter said*
> *And all the saints alive and dead*
> *Swore she had the sweetest head,*
> *Bonnie, bonnie Bride of the yellow, yellow hair.*

Grandmother knew that the secret of her other self was safe in the
keeping of the black pig and Janie. Neither of them thought it in any
way odd for Grandmother to kilt up her apron and trip sedately round
the sty to her own singing:

> *And she slept for a hundred years,*
> *YEARS, YEARS.*
> *And she slept for a hundred years,*
> *A hundred years.*
> *Till Prince Charming came and kissed her*
> *Long ago.*

They stepped easily into this other world, the child and the
Grandmother. Pondering over a new word for meadow. Musko-

day. Musk in the garden now. And small, yellow musk roses waiting to come in summer. High afternoon, the stables doors open, the stables empty. No great, black wood horses there now, to flick their tails, and stamp their feet, and roll their wild and searching eyes round at a visitor. The whitewashed byre, dark stone drinking troughs. An intruding hen whirred out of her nest in the manger, cackling her resentment, and rousing the sleeping afternoon. 'We'll go in bye now,' Grandmother said, 'I'll make a baking of scones for our tea. You can have a hot one with milk. Hot scones are ill for the belly they say, but I never died of eating one yet. And, for an ill thing, a hot scone's got an unco fine taste.'

The bellows roared the fire into redness. Grandmother, huge and hurried in her white baking apron, had become old and wise again.

2.   Aberdeenshire pre-1914

My grandmother always raised a lot of poultry, which must have been a great help towards the housekeeping, though the Old Man, like every other farmer then, despised poultry as parasites and worse. I used to help my grandmother with the hens, particularly at hatching time, for I was fascinated by the miracle of the chicken in the egg. The old woman had a trick of placing the egg to her ear, and of being able to tell whether or not it would produce a live chicken. Those eggs that were infertile she placed aside, and I was allowed to break them against the midden wall, a much cherished privilege. Well, one afternoon when I was making a round of the nesting shed alone, it occurred to me that I too might test a few of the eggs. So I unseated a friendly old hen (as a rule the brooders were very kittle cattle) and sounded the eggs. I did not seem to have the knack of it, for though I held them to either ear, I could not decide one way or the other. The passion of scientific inquiry now ran away with me. I just had to know what was inside the eggs. I employed the traditional method. It was great fun – at least to me – but it may have been otherwise to my grandmother who came in to find me breaking up the last nestful, while the dispossessed hens stood disconsolately in a gigantic omelet on the floor, lamenting dolefully. I am told that I looked up with my most innocent round-faced smile and said:

'I wis jist seein' if there wis ony chuckies in them.'

My grandmother looked sadly at the ruins and thought of all the chuckies she had counted before they were hatched.

'Aw weel,' she said, 'we fairly ken noo.'

That was all she ever said about it, but I did not need the business discussed as man to man. The look on her face told me that the spirit of scientific inquiry must be tempered with discretion. Life becomes very difficult about the age of six.

3.   Nairn 1928

I suppose Granma had kind and gentle qualities – she was my mother's mother – and I suppose she could speak in an ordinary calm voice and have conversations with friends – she had after all brought up three daughters and a son renowned for their liveliness, intelligence and wit – yet after those three years of living with her, from the age of eleven to fourteen I can remember nothing but acerbity issuing from her tight mouth. Perhaps the premature death of her husband had sunk her spirits so low that during the ensuing years they became entirely hidden, until by the time I knew her they were lost to her entirely, buried deep in her unconscious mind as a protection against pain.

I cannot remember ever hearing her use my Christian name in the vocative once during these three years.

— Do not take so much salt to your meat. It is uncomplimentary. Janet's cooking is adequate.

— If you must take salt, do not splatter it. Place half a spoonful on the side of your plate.

— Does salt cost a lot then, Granma?

The granite stare. Grey granite.

— I cannot bear to sit beside you. You have not washed your hands.

— I did wash them, Granma. It hasn't all come off.

— Then leave the table and wash them properly.

The dung from the byre and stable had come off easily before dinner with ordinary soap, but there was no green soft soap in the lavatory and yellow grease and black oil from ploughs and harrows were indelible; and then, from grooming horses, every pore on my fingers and the backs of my hands was ingrained with fine, grey scurf; and as I never bothered to wash after milking my hands began to smell sour soon afterwards. Sour milk wins against hurried soaping.

Cleanliness is godliness, love is a paltry ridiculous joke, sex, even thoughts of it, are wicked and filthy; dance, song and pictures are the work of Satan. Scotch morality is filled with such perverted notions and even though Granma adhered to the Episcopal Church, which is said to be less puritanical than the others, she abode by them all. The vice of meanness, condemned in every other country, is in Scotland translated into a virtue called 'thrift'. Granma was thrifty. The downstairs rooms of Tigh-na-Rosan were lit by gas, by wall-bracket lamps that gave a good light. But the only light in my bedroom was one candle which burned in an ordinary saucer-shaped candlestick. I was supposed to bring it down every morning and put it into the pantry so that I could put a match to it in the evening and light my way upstairs to bed. But often I forgot to bring it down.

One evening when I went to the pantry and saw I had forgotten it, I remembered that I had used my last match on the night before. I went back to the drawing room to ask Granma for a new box.
— Bring your box, she said.
So I had to grope my way upstairs in the dark and feel about my bedroom till I found the empty box. Granma unlocked a drawer of her writing table, took a full box out and placed four matches in my empty box.

4.   *c.* 1990

ARRAHEIDS

See thon raws o flint arraheids
in oor gret museums o antiquities
awful grand in Embro –
Dae'ye near'n daur wunner at wur histrie?
Weel then, Bewaur!
The museums of Scotland are wrang.
They urnae arraheids
but a show o grannie's tongues,
the hard tongues o grannies
aa deid an gaun
back to thur peat and burns,

but for thur sherp
chert tongues, that lee
fur generations in the land
like wicked cherms, that lee
aa douce in the glessy cases in the gloom
o oor museums, an
they arenae lettin oan. But if you daur
sorn aboot an fancy
the vanished hunter, the wise deer runnin on:
wheesh . . . an you'll hear them,
fur they cannae keep fae muttering
ye arenae here tae wonder,
whae dae ye think ye ur?

5.   Glasgow 1950s/1960s

. . . on Ash Wednesday Nan [my mother] and I had come through
from Drumchapel to see Peggy [my aunt] and the baby, stopping at St
Philomena's church first, so that I could have the ritual dab of ashes on
my forehead. All Catholics knew that the ashes were sacred, to remove
them was a great sin for which I knew I would be struck instantly
dead.

Nan was shopping and I'd run on ahead because I wanted to see the
baby. When I got to the house, one of [my grandmother] Maw Clark's
cronies was with her, a woman I knew as Auld Broon, and another
strong supporter of the Orange Lodge. Peggy was changing the baby
and suddenly Maw Clark leaned over, grabbed hold of me, snatched
the dirty nappy and wiped it across my face, removing the ashes from
my forehead. Then she and Auld Broon fell about cackling with
delight.

Poor Peggy was embarrassed and took me into the kitchen, offering
to replace the ashes with some from the fireplace, which was doubtless
where the priest had got them from in the first place. But she didn't
understand! The ashes were HOLY, they were BLESSED, and now I
would be struck dead before finishing primary school as punishment
for letting them be removed!

When Nan arrived Peggy motioned her into the kitchen and
whispered what had happened, and the two of them entered into

a conspiracy to calm me down by convincing me that the ashes put on my head by the priest had somehow survived. Then Nan went into the living-room and told Maw Clark off while Peggy kept me in the kitchen and gave me a special treat, some of the baby's National Orange Juice . . . When we left, Nan was still angry enough to burst. I asked why Maw Clark had done it and Nan replied, 'Sometimes yer Maw's no' a very nice wumman, hen, in fact maist o' the time she's no' a nice wumman! She's ma ain mither, bit she's common. Noo don't you go tellin' anybody that!'

6.   Glasgow 1920s

Somehow I was never awake at the precise moment when Grannie came into bed. One moment I was drowsily gazing at the gas mantle, blinking my lashes against its soft radiance and making rainbows with my flickering eyelids and its glowing globe, and the next moment it was dark and Grannie was pulling the blankets round her, and easing herself into the hollow in front of her. As I cooried in closer, to keep my share of the bedclothes, she would reach out a hand to push my knees down. 'Your banes are like sticks,' she would complain. 'Streetch them doon noo. They're that sherp, they're cuttin' intae auld Grannie's back.' Sleepily, obediently, I would straiten out my legs, and I would drift with a drowsy smile as I prodded with a small hand my offending knees. How could Grannie think they were sharp enough to hurt her? I wondered. They felt soft and ordinary enough to me. But then I was only three years old and Grannie was, oh maybe a hundred, for, after all, she was my mother's mother, and my mother was twenty-one, for she had told us so when we asked her.

I couldn't remember a time when I hadn't slept in the hurley bed with Grannie. This was a bed on casters, which 'hurled' under the big recess bed out of sight during the day, and was hidden tidily out of sight behind the bed-pawn, ready to be pulled out at a touch whenever it was my bed-time. It was only about a foot off the floor, so that it could be hurled away fully made up with its sheets and pillows and blankets, and was probably made by a neighbour who was a handyman joiner, and who grasped at once the necessity for using every inch of space in a room and kitchen which had to accommodate five people.

There was my grannie, my mother, my two brothers and myself. Away, way back I had a dream-like memory of a man who refused to pick me up and carry me when we had been out visiting one bitterly cold Sunday, and it was very late, and we couldn't find a tramcar. 'Give her a carry,' my mother's voice said. 'She's only a baby.' 'She can walk,' came the man's voice. 'There's nothing wrong with her legs.' There was no spoiling for me. That must have been my father. A father who only lived long enough to sire three children. Four if you count the little sister who died in infancy, and whom he quickly followed, leaving my mother to bring the three of us up without anyone's help except that given by Grannie. Grannie gave up her own wee single end, and came to live with us. I never missed my father. For, filling every corner of my world was Grannie. From the minute I opened my eyes in the hurley bed in the morning, she tormented me, disciplined me, taught me, laughed at me, loved me, and tied me to her forever, though I didn't know it at the time.

PLAY, ADVENTURE
AND DISCOVERY

taken from

1.   1767

OF KEEPING COMPANY WITH OTHER BOYS

1. CHUSE for your Companions, the most decent, genteel, and good-
humoured of your Schoolfellows.
2. Avoid all such as are clownish, dirty, rude, or cruel.
3. Never join a party in any Mischief.
4. Never mix with those who torment dumb Creatures in Sport.
5. Be willing to oblige every one; but not ready to take Offence at
any.
6. If any one uses you unkindly, despise him; and do not keep
Company with him afterwards.
7. Never quarrel, for it is the Practice of vulgar cowardly Boys.

19. Never engage in any dirty Diversions.

2.   'County of Edinburgh' c. 1790

. . . The old ale-house at Heriot was the first inn I ever entered. My
father, who, I think, was then convener of the county of Edinburgh,
went out to attend some meeting of road trustees, and he took a parcel
of us with him. He rode; and we had a chaise to ourselves – happiness
enough for boys. But more was in store for us. For he remained at the
mansion house of Middleton with his friend Mr Hepburn, and we
went on, about four miles further, to Heriot House, where we
breakfasted and passed the day, fishing, bathing, and rioting. It
was the first inn of most of the party.
    What delight! A house to ourselves, on a moor; a burn; nobody to
interfere with us; the power of ringing the bell when we chose; the
ordering of our own dinner; blowing the peat fire; laughing as often
and as loud as we liked. What a day! We rang the hand bell for the
pure pleasure of ringing, and enjoyed our independence by always
going in and out by the window. This dear little inn does not now

exist, but its place is marked by a square of ash trees. It was a bright, beautiful August day.

We returned to the inn of Middleton, on our way home, about seven in the evening; and there we saw another scene. People sometimes say that there is no probability in Scott's making the party in 'Waverley' retire from the Castle to the Howf; but these people were not with me at the inn at Middleton, about forty years ago. The Duke of Buccleuch was living at Dalkeith; Henry Dundas at Melville; Robert Dundas, the Lord Advocate, at Arniston; Hepburn of Clerkington at Middleton; and several of the rest of the aristocracy of Midlothian within a few miles; all with their families, and luxurious houses; yet had they, to the number of twelve or sixteen, congregated in this wretched ale-house for a day of freedom and jollity.

We found them roaring and singing and laughing, in a low-roofed room scarcely large enough to hold them, with wooden chairs and a sanded floor. . . . There was plenty of wine, particularly claret, in rapid circulation on the table; but my eye was chiefly attracted by a huge bowl of whisky punch, the steam of which was almost dropping from the roof, while the odour was enough to perfume the whole parish. We were called in, and made to partake, and were very kindly used, particularly by my uncle Harry Dundas. How they did joke and laugh! with songs, and toasts, and disputation, and no want of practical fun. I don't remember anything they said, and probably did not understand it. But the noise, and the heat, and the uproarious mirth I think I hear and feel them yet.

3.   Edinburgh *c.* 1860

When my cousin and I took our porridge of a morning, we had a device to enliven the course of the meal. He ate his with sugar, and explained it to be a country continually buried under snow. I took mine with milk, and explained it to be a country suffering gradual inundation. You can imagine us exchanging bulletins; how here was an island still unsubmerged, here a valley not yet covered with snow; what inventions were made; how his population lived in cabins on perches and travelled on stilts, and how mine was always in boats; how the interest grew furious, as the last corner of safe ground was cut off on all sides and grew smaller every moment; and how in fine, the food was of altogether secondary importance, and might even have been nauseous, so long as we seasoned it with these dreams. But perhaps the most exciting moments I ever had over a meal, were in the case of calves'-feet jelly. It was hardly possible not to believe – and you may be sure, so far from trying, I did all I could to favour the illusion – that some part of it was hollow, and that sooner or later my spoon would lay open the secret tabernacle of the golden rock. There might some miniature *Red Beard* await his hour; there, might one find the treasures of the *Forty Thieves*, and bewildered Cassim beating about the walls. And so I quarried on slowly, with bated breath, savouring the interest. Believe me, I had little palate left for the jelly; and though I preferred the taste when I took cream with it, I used often to go without, because the cream dimmed the transparent fractures.

Even with games, this spirit is authoritative with right-minded children. It is thus that hide-and-seek has so pre-eminent an authority, for it is the well-spring of romance, and the actions and the excitement to which it gives rise lend themselves to almost any sort of fable. And thus cricket, which is a mere matter of dexterity, palpably about nothing and for no end, often fails to satisfy infantile craving. It is a game, if you like, but not a game of play. You cannot tell yourself a story about cricket; and the activity it calls forth can be justified on no rational theory. Even football, although it admirably simulates the tug and the ebb and flow of battle, has presented difficulties to the mind of young sticklers after verisimilitude; and I know one little boy who was mightily exercised by the presence of the ball, and had to spirit himself up, whenever he came to play, with an elaborate story of enchantment, and take the missile as a sort of talisman bandied about in conflict between two Arabian nations.

4.   Edinburgh twentieth century

FI'BAW IN THE STREET

Shote! here's the poliss,
the Gayfield poliss,
    and thull pi'is in the nick fir
    pleyan fi'baw in the street!
Yin o thum's a faw'y

like a muckle foazie taw'y,
   bi' the ither's lang and skinnylike,
   wi umburrelly feet.
Ach, awaw, says Tammy Curtis,
fir thir baith owre blate tae hurt iz,
   thir a glaikit pair o Teuchters
   an as Hielant as a peat.
Shote! thayr thir comin
wi the hurdygurdy wummin
   that we coupit wi her puggy
   pleyan fi'baw in the street.

Sae wir aff by Cockie-Dudgeons and
the Sandies and the Coup,
   an wir owre a dizzen fences tha'
   the coppers canny loup,
an wir in an ou' o backgreens an
wir dreepan muckle dikes,
   an we tear ir claes on railins
   full o nesty iron spikes.
An aw the time the skinnylinky
copper's a' ir heels,
   though the faw'y's deid ir deean
   this yin seems ti rin on wheels:
noo he's stickit on a railin wi
his helmet on a spike,
   noo he's up and owre and rinnan, did
   ye iver see the like?

Bi' we stour awa ti Puddocky
(That's doon by Logie Green)
   an wir roon by Beaverhaw whayr
   deil a beaver's iver seen;
noo wir aff wi buitts and stockins
and wir wadin roon a fence
   (it sticks oot inty the wa'er, bi
   tha' nithin if ye've sense)
syne we cooshy doon thegither
jist like choockies wi a hen

in a bonny wee-bit bunky-hole
tha' bobbies dinna ken.
Bi' ma knees is skint and bluddan,
an ma breeks they want the seat
jings! ye git mair nir ye're eftir,
pleyan fi'baw in the street.

5.   North-East *c.* 1830

. . . there was pleasure enough in the company and devices of the
cowherd, a freckle-face, white-haired, weak-eyed boy of ten, named – I
forget his real name: we always called him Turkey, because his nose was
the colour of a turkey's egg. Who but Turkey knew mushrooms from
toadstools? Who but Turkey could detect earth-nuts – and that with the
certainty of a truffle-hunting dog? Who but Turkey knew the note and
the form and the nest and the eggs of every bird in the country? Who but
Turkey, with his little whip and its lash of brass wire, would encounter
the angriest bull in Christendom, provided he carried, like the bulls of
Scotland, his most sensitive part, the nose, forward?

In our eyes Turkey was a hero. Who but Turkey could discover
the nests of hens whose maternal anxiety had eluded the *finesse* of
Kirsty? and who so well as he could roast the egg with which she
always rewarded such a discovery? Words are feeble before the
delight we experienced on such an occasion, when Turkey, proceeding to light a fire against one of the earthen walls which divided the
fields, would send us abroad to gather sticks and straws and whatever
outcast combustibles we could find, of which there was a great
scarcity, there being no woods or hedges within reach. Who like
Turkey could rob a wild bee's nest? And who could be more just than
he in distributing the luscious prize? In fine, his accomplishments
were innumerable. Short of flying, we believed him capable of
everything imaginable.

6.   Perthshire 1880s

In the cottage an old couple were installed to bake for us, make butter
and grow vegetables. From the man I learned to milk. But we had no

duties, no tasks, no prohibitions. I can recall no single rule, injunction nor warning. A big brass bell was rung on the lawn to announce meals. Otherwise, except on Sundays, we followed our own devices. No matter how torn, bruised or muddy we might return we were subjected to none but helpful, immediately practical questioning. Scoldings and smacks were unknown, punishments rare and without spite. Neither in town nor in the country can I remember a single instance of ill-temper. It was shock in after-life to find that people otherwise well conditioned should get angry over trifles.

. . . In town we were dressed with care and expense, and – to me at least, for I did not well tolerate the slightest constriction – sometimes with acute malaise, especially on Sundays. Twice in the year we spent long, weary hours at the dressmaker, my mother having to be awakened at intervals, while my sister took the lead in choosing styles, colours, embroideries.

But at Mount Quharrie, except on Sundays, we discarded our mass of starched, frilled underclothes, and wore old sailor suits or check gingham frocks so that we might climb and scramble without danger except to our skins. The resumption of town clothes, expecially of shoes and stockings, used to cause me an affliction almost past bearing. For some weeks I felt trapped, harnessed, desperate; and the pavements hurt my feet. But a price had to be paid for the months of wild glory. Besides, when one grew accustomed to it again, Glasgow was not without its peculiar attractions which, if sordid, were possibly more conducive to mental development and to knowledge of the human world.

Even in town we were allowed the utmost freedom in almost every direction, and I cannot remember a time when we did not play in the streets as and with whom we pleased, so long as our comings and goings did not impinge on the simple home routine of meals, lessons, prayers and bedtime. We made our forays unburdened by warnings, moral instructions or questioning. So we were usually ready to babble of our doings. Glasgow, often known as 'the second city of the empire', might have been our village of Abernethy for all the nervousness displayed in trusting us to the life of the pavements.

In permitting such liberty as a matter of course, and in confiding in our decent behaviour, our parents followed a fashion of life once common but already discarded by those who prided themselves on gentility. Many, I think most, of the families in our acquaintance forbade their children the streets as a playground. We were sorry (and I still am) for these guarded children. They missed endless fun. And how we despised their parents.

We did not only play at tops, marbles, 'peever', hoop-running (insisting upon iron hoops and hooks to match those of our street boy friends), ball, and road games, each in their season and correct circumstance; we fought in gangs with peashooters and catapults, rode madly on a tricycle horse, tore about on roller skates or trundling a cane 'mail-cart' crammed with passengers; we coasted the steep hills on wheels or sledges. We fished down gratings for queer objects; we scoured waste lands, dodged policemen, hung on the back rails of horse trams, four-wheelers and lorries in the traffic of Sauchiehall Street. There were, of course, no motor vehicles, but the traffic was brisk. We followed with mimicry and absurd gestures any passer-by who appeared to us over-dressed or 'stuck-up'. I can still feel this impulse come over me at times in fashionable surroundings. Though we returned often with torn clothes and broken knees, and always with dirty faces, we never came to any serious accident. Nor did we ever choose to go farther than a quarter of a mile or so in any direction from our own doorstep. My own habit was to rush home at intervals, ring the front-door bell, inquire of the housemaid who opened it, 'Is Mother in?' – and on being told that she was – to run off again, as often as not without entering the house.

Later on, when we moved to a house in a west-end square with large railinged 'gardens' in the middle, I felt no desire to seek amusement in the formal and cultured space thus provided.

So far as street playing went, I must say that my parents were justified in their trustingness. We were often rude, and our companions, who were mostly boys and girls we should not otherwise have met, were as often both rude and rough. We trespassed, we sometimes came into conflict with the police. We fought pitched battles, encountered crude facts, learned to be wary. But there must have been far more vice, both flagrant and insidious, in my sister's expensive and 'select' Edinburgh boarding school, by her accounts, than in the maze of somewhat low thoroughfares and the very dark closes round Renfrew Street.

7.   Dumfriesshire *c.* 1900

After journeying over most of Scotland, England and central, southern and eastern Europe, as well as America, Siberia and China, I am of the opinion that 'my native place' – the Muckle Toon of Langholm, in Dumfriesshire – is the bonniest place I know: by virtue not of the little burgh in itself (though that has its treasurable aspects, and on nights when, as boys, we used to thread its dim streets playing 'Jock, Shine the Light', and race over the one bridge, past the factory, and over the other, with the lamp reflections wriggling like eels at intervals in the racing water, had an indubitable magic of its own), but by virtue of the wonderful variety and quality of the scenery in which it is set. The delights of sledging on the Lamb Hill or Murtholm Brae; of gathering hines in the Langfall; of going through the fields of Baggara hedged in honeysuckle and wild roses, through knee-deep meadow-sweet to the Scrog Nut Wood and gathering the nuts or crab-apples there; of blaeberrying on Warblaw or the Castle Hill; of dookin' and guddlin' or making islands in the Esk or Ewes or Wauchope and lighting stick fires on them and cooking potatoes in tin cans – these are only a few of the joys I knew, in addition to general ones of hill-climbing and penetrating the five glens which (each with its distinct character) converge upon or encircle the town – Eskdale, Wauchopedale, Tarrasdale, Ewesdale and, below the town Carlislewards, the Dean Banks.

As I grew into my early teens I ranged further afield, and soon all the Borders were within my ken. Many places had their special beauties or points of interest and advantage; but none had the variety of beauty centred round Langholm itself – none seemed so complete a microcosm of the entire Borderland. I knew where to find not only the common delights of hill and forest and waterside (and chiefest of all these to me were the chestnut trees at the sawmill – even now it thrills me to remember the beautiful chestnuts, large and luxurious as horses' eyes, which so surprisingly displayed themselves when we cracked open the prickly green shells, and I remember many huge strops of them I strung and a fierce competition at Conquerors), but also the various kinds of orchises, and butterwort, sundew, and the like; the various nests – including Terrona crags where ravens nested; how to deal with adders and smoke out wasp's 'bikes', and much other lore of that sort. In short, a boyhood full of country sights and sounds – healthy and happy and able to satisfy its hunger with juicy slices of a big yellow neep stolen from an adjoining field.

8.   Perthshire *c.* 1915

. . . We rowed on the loch in a rotten leaky boat; we traversed deep water on ice that threatened to give way at every timorous slip; we climbed out on the dead limbs of trees after birds' nests and later breathed with relief that the branch hadn't snapped under our weight and flung us thirty or forty feet to the ground.

Wet or dry, cold or warm, we had always several choices by way of recreation. I can remember no time when the feeling of having nothing to do or having nowhere to go hung heavily on our hands . . .

Perhaps we were young barbarians. We were incapable of polished manners. We knew nothing of social etiquette; we hated new clothes and the feeling of being dressed was purgatory. We weren't overmuch enamoured of soap and water. Our one sartorial ambition was to own and keep in good condition a great pair of tacketty steel-tipped boots and we preferred dubbin to boot polish. We loved an old jacket so that we could use every inch of space between the lining and the cloth to stuff away our equipment of string, nails, knives, wire, slings, peeries, bools, candle stumps, matches, bootlaces, magnifying glasses, boxes for birds' eggs and all the incredible junk we found so useful at one time or another. We had to be prepared for every contingency: climbing trees or barbed wire fences; crawling into the caverns of rhododendron clumps; cleaning turnips; mucking byres and loose boxes; riding in muddy carts; playing among clay, sand and lime; and generally no thought of clothes or cleanliness prevented us from indulging in whatever work, game or ploy took our fancy.

9. North-East Highlands *c.* 1910

. . . In this little Highland community young boys were not sent to bed early. Kenn was barely nine years old, and though he might be shouted at to take himself off at ten o'clock, he would often hang out till eleven. Last night it had been nearly midnight before sleep had curled him up in a corner of the kitchen, and his father had had to carry him to bed.

It was only when his mother's voice said something about the boats going away that he knew he must get up, so he muttered, 'What are you wanting?' His mother told him she wanted fresh water from the well. What an excuse for wakening a fellow! He could almost have cried. And when he did stagger out of bed and found from the greyness of the light that it could not be much more than six o'clock, his vexation became bitter. He stood in his shirt, whimpered moodily as he scratched himself, then slowly pulled on his trousers and his blue fisherman's gansey.

In the kitchen his father and mother were talking. He paid no attention to them but picked up the bright tin pail and made it clatter against the jamb of the door as he went out.

The dawn air was cold and the touch of frost on the ground was such a shock to his bare feet that he nearly cried out. He should have put on his boots, holed as they were. He hoped his parents were watching him through the window and seeing what he had to endure.

In this mood he arrived at the well, which was at the foot of a steep bank by the side of the river. Carelessly he bumped the pail down on the flat stone, and at the sound, as at a signal in a weird fairy tale, the whole world changed. His moodiness leapt right out of him and fear had him by the throat.

For from his very feet a great fish had started ploughing its way across the river, the king of fish, the living salmon.

Kenn had never seen a living salmon before, and of those he had seen dead this was beyond doubt the all-father.

When the waves faded out on the far side of the stream, where the bed was three feet deep, Kenn felt the great silence that lay upon the world and stood in the midst of it trembling like a hunted hare.

So intensely did he listen to the silence that he might well have caught a footfall a mile away. But there was no slightest sound anywhere. His eyes shot hither and thither, along horizons, down braes, across fields and wooded river-flats. No life moved; no face was watching.

Out of that noiseless world in the grey of the morning, all his ancestors came at him. They tapped his breast until the bird inside it fluttered madly; they drew a hand across his hair until the scalp crinkled; they made the blood within him tingle to a dance that had him leaping from boulder to boulder before he rightly knew to what desperate venture he was committed.

For it was all in a way a sort of madness. The fear was fear of the fish itself, of its monstrous reality, primal fear; but it was also infinitely complicated by fear of gamekeepers, of the horror and violence of law-courts, of our modern social fear. Not only did his hunting ancestors of the Caledonian Forest come at him, but his grown-up brothers and his brothers' friends, with their wild forays and epic stories, a constant running the gauntlet against enemy forces, for the glory of fun and laughter and daring – and the silver gift of the salmon. A thousand influences had his young body taut as a bow, when at last, bending over a boulder of the old red sandstone, he saw again the salmon.

Fear rose at him afresh, for there was a greyness in its dark-blue back that was menacing and ghostly. An apparition, an uncanny beast, from which instinct urged him to fly on tiptoe. The strength of his will holding him there brought a faint sickness to his throat. He could see the eyes on each side of the shapely head and knew the eyes must see him. Still as a rock and in some mysterious way as unheeding, the salmon lay beneath him. Slowly he drew his head back until at last the boulder shut off sight of the salmon and released his breath.

As before, he looked all around him, but now with a more conscious cunning. A pulse was spiriting in his neck. There was colour in his sensitive features and a feverish brilliance in the dark-brown eyes beneath the straight fringe of darker hair. Tiptoeing away from the boulder, he went searching downstream until he found a large flattish stone, and returned with it pressed against his stomach.

When he had got the best grip, he raised it above his head, and, staggering to the upper edge of the sandstone boulder, poised it in aim. Then he did not let it drop so much as contrive, with the last grain of his strength, to hurl it down on the fish.

Though untouched, the salmon was very clearly astonished and, before the stone had come to rest, had the pool in a splendid tumult . . .

It was a sea-trout rather than a salmon pool, as became apparent in that first blind rush, when the fish thrashed the water to froth in a terrific boil on top of the gravel bank, cleared the bank, and, with back fin showing, shot across the calm water towards the well where he had been resting. So headlong was his speed that he beached himself not two yards from Kenn's pail. Curving from nose to tail, the great body walloped the stones with resounding whacks. So hypnotised was Kenn by this extraordinary spectacle, that he remained stiff and powerless, but inwardly a madness was already rising in him, an urgency to rush, to hit, to kill. The salmon was back in the shallow water, lashing it, and in a moment, released, was coming straight for him. Right at his feet there was a swirl, a spitting of drops into his face. The fish saw him and, as if possessed by a thousand otters, flashed up the deep water and launched himself, flailing wildly, in the rushing shallows of the neck.

And then Kenn went into action, caution and fear forgotten. It was in truth a madness not unlike the salmon's. In his blind panic, the fish had no regard for bodily stress; in his blind exaltation, neither had Kenn.

Less than a hundred yards beyond the shallows of the neck was a long dark pool, and in it lay escape. If the brute had been calm, been travelling by night, it could have made the passage with ease. But now, having lost its head, it defeated itself with its own strength and added to its panic by bashing its nose against boulders.

Kenn approached the scene with such speed that before one toe could slip on slime the other was forward to thrust him on. Landing knee-deep in the final jump, he tore a stone from the bed of the stream and, blinded by the salmon's lashings, let drive.

He missed by over a foot and there followed a jumble in which, in his excitement, he not only threw guttural challenges but lunged fiercely and recklessly, to be left grovelling on his back as the salmon shot downward.

In his leap for the bank Kenn stumbled and was thrown severely. But he had no consciousness of pain; only of loss of time, of awful fear lest the salmon should escape.

And running down the bank it seemed to him as if the salmon had escaped. No trace of 'way' on the pool. Nothing . . . Was that a swirl – far down? Making his way out of the pool!

On his toes again, Kenn sped downward, came in below the fish, and picking up a stone half the size of his head, went straight to the attack.

The water was now growing narrower and deeper, but it was tortured by boulders and sloping flagstones. The passage to the sea was easy and hardly half a mile long, but Kenn complicated the boulder pattern by adding with violence small boulders of his own. Twice the salmon flashed past him, and now Kenn was not merely wading into the water, but falling and crawling and choking in it, yet ever with his dark head rising indomitably.

. . . A rush and a heave and the salmon bared his girth on a sloping flagstone. From the bottom, Kenn had raked a stone barely the size of his small fist, but he threw it with all his vigour and it scored a first direct hit by stinging smartly blue cheek against red gills.

Back off the flagstone came the salmon with his nose pointing upstream, and he followed his nose. At the best of times it is awkward for a salmon to go downstream, but upstream, given depth and shoulder room, speed becomes a frenzy. This fish turned it into a debauch and reached the well pool like a demented torpedo.

Kenn had chosen his battleground and laid down the conditions of the fight.

*

And it was a saga of a fight, for of all that befell Kenn afterwards, of war and horror and love and scientific triumphs, nothing ever had quite the splendour and glory of that struggle by the Well Pool, while the tin pail that the tinkers had made watched with bright face from the kneeling-stone and his mother, murmuring in her anger, put last night's water in the kettle.

For Kenn had no weapons of attack other than his little fists and what they could grab from the river bottom; no rod, hook, net, or implement of constraint or explosion. It was a war between an immature human body on the one side, and a superbly matured body of incredible swiftness and strength on the other. In physical length, laid out side by side, there would have been little difference between them.

But neither of them was laid out yet! Indeed so far there had been little more than the courteous slap on the cheek as gauge of battle, and it had been delivered by Kenn.

The initial strategy, however, for such warfare was his, not from learning or experience but out of instinct, and it could be summed up in the words 'keep him on the run'. All his tactics brought this about as their natural result, whether he was careering wildly up and down the bank, pausing to hurl a stone, or dashing into shallows to get at close quarters. The frenzy of both had first to be worn down, before the cunning brain could stalk the tired body.

. . . several times Kenn had his heart in his mouth when it seemed that the salmon had altogether vanished. In the dark shadow of a leaning stone where the amber water gurgled past, a dark-blue back was but a darker shadow. Then Kenn would spot the tail or the curve of the nose or the pallor of a fin; would be overcome with an emotion keener in its thrust than ever; would back away and hunt his stone. Splash! and the salmon was on its journey once more, betrayed by its great size.

This phase of the battle went on for a long time, until Kenn knew all the resting places and there began to grow in him a terrible feeling of power, terrible in its excitement, in his realisation that he might be successful, and even more terrible in its longing.

There came a time when Kenn, having got the fish resting where he wanted him, went downstream to choose his stone, but no longer in blind urgency. He handled two or three before lifting one against his breast.

The salmon lay by the outer edge of a greenish underwater slab. By approaching it on a slant towards its tail, he could keep its head out of sight. Warily he did this until he came to the edge of the stream. But now he knew that however he stooped while wading in, the eyes would be disclosed. He did not hesitate; he let himself down into the water and, the stone against his stomach, slithered over the gravelly bottom on his stern. It was an autumn morning, after a night of hoarfrost, but when the water got fully about his body he felt it warm. Foot by foot he thrust himself on, until at last the could have put out a hand and touched the tail; and the tail was as deep as his face and as taut.

Slowly he reared up on his knees, fighting down the sinking sensation that beset him, his hands fiercely gripping the stone. Anxiety now started shouting in him to heave the stone and be done, but, though trembling, he rose with infinite care, little by little, disclosing the back fin, the nape of the neck where the otter bites, and at last the near eye. The fish did not move. Inch by inch the stone went up until at last his own eyes were looking from underneath it. Then in one thrust he launched stone and body at the fish.

The thud of the stone on the great back was a sound of such

potency that even in that wild drenching moment it sang above all else. For the stone had landed; the stone had got him! Spewing the river water forth, stumbling and falling, he reached the bank. Then both of them went berserk.

This great fish had not the slippery cunning, the evasiveness of a small salmon or grilse. It tore around like a bull in a ring. Kenn began to score direct hits more and more often. He was learning the way. He could throw a stone ahead; he could madden; he could stalk warily and hear ever more exultingly the stinging thud.

The fatal part for a salmon is the nape of the neck. The time came when Kenn landed there heavily with the narrow stone edge; the salmon circled and thrashed as if half paralysed or blinded; Kenn with no more stones at hand launched a body attack and received one wallop from the tail that sent him flat on his back; the salmon was off again.

The end came near the neck of the pool on the side opposite the well. Here the low bank of the river widened out into a grassy field. The tired fish, with pale mouth gaping every now and then, went nosing into shallow water, where some upended flagstones might provide a new and dark retreat. But there was no hidden retreat there and Kenn, well down the pool, waited with wild hope. If it lay anywhere thereabouts until he got up, it would be finished! And it lay.

It actually lay in full view between two stone edges, its back fin barely covered. Kenn hit it as it moved and then fell on it.

His hands went straight for the gills; one found a grip under a cheek, the other, slipping, tried for a hold on the body, and there and then began the oddest tussle that that river could ever have seen.

Under the burning grip of human hands, the salmon went frantic and threw Kenn about as if he were a streamer tied to its neck; the upended stones bashed his arms, his legs, the back of his head; the bony cheek dug into his wrist; but nothing could now dim the relentless instinct in him to roll both bodies from the shallow water on to dry land.

And this in time he accomplished. When his hand was shot from behind the cheek it drew gills with it.

The salmon flailed the dry stones with desperate violence, but Kenn was now in his own element, and ever he brought his body behind the body of the fish and shored it upwards, thrusting at the gills until his hands were lacerated and bleeding.

He dragged that fish over fifty yards into the grass park before he laid it down. And when it heaved in a last convulsive shudder, he at once fell upon it as if the river of escape still lapped its tail.

And now on this busy morning, angered against him for not returning with the well water, [his mother] suddenly saw him rounding the corner of the house towards the door of the back porch, face down, hands knotted behind his head, dripping wet and staggering. The salmon's nose was under his right ear, its tail was sweeping the ground behind. She gave way to him as he lurched in. Releasing his crooked fingers and heaving with a shoulder, he set the great fish with a mighty thump on the smooth blue flagstone at her feet . . .

She looked at the frightening size of the fish on the floor; she looked at her son. His dark hair was flattened to rat tails; his brown eyes were black against the excited pallor of his face; water seeped from his clothes; his body seemed no longer boyish but immature and fragile, his bones thin brittle stalks. Yet there was a flame, an intolerant fighting spirit, that knit him together, and separated him from her in a way that suddenly pulled at her heart.

She looked back to the fish and whispered, 'Where did you get that?'

10.   Edinburgh 1920s

Sandy had the feeling at the time that they were supposed to be the happiest days of her life, and on her tenth birthday she said so to her best friend Jenny Gray who had been asked to tea at Sandy's house. The speciality of the feast was pineapple cubes with cream, and the speciality of the day was that they were left to themselves. To Sandy the unfamiliar pineapple had the authentic taste and appearance of happiness and she focused her small eyes on the pale gold cubes before she scooped them up in her spoon, and she thought the sharp taste on her tongue was that of a special happiness, which was nothing to do with eating, and was different from the happiness of play that one enjoyed unawares. Both girls saved the cream to the last, then ate it in spoonfuls.

'Little girls, you are going to be the the the crème de la crème,' said Sandy, and Jenny spluttered her cream into her handkerchief.

'You know,' Sandy said, 'these are supposed to be the happiest days of our lives.'

'Yes, they are always saying that,' Jenny said. 'They say, make the most of your schooldays because you never know what lies ahead of you.'

'Miss Brodie says prime is best,' Sandy said.

'Yes, but she never got married like our mothers and fathers.'

'They don't have primes,' said Sandy.

'They have sexual intercourse,' Jenny said.

The little girls paused, because this was still a stupendous thought, and one which they had only lately lit upon; the very phrase and its meaning were new. It was quite unbelievable. Sandy said, then, 'Mr Lloyd had a baby last week. He must have committed sex with his wife.' This idea was easier to cope with and they laughed screamingly into their pink paper napkins. Mr Lloyd was the Art master to the Senior girls.

'Can you *see* it happening?' Jenny whispered.

Sandy screwed her eyes even smaller in the effort of seeing with her mind. 'He would be wearing his pyjamas,' she whispered back.

The girls rocked with mirth, thinking of one-armed Mr Lloyd, in his solemnity, striding into the school.

Then Jenny said, 'You do it on the spur of the moment. That's how it happens.'

Jenny was a reliable source of information, because a girl employed by her father in his grocer shop had recently been found to be pregnant, and Jenny had picked up some fragments of the ensuing fuss. Having confided her finds to Sandy, they had embarked on a course of research which they called 'research', piecing together clues from remembered conversations illicitly overheard, and passages from the big dictionaries.

'It all happens in a flash,' Jenny said. 'It happened to Teenie when she was out walking at Puddocky with her boy friend. Then they had to get married.'

'You would think the urge would have passed by the time she got her *clothes* off,' Sandy said. By 'clothes' she definitely meant to imply 'knickers', but 'knickers' was rude in this scientific context.

'Yes, that's what I can't understand,' said Jenny.

Sandy's mother looked round the door and said, 'Enjoying yourselves, darlings?' Over her shoulder appeared the head of

Jenny's mother. 'My word,' said Jenny's mother, looking at the tea-table, 'they've been tucking in!'

Sandy felt offended and belittled by this; it was as if the main idea of the party had been the food.

'What would you like to do now?' Sandy's mother said.

Sandy gave her mother a look of secret ferocity which meant: you promised to leave us all on our own, and a promise is a promise, you know it's very bad to break a promise to a child, you might ruin all my life by breaking your promise, it's my birthday.

Sandy's mother backed away bearing Jenny's mother with her. 'Let's leave them to themselves,' she said. 'Just enjoy yourselves, darlings.'

Sandy was sometimes embarrassed by her mother being English and calling her 'darling', not like the mothers of Edinburgh who said 'dear'. Sandy's mother had a flashy winter coat trimmed with fluffy fox fur like the Duchess of York's, while other mothers wore tweed or, at the most, musquash that would do them all their days.

HOMES FROM HOME

taken from

The Home was commenced in a large room in Renfrew Lane, intended for a workshop, a kitchen partitioned off and the bare brick walls brightened with Scripture texts, etc. On the 18th of November, 1871, the first boy, jacketless and shoeless, came in. We well remember his suspicious look as he inquired whether any more boys would sleep there that night for, if not, he would rather go back to the [Shoe-Black] Brigade. Enticed by the genial warmth of the fire, stripped of his dripping rags, and comfortably clothed, he soon began to feel more at home. But Andrew had no love for solitude, and, in a day or two, he gladly welcomed his first companion, Willie D., a poor orphan boy in a miserable state of rags and vermin. Looking as he is now, bright and happy, though somewhat hasty still, we can hardly realise that it is the same boy whose fearful outbursts of passion, in those early days of our work, filled us with dismay.

. . . It was a great pleasure to the boys when the first little girl was brought into the home, Sarah P., a poor, frightened-looking child of six, who all day long had been shut in a room alone since her mother's death three months before. [Another girl], Maggie T., was a little *Citizen* seller of ten years of age, shaggy and uncouth, but with a yearning to be loved and cared for that made her beg to be taken in weeks before we could do so. There are two little sisters, Helen and Isabella M., whose story is a very touching one. Their father was killed some two years ago, when employed building the new College, and, strangely enough, their mother dropped down dead when cleaning one of the rooms of the same building a few weeks ago. The passionate grief of Helen (nine years old) when brought in was very sad to see, and she is still suffering in health from what she then passed through, though much comforted now by the presence of the little four-year-old, Bella, and by feeling that she is again in a real home. One day she brought tears to the Matron's eyes by telling how the minister broke to her the news of her mother's death, saying the Good Shepherd had taken her mother home to Himself, but if she loved Him He would take care of her. 'And it has come true,' Helen said, 'for He had brought me here.'

One of our boys had, for three weeks after his mother's death, wandered homeless in the streets, sleeping on stairs, till he was found at a mission meeting, crying with hunger, and brought to the Home. Two others had been 'dawsing', *i.e.*, 'sleeping out' among the egg boxes on the quay, when they heard of the Home, and begged to be taken in. Two brothers and a sister were brought by a Bible-woman from the High Street, so attenuated with starvation that we could hardly look at them without tears.

2.   North-East 1920s

The Orphanage of Skeyne folds itself back from the main road, withdrawing into a huddle of trees. Tall trees, top-heavy and shaggy with crow's nests, loud with their rancour. Trees that shuddered and whined throughout Janie's first night in the Orphanage, twining their shadows across the walls of the dormitory.

It had been a long day. Still spring. But it seemed to have been spring in Grandmother's country ages ago. A white, quiet spring, then. Now it was loud and yellow. The glare of daffodils crowding out the Orphanage garden still beat hotly under Janie's heavy eyelids; the smell of them hovered through her senses. The suddenness of their impact had imprinted itself in her being. I'll never smell a daffodil in all my life again without minding how I first saw the Orphanage.

So many things lay in mind. Urgent, elusive scraps. The sense of lostness when the train screamed past Loch Na Boune, the last known landmark in Janie's world. Screaming out of time and place altogether. I'm leaving my Mam. I'm leaving my Mam, it had panted. A loud thing in a living hurry. The places it had flashed through focusing in fragments now. Bending boulders like old men groping round a high hill. Dead Man's Bells fleeing whitely from their own wood, shivering down the banks, bowing the train out and past. OYNE in big white letters on a small, black station. A strange name for a place, the only name I remember now. I'm sure I saw it though. Some day I'll go back to see if it's real.

All things seemed unreal to Janie. The dormitory most of all. She looked anxiously over to the chair beside her bed. Her new hat lay

safely. So huge that it hid her small bundle of underclothes. She felt
her head, still with a small sense of shock, although it had been shaved
hours ago, after she left the Courthouse. This morning. Or was it
yesterday morning? Time had leapt out of bounds. She lay trying to
catch time and return it to its proper place. Its hours eluded her. How
enviably Peggy's long hair scattered itself on the pillow there. If I got
one wish I'd just ask for all my hair back again. No I wouldn't. I'd just
ask to get home to my Mam again. Not having any hair wouldn't
matter if I could just get home again.

But home lay too raw and tender to the piercing touch of thought
yet. There was escape from thought in listening to the whispers flitting
frighteningly like small bats through the dim dormitory.

'Did you have to read the inscription above the front door, Janie?'
'Yes.'

'You've got to remember it by heart as well, though.'

'I do. "Proctor's Orphan Training Home 1891".'

'If ever you don't do your work right, Mrs Thane will take you
round to the front door to read it again.'

'She makes you say "training" three times. That's so you'll never
forget.'

'And you've got to learn Table Manners off the Card as well, Janie.
But you'll get a week to learn them in.'

'I've learned a bit of them already:-

> *I must not talk about my food,*
> *Nor fret if I don't think it good.*'

'Do you know something, Janie? We get porridge for breakfast
every morning except Sundays.'

'And we get fish on Sundays. Haddocks. I just can't abide them.
You get an egg on Easter Sunday, though, Janie.'

'And an egg on Christmas morning. Don't forget, Peggy, we get an
egg on Christmas morning.'

A panic seized Janie and forced her upright in bed:

'When will I get home? I've asked everybody. The Court Man and
the Vigilance Officer and Mrs Thane and just everybody. They all let
on they don't hear me. But somebody must know *when*?'

'When you're sixteen, most likely.' Peggy's casualness distressed
Janie. 'At least that's when I'm getting home. When I'm sixteen.'

'But that's ages!' Janie's distress increased. 'That's just years and years. I'm not nine yet. Not till October. I'll have to stay here for eight years.'

'Only seven and a half years, Janie,' Peggy corrected. 'If you're eight and a half now.'

'But it's still years and years.' Janie was disconsolate. 'My Mam could die by that time.'

3.   North-East *c.* 1930

The clock was changed, the dark nights came, and gases were lit in the dayrooms. Meta and I sat together, her jaws going munch, munch on my jammy crusts, while I licked my lips, pretending not to be hungry, and listened to the girls singing.

> 'I am a poor wee orphanage girl,
> My mother she is dead,
> My father he is far away
> And cannot buy me bread.
> Alone I stand at the window
> To hear the church bells ring,
> God bless my dear old mother,
> She's dead and in her grave.
> Ding, dong, my castle bell!
> Farewell, my mother!
> Bury me in the old churchyard
> Beside my eldest brother . . .'

We always sang in the evenings. The gases burned green, the black windows showed nothing but our own scared reflections, and our songs were about fearful things, as we got on with our eternal mending. Our hands were muffled in long black stockings, our darning needles flicked silver, and one song followed another as the gas hissed and the fire died down towards eight o'clock.

We did not pause in our darning. The knitting women at the guillotine could not have been more intent. We were not consciously miserable in our singing, but we could not get away from blood and grief.

'But something wi' ma hert gaed wrang.
A vessel burst, and blood outsprang.
My days on earth will no' be lang,
For noo's my time, and I maun gang.'

By this time, we had worked ourselves into a fine emotional mood. Ham actors, the lot of us, we sang on our knees, our hands stretched out appealingly.

'There are many, sad and weary,
In this pleasant world of ours,
Crying every night so sadly,
"Won't you buy my pretty flowers?"'

'I stabbed her and I stabbed her
Till the blood did overflow,
And buried her body
In the valley below.'

And, for sheer haunting inanity,

'Last night in Tokyo,
I met a man without a toe.
His toe was sore, he cried no more,
Last night in Tokyo.'

The reason for this preoccupation with death and dying lay, I think, in our collective past. Our music was just what one would expect from deprived and cloistered humanity. Even the more fortunate children were influenced by something beyond them, some mass memory which brought to their minds terrors they had never known . . .

The gas flared, it was time to put away our mending, and go down the dark passages to bed, under the fish-tail burners, in and out of the pools of shadow; and late at night, when the matrons had gone to their rooms, and the doors were locked, so that we couldn't escape, Miss McKee, the Lady Superintendent, would pace the corridors, turning out the gases, one by one – how did we *know* it was Miss McKee? And

what would happen when the last jet dwindled to black? Someone
with black gloves would go creep, creep, turning the gases on again,
but *not lighting them* . . .

> Oh – !
> I want to go home!
> I want to go home!
> I'm no gonnie stay in the orphanage no more,
> The place where the matrons are always indoor.
> Take me over the sea.
> The matron'll never catch me.
> Oh my, I think I shall die
> If you don't *take me home*!'

4.   1960s/1970s

CHAPTER SIX: THE TELLING PART

Ma mammy bot me oot a shop
Ma mammy says I was a luvly baby

Ma mammy picked me (I wiz the best)
your mammy had to take you (she'd no choice)

Ma mammy says she's no really ma mammy
(just kid on)

It's a bit like a part you've rehearsed so well
you can't play it on the opening night
She says my real mammy is away far away
Mammy why aren't you and me the same colour
But I love my mammy whether she's real or no
My heart started rat tat tat like a tin drum
all the words took off to another planet
Why

But I love ma mammy whether she's real or no

I could hear the upset in her voice
I say *I'm not your real mother*,
though Christ knows why I said that,
If I'm not who is, but all my planned speech
went out the window

She took me when I'd nowhere to go
my mammy is the best mammy in the world OK.

After mammy telt me she wisnae my real mammy
I was scared to death she was gonnie melt
or something or mibbe disappear in the dead
of night and somebody would say she wis a fairy
godmother. So the next morning I felt her skin
to check it was flesh, but mibbe it was just
a good imitation. How could I tell if my mammy
was a dummy with a voice spoken by someone else?
So I searches the whole house for clues
but I never found nothing. Anyhow a day after
I got my guinea pig and forgot all about it.

I always believed in the telling anyhow.
You can't keep something like that secret
I wanted her to think of her other mother
out there, thinking that child I had will be
seven today eight today all the way up to
god knows when. I told my daughter –
I bet your mother's never missed your birthday,
how could she?

Mammy's face is cherries.
She is stirring the big pot of mutton soup
singing *I gave my love a cherry*
it had no stone.
I am up to her apron.
I jump onto her feet and grab her legs
like a huge pair of trousers,
she walks round the kitchen lifting me up.

Suddenly I fall off her feet.
And mammy falls to the floor.
She won't stop the song
I gave my love a chicken it had no bone.
I run next door for help.
When me and Uncle Alec come back
Mammy's skin is toffee stuck to the floor.
And her bones are all scattered like toys.

Now when people say 'ah but
it's not like having your own child though is it',
I say of course it is, what else is it?
she's my child, I have told her stories
wept at her losses, laughed at her pleasures,
she is mine.

I was always the first to hear her in the night
all this umbilical knot business is nonsense
– the men can afford deeper sleep that's all.
I listened to hear her talk,
and when she did I heard my voice under hers
and now some of her mannerisms crack me up

Me and my best pal
don't have Donny Osmond or David Cassidy
on our walls and we don't wear Starsky and Hutch
jumpers either. Round at her house we put on
the old record player and mime to Pearl Bailey
Tired of the life I lead, tired of the blues I breed
and Bessie Smith I can't do without my kitchen man.
Then we practice ballroom dancing giggling,
everyone thinks we're dead old-fashioned.

FOOD AND CLOTHES

taken from

1.   Edinburgh mid-nineteenth century

. . . with two intact silver shillings in his hand, Cleg went and bought
twopence worth of meat from the neck and a penny bone for boiling, a
pennyworth of carrots, a halfpenny cabbage, a large four-pound loaf,
and twopence worth of the best milk. To this he added two apples and
an orange for Hugh, so that he might have a foretaste of the golden
time when dadda should come home.

2.   Aberdeenshire 1914–1918

I have no recollection of the rationing of bacon, but then I have only
the remotest recollection of bacon itself; it was always at the other end
of the table on my father's plate. It was one of those things you
graduated to when you were grown up. Until then you had to be
content with an occasional slice of bread fried in the fat from your
father's bacon. I am not sure indeed that the word 'bacon' was even in
my vocabulary then; it was an English-sounding word, a bit foreign. I
think that anything that came from a pig, if it was not trotters, brains or
pork, was to us just ham. Pig's trotters or brains were not, however, on
our menu.

So there you have a picture of my father with his bacon at one end
of the table and me at the other without. I must quickly add, however,
that this does not show my father up as being a mean man, but rather a
combination of Victorian parent and Calvinist or, perhaps, vestigial
Plymouth Brother . . . Father had his own special gooseberry-bush
with bigger berries than any of the other bushes in the garden and they
tasted better than any of the others if only because when you helped
yourself to one it was as good as an apple stolen from the laird's walled
garden. When the strawberry jam was running low, he was the one for
whom the last jar or two was reserved. But all this did not denote
selfishness unadulterated; it was the way things went in a society that
had not ceased to be patriarchal. And now that I think of it – and this is
one of the insights that writing these books brings – it was never he

who referred to these privileges. He never spoke about 'my gooseberry bush', 'my strawberry jam', or 'my ham'; it was always Mother who would say 'Hoo aften have I tell't ye tae leave yer father's gooseberry bush alane!' or 'No. There's nae strawberry jam for ye the day. That's the last jar and it's yer father's' or 'Ay, it dis smell fine. A'll pit a slice o' loaf in't for frying aifter yer father has had 'is ham.'

Nor would I have you think that we children went hungry while Father lived on the ham of the land. We did not. Mother would have regarded herself as failing in her duty if at dinner-time she had not cooked enough for anyone who wanted it to have a second helping. Sometimes the second helping was of something re-cooked, not merely re-heated, from the day before. I preferred food that had been cooked twice. Father on the other hand would as soon have eaten a raw onion as touch anything that had been cooked for two days running.

3.   Perthshire *c.* 1915

There was always plenty of food at Tulliallan. Having the dairy, there were always lashings of milk and cream and butter. Sir James Sievewright and his friends may have gone short of these [due to wartime rationing?], but the dairymaid's family never.

Mother made food part of her religion. She insisted on us eating the maximum of plain wholesome food and had nothing but contempt, in those days, for 'they dirt o' cakes and buns'. She had a love of words that Sir Thomas Urquhart would have delighted in. The delicacies of the confectioners' and bakers' arts she described as 'turks and pasheries'.

She was an excellent baker of scones and baked every day. She excelled in oatcakes, soda scones, treacle scones, sweet scones, potato scones, potato-meal scones and pancakes. When the table was heaped up with these at meal times it literally groaned. I'd give a lot to taste again those potato scones fried for breakfast. The kind the shops sell taste as if they had been made with floor sweepings: and mostly are.

There was never much butcher meat in the house: that couldn't be afforded. But occasionally there was mince; and herring new drawn frae the Forth were plentiful in season. And there was always a side of bacon and home-made white puddings.

But what need was there for meat when to half-a-dozen big mealy potatoes could be added a quarter of a pound of good butter – the whole washed down with a half-pint of rich fresh milk? And when the potatoes were preceded by a plateful of thick Scotch broth, pea, lentil or chicken soup and rounded off with a plate of baked rice swimming in melted golden butter to which a gill of rich skimmed cream was added, it will be understood that butcher meat would have been little short of an impertinence.

4.   North-East 1920s

Mealtimes held another ever-present fear – that of not getting enough to eat. At the Home Farm – the one that existed for the sole purpose of supplying the castle with produce – the fat cows lowed in their stalls, letting down steady streams of rich, creamy milk, while in the five-acre kitchen garden, gardeners laboured over regimented lines of peas and beans, lettuces and cucumbers and asparagus, cabbages and spinach. Raspberries and strawberries and plums and damsons and cherries and grapes poured into the castle every summer morning, carried shoulder-high by barefoot garden boys, while in the shooting season the gamekeepers, their tweed breeches stained by the blood of their victims, impaled on the sharp hooks of the game larder the delicately-muscled legs of deer and hare, and hung, on nails hammered into the rafters, great clusters of pheasant, partridge, snipe, duck and grouse; the dead birds' heads, beaks agape, lolled sideways, the cords that circled the radiantly-feathered throats giving each plump body an undeserved air of pendulated felony. Salmon were hauled from the river – struggling on the pointed steel of the gaffs – with such frequency that servants, disdaining the tender pink flesh, insisted that their contracts of service included a clause guaranteeing that salmon would not be served to them more than once a week. Towards the sea rolled the fields of oats, to be ground in autumn between the flat stones of the village mill; in winter, potatoes and turnips and carrots lay heaped in earth-covered mounds, while all the year round pigs and calves died, protesting noisily, in murky farmyard pens. Almost all this activity was for the purpose of feeding the people in the castle, yet we children seemed perpetually hungry. Our mother never took all six of us to the same children's party, partly because, if there were competitions, our sheer exuberance caused us to carry off an unfair share of the prizes, but also because between us we would have wolfed down all the trifles and jellies and éclairs. But it never seemed to occur to her that we might have welcomed more food at home.

At luncheon in the dining room, the hall-boy would carry in a tray of heavy silver dishes, and the butler and footmen, one behind the other would advance on the table. As the first dish was handed to my mother, six anxious pairs of eyes would assess the quantity that it held. Nine small rissoles of leftover meat. Well, at least that was fair – one each (our governess ate lunch with us). Then came the potatoes – misery, there were only sixteen. Which of us would get two, and which only one? My mother took a single potato – oh, good. But then my father took four, and gloom descended on those children who were waiting to be served after him. Even the quantity of green peas was avidly estimated, and though we would never have dared to complain while actually at table, the post mortems that took place after meals were acrimonious.

'You took two spoonfuls of peas – I saw you!'

'I didn't.'

'You *did*.'

'Well, perhaps I *did* have a very small second spoonful, but some of my first spoonful were maggotty.'

'Greedy pig.'

'I'm *not*.'

'You *are*.'

And everyone would fall on the floor, fighting.

My parents, who had our welfare very much at heart, cannot have intended us to go hungry, but my mother's upbringing had been very religious and had instilled into her a firm conviction that it was sinful to pay attention to such wordly things as food. She had been taught that a true Christian ate what was put in front of him and thanked God for it both before and after the meal; to question the taste of what one ate – or, worse, to be interested in the quantity – was almost as wicked as studying one's own face in the glass to find out whether or not one was pretty. As for my father, he thought that to be greedy showed weakness of character – something not to be tolerated either in oneself or in one's children.

At our table, food was never wasted. 'Eat up, child,' my father commanded, if one of us should leave a bit of gristle or fat. (He hardly ever addressed us by name, and when he did he as often as not used the wrong one.) Mournfully, the culprit would force the unappetising morsel into his mouth; if my father suspected that it was not actually swallowed but simply parked behind a tooth to be spat out later, he would order the child to open his mouth for inspection.

What we lacked at luncheon or dinner, though, we made up at the more informal meals of breakfast and tea. Dining room breakfast began with porridge, liberally doused with cream; after the porridge, one could take one's pick of eggs, bacon, finnan haddie, sausages, kedgeree or grilled kidneys served from lidded silver dishes warmed by heating lamps, and finish with baps or toast or oatcakes, spread thickly with butter and home-made marmalade. Tea was equally lavish. Although between the six of us we were only allowed one cake a week – this vanishing, down to the last crumb, within minutes of being put on the table – there was always an ample supply of freshly baked scones and drop-scones, sticky treacly bread and large biscuits known, because of the raisins and sultanas they contained, as 'squashed flies'. Both at breakfast and tea – except for my mother and the governess – everyone, incuding my father, drank milk.

5.   1767

OF BEHAVIOUR AT MEALS

1. NOTHING shews the Difference between a young Gentleman and a vulgar Boy so much as the Behaviour in eating.
2. Know the Time of Dinner, and be ready a Quarter of an Hour before.
3. Never come to the Table hot, nor in a hurry.
4. Be in the Room dressed, and ready before the Company come in.
5. Advance to the Table when Grace is to be said, and go to the Lower End.

10. Never attempt to help yourself to any Thing.
11. Do not ask till you see the Company are all helped; then, if it happens you have been forgot, you will be served.
12. Whatever is given you, be satisfied it is good, and desire no other.

13. Eat soberly and decently; and take great care to be cleanly.

14. Never speak when you are eating.

15. If you want any Thing of the Servant, wait till he is at Leisure; never call when he is waiting on some other Person.

16. Eat with your Knife and Fork, and never touch your Meat with your Fingers.

17. Never eat large Mouthfuls, nor greedily.

18. Never desire more, after your Parents tell you, you have enough.

20. Eat silently and decently, not making a Noise with your Lips, or Mouth, as vulgar Boys do.

22. Wipe your Mouth often, that it be not greasy; and lay your Knife and Fork upon your Plate, that you do not soil the Cloth.

23. Cut your Bread, and break it, for it is vulgar to bite or gnaw it.

24. Take Salt with the Salt Spoon, or else with a clean Knife, not with that you are eating with, for that will foul the rest.

25. Sit upright in your Chair; and never loiter in it, nor lean upon the Table.

26. Do not laugh at Table, much less sneeze, cough, or yawn; but if you cannot avoid it, hold up the Napkin, or Table Cloth, before your Face, and turn aside from the Table.

27. If what is given you be too hot, wait patiently for its cooling, that you may eat it with Decency.

28. Pick Bones clean, and leave them on your Plate; they must not be thrown down, nor given to Dogs in the Room.

29. In eating Fruit, do not swallow the Stones, but lay them on one Side of your Plate, laying one of the Leaves that came with the Fruit over them.

30. When you drink, bow to some one of the Company, and say, Sir, or Madam.

31. Stoop a little to your Plate as you take each Mouthful; it prevents greasing yourself or the Cloth.

32. Never regard what another has on his Plate; it looks as if you wanted it.

33. Do not fix your Eyes upon those who are eating; it is unmannerly.

34. Before you drink entirely empty your Mouth, and do the same before you speak.

35. Always wipe your Mouth as soon as you have drank.

36. Chew your Meat well before you swallow it; but do this decently without making Faces.

37. Let one Mouthful be swallowed before you take up another.

38. If a Bone hurts your Mouth, or any Thing sticks in your Teeth, hold up your Napkin with your Left-Hand while you take it away with the other.

39. When you have dined with Cleanliness, get up with Decency; you are not to sit at the Table so long as the Company.

40. When you are got from your Seat make a bow, and go to the Servant, who will lead you out of the Room, unless it is the Pleasure of your Parents you should stay longer.

6.   Oban 1950s

We all come home for dinner. That's our main meal. Mashed potatoes and something. Mince or grated cheese or corned beef or fish, with tinned peas on the side and bread to fill up with. Sometimes the potatoes are put through the strainer and made into soup with tinned tomatoes or leeks, and grated cheese on top. My father can eat four plates of that. I like it too, but it's disastrous if we have gym in the afternoon. It disappears and leaves you gibbering with hunger. I keep telling my mother, but she can never remember which days we have gym. Most of all I hate it when my mother makes rehash. That's her word for anything made out of yesterday's dinner with something added – a tin of mixed vegetables or spaghetti or beans, or Sunday's meat put through the mincer. For pudding they eat something milky (custard or rice or semolina) with stewed apples or rhubarb or tinned mandarins or guavas. I only like the mandarins but my granny loves her pudding. She used to make fiendish things like bread-and-butter pudding or treacle tart, but nowadays she can barely manage custard – sometimes it's all watery with lumps. Not that I care anyway. She can't understand why I won't eat milk puddings. Whatever's the matter with Mary Jane, she isn't sick and she hasn't a pain and there's lovely rice-pudding for dinner again, whatever's the matter with Mary Jane. If she says that once again I'll murder her.

For tea it's usually whatever's in the cupboard. Eggs, spaghetti on toast, sardines, tomato fritters, mock crab, toasted cheese. I'm sure Real People don't have things like that. They have lamb chops and black pudding and tattie scones and dumpling. And plain bread. Personally I could live on tomatoes boiled in marge but There's Absolutely No Nutritional Value in That, Mary. Sometimes on a Sunday afternoon my mother makes pancakes on the girdle. I love that. It makes me feel like she's a Proper Mother. I always make wee totty pancakes round the edges, and we usually have them all eaten up before they can reach the table. You can use preserved eggs in pancakes. You can't risk boiling them. My mother also makes jam – bramble and apple, strawberry, plum, goose-gog, marmalade, lemon curd. But I don't like jam very much. Or lemon curd. I'd rather eat the fruit. In the summer holidays I make the puddings . . . The first time I made a rhubarb pie I put a plastic egg-cup in the middle instead of china, and it melted. My brother nearly killed himself laughing. I was terribly upset.

7.   St Kilda nineteenth and twentieth centuries

Breakfast normally consisted of porridge and milk, with a puffin boiled in with the oats to give flavour. The main meal of the day, taken at about lunch-time, comprised potatoes and the flesh of fulmars.

Nearly all the food on Hirta had to be boiled or stewed. To the outsider, food tasted rather bland, and a lack of proper fuel meant that it was usually undercooked and never served very hot. The flesh of the fulmar is white. In the older birds, it is a mixture of fat and meat, while the young birds are nearly all fat. When cooked, the fulmar tasted somewhat like beef, and Heathcote, having eaten a meal with the St Kildans [1900–1901], remarked, 'I must say we were agreeably surprised. We had expected something nasty, but it was not nasty. It was oleaginous, but distinctly tasty.'

'The gannets we ate,' recalls Neil Ferguson (1855), 'tasted fishy and salty.' Like the fulmar, the gannet was normally salted down for eating in winter. Ferguson recalls: 'You had to steep them in water for twenty-four hours to take the salt out of them, and then boil them with tatties for your dinner.'

The islanders also ate large quantities of eggs, which, one visitor remarked, 'they just eat as the peasantry eat potatoes'. Gathered in the spring months, the eggs were boiled and eaten immediately, or else preserved in barrels. The St Kildans were never too fussy about the freshness of the eggs, often keeping them for six to eight weeks before eating them because, they said, time added to their flavour.

8.   Perthshire 1880s

Our fare, though ample and honest, was so simple that visitors from the Glasgow slums turned from it in disgust. They longed so much for their pastries, fish-and-chips, and ice-creams that I have known visits cut short on this account. My father had a passion for rice-and-milk soup; served in a gigantic tureen, the rice boiled in salted milk containing chopped parsley and onion. Often this would be our main dish. But he was a good shot and, when he was there with us, we would eat the game he brought. There was tremendous excitement once when he arrived from Glasgow bringing with him specimens of two fruits we had never seen before. One was a tomato, the other a banana.

9.   Glasgow 1920s

In winter, our Tallie went over [from ice-cream] to hot peas, and no peas cooked at home ever tasted half as good as those bought in that wee shop. A penny bought a cup of 'pea brae', which was actually the thickened water in which the peas had been boiled, liberally seasoned with pepper and a good dash of vinegar. There was always the excitement of maybe finding a few squashed peas at the bottom of the cup, and we would feel about with our spoon, eyes lighting with joy if we found something solid and knew we had struck gold. How we dallied over each spoonful so that we could enjoy the wamth and camaraderie of the clean little shop as long as possible, for now it was cosy and heated, and steaming with cooking peas. The lordly ones seated at the tables consumed threepenny plates of peas, which made us sick with envy, but when the day arrived when we were big enough and rich enough to spend threepence in one go, I found to my surprise and disappointment that I preferred the penny 'pea brae'.

There were four fish-and-chip shops with ten minutes' walking distance of our house (or six minutes if we ran, as we usually did). Each had a subtle advantage over the others, which made choice agonizing when one's mother forgot to say which shop was to be patronized.

If it was your own pocket money, of course, the choice of shop was dictated by the amount of cash in hand. When it was a ha'penny, Jimmy's was the only possible choice, for he alone understood infant economics, and he saved all the wee hard bits of potato which floated to the top of the fryer, and kept them in a separate partition, hot, crisp and greasy, ready to be served out by the fistful at a ha'penny a time, when we hungrily demanded, 'Ony crimps, Jimmy?' We were allowed to salt them but no vinegar was provided. As he reasonably pointed out, he couldn't make any profit at all if he supplied vinegar on ha'penny sales, an argument which we felt was quite sound.

A penny in our pockets saw us deserting generous Jimmy for the shop at the bend of the road, where the marble counter reached to our noses, and where they sold the most mouth-watering potato fritters for three a penny. What pleasure to crunch through the thin layer of batter and reach the steaming potato in the centre.

When we had the rich sum of tuppence we went round the corner to the shop where they sold pies and black puddings. We had no intention of buying such delicacies for ourselves – tuppence wouldn't have stretched so far – but we went for the sheer thrill of listening to the plutocrats who *could* order such foods, and for the pleasure we derived from watching the assistant lower pie or pudding into the hot fat. We admired his judgment in knowing the moment to whisk out pie or pudding, glistening and rich with fat. Sometimes a purchaser would demand tuppence worth of pickles to enhance the feast, and we gazed at each other with smiles of delight that we were in the presence of such extravagant living.

Across the road and round the far corner was the fourth shop, to which our mothers sent us when we could coax them to buy chips for supper. 'Very clean,' my mother would say, 'everything spotless.' We weren't all that impressed with this praise, because the bags in which the chips were daintily shovelled were scandalously small, but we didn't dare disobey and go where the helpings were bigger, because at that time this was the only shop using those wee bags.

10.   Glasgow 1972

LAMENT FOR A LOST DINNER TICKET

See ma mammy
See ma dinner ticket
A pititnma
Pokit an she pititny
Washnmachine.

See thon burnty
Up wherra firewiz
Ma mammy says Am no tellnyagain
No'y playnit.
A jist wen'y eat ma
Pokacrisps furma dinner
Nabigwoffldoon.

The wumman sed Aver near
Clapsd
Jistur heednur
Wee wellies sticknoot.

They sed Wot heppind?
Nme'nma belly
na bedna hospital.
A sed A pititnma
Pokit and she pititny
Washnmachine.

They sed Ees thees chaild eb slootly
Non verbal?
A sed MA BUMSAIR
Nwen'y sleep.

11.   Banffshire *c.* 1930

Remembering that there was a depression going on outside, we at
Aberlour [Orphanage], if only we had realised it, were pretty well

done by. Meals were plain but generous, we had a bed apiece, with warm blankets and a heated dormitory . . .

Every afternoon there was a compulsory walk. If it was Sunday, or if we were going for an extra long distance, we were allowed to put our boots on, but mostly we got along on our bare feet. On very hot days our matrons were inclined to take us to the nearest convenient spot, and then leave us to explore or play on our own, and these explorations always ended in a search for food.

We ate everything we could lay our hands on, and quite a few things which should have poisoned us but didn't. We were chewing rose-hips long before rose-hip syrup was thought of, we ate handfuls of wood-sorrel, and we picked thistles and ate the banana-like kernel under the prickles. Beech nuts, hips and haws, grains of wheat and burdock stalks – we tried them all, and came to no harm. There was a tree in the drive which gave 'henny-yackles', a fruit like a cherry with a soft inside like a pulpy apple. I have tried since to identify this fruit, but the best guess I can make is that it was a gean, or wild cherry.

Equally elusive was the bush which gave 'cough mixtures' or 'nippies'. This is another plant I haven't seen since. It grew near the water, looked something like cow parsley, and had bunches of pods, like clumps of bananas, which tasted of liquorice or aniseed, and turned your teeth black if you ate too much.

But the best feasts came from the wild raspberries. They were ripe and red and luxurious, and when we came home our pinafores were stained and we smelt like a jam factory. Later on there were blaeberries and brambles, and hardly a day passed without somebody knocking off a turnip from somebody's field. It wasn't that we needed the food, but our meals were so predictable, day after day, and we could not, like other children, run in at any old time and ask for a piece. What we ate probably did us less harm than a concentration of carbohydrate.

hennie apple: the fruit of the service tree (Concise Scots Dictionary)

12.   North-East *c.* 1910

From my early days at school I did all the shopping. I was the oldest and there was just about fourteen months atween the nine of us.

On Saturday I would go to William Benzies in the Broch [Fraserburgh] and asked 'a secht o ganzies' and the lassie would bring out a pile of jerseys and I would pick out maybe two, whatever I thought would do and take them home. The next week I would pay for the ones I had got last week and put back any mother didn't want and I might get some trousers or skirts next time. She bought something near every week and paid the next week.

Right from starting school, I suppose, I never slept later than five o'clock. The baker, that was Thomson in Cross Street, opened at six but you could go round to the bakehouse before that and for me they always put in one or two extra biscuits ['softies' – soft floury white rolls]. There was a dairy along the shore and when I got back from the bakery I took up a flagon [small tin can] and went down for tuppence of milk. Back home I had to help dress the younger ones. My mother worked in the herrin. She was a packer and worked with two gutters. The man opened the front door and yelled up. 'Noble! the herrin's in,' and she would get ready for work. I had to tie the clooties on her fingers to stop them gettin cut and the salt gettin in. If the boats had come back at night she would have to work from about nine until around six in the morning. I had to look after all the littler ones. On Friday I had to carry the washtub up and put on the big kettle and broth-pot to heat water. I had to bath them all then put in the girls' papers for at that time girls wore their hair long and curled in ringlets. When the bairns were beddit I made a pot of tea for the three women in her crew and maybe a loaf and jam. There were no thermos flasks so I just put the tea in a flagon and packed the basket and with that over my arm I went down to the shore. It would be pitch dark, the only light came from those bubbly lamps, and down to the herrin yards where I would wait until they had drunk all the tea and had their piece then I took the flagon back home.

My brother would collect fish that had dropped while they were unloading the boats and loading up the carts. He would put one on each finger through the gills to carry them. He went round the doors with them and got tuppence a dozen for his herrin and that was all profit since he hadn't had to pay for them. Everybody had a barrel of salt herrin for the winter, often a little forty [quarter sized] barrelie at their door.

13.   Angus *c.* 1930

Mother didn't know about the embarrassment I endured when I went
to the gym. All the other girls had sandshoes and shorts but me, I had
clog-like tackety boots, and my stockings were either doubled down
under my feet or with my toes sticking through them. The gym teacher
had asked me to take the boots off but I had refused. She was a young
French girl and was always teaching us country dancing. So you can
imagine what I looked and felt like, clattering up and down doing Strip
the Willow or some other such thing.

This year it would be worse. The High School girls all wore
uniform – green gym slip, maroon blazer, black stockings. I had seen
them often. Then there would also be hockey sticks, tennis rackets,
sewing material, knitting wool, and things for cooking. All of these had
to be your own at that time, and if there is any person more cruel and
sarcastic than the High School girls of that time I have yet to meet him
or her. I never talked to Mother about these things, and it never
occured to me to darn my stockings. We were still very primitive, I'm
afraid. At that time I considered the 'country hantle' to be some kind
of God-like people who could do wonders that we [travelling people/
pearl fishers] couldn't do. I just didn't want to be with them in the way
we were at school, or any other way.

14.   North-East 1920s

The pearl poachers had been ragged, but so, too, were we children.
Practically no attention was paid to what we wore during the daytime.
One new set of male or female garments was bought whenever the
oldest boy or girl grew out of what he or she was wearing; as there
were two big boys and two big girls, this meant that the elder members
of the family had, at least, the correct clothes for their sex. The boys
always wore kilts and the girls either tweed or tartan skirts. But my
nearest sister and I, at the tail end of the family, had to wear whatever
fitted us. This was all right when the handed-down boy's garment was
a kilt, but not so good when it was grey flannel trousers or striped
football socks brought back from a boarding school in England.
Rough hand-knitted jerseys, their snagged stitches cascading from
neck to hem, were gathered around our small waists by large dog

collars, the brass labels of which proclaimed our names to be Rover or Thunder or Trust. When we got larger and one collar would no longer do, two collars were buckled together to make the belt. On our heads we wore ancient felt hats discarded even by my frugal father as being too shapeless to wear; they looked like wilting mushrooms and were decorated around the brims by mangled collections of fishing flies. On our feet, in winter, we wore heavy black boots made by the village shoemaker, their soles almost solid with nails; in summer, unless the weather was particularly bad, we went barefoot. During a cold summer we wore tennis shoes, but these were not replaced when our feet grew; instead a section of the canvas was cut away to allow our toes to poke out.

In contrast, our evening dress was very formal. When we graduated from the nursery to the schoolroom, substituting for a bedtime snack of milk and biscuits a five-course dinner with our parents, we stopped wearing the short skirts of our babyhood and put on long dresses that might have come out of the family portraits that gazed down on us as we ate. There was one dinner dress of which I was particularly fond, a grass-green velvet, with a wide lace collar. True, it was the only one I had, and it had been worn before me by all my sisters, but I knew it to be the most beautiful thing I had ever put on. To give it variety – for I wore it almost every night for a year – I made wreaths from the troughs of hothouse flowers that stood around the Big Drawing Room, crowning myself with a different selection each evening. Remembering how we were discouraged from any show of vanity, I sometimes wonder how I got away with this. Perhaps nobody noticed.

My brothers, who during the day looked more untidy than the village children, came down to dinner in immaculately pressed scarlet kilts, lace-edged shirts and velvet jackets, the silver buttons of which were embossed with our family crest. Into the tops of their tartan stockings were stuck cairngorm-crowned skeandhus – ridge-backed knives capable not only of killing a man but of ripping him up in the process. The silver buckles on their shoes flashed when, late as usual for the meal, they swung themselves down the rope of the spiral stairs; they dashed into the anteroom just as my father was finishing his piece on the xylophone.

91

My mother bought the kilt from a second-hand clothes dealer called Lumhat Broon. It had once belonged to a boy whose father was a director of Stewart's of Gantock, the shipbuilding company for which my 'father' (the honourable good-hearted champion quoiter John Lamont, whose name is on my birth certificate) worked as a joiner, and my maternal grandfather, Donald McGilvray, as chief pay-clerk. The tartan was the dress McLeod.

She had seen the kilt in the window, beside the tile hat; but she had not gone into the shop to buy it, she had gone in to avoid Mrs Maitland and Mrs Blanie who were coming along the street. She had been so agitated when asking Lumhat to show us the kilt that I was too worried to object.

In the house, with this yellow and black kilt spread out over her lilac lap, my mother, twenty-six years old, pale-cheeked and red-haired, urged me, with a passion I thought extravagant and unfair, to put it on.

I kept muttering dourly: 'They'd a' ca' me a jessie.' I had seen boys in kilts before, toffs from the villa'd West End, as remote from us in tenemented Lomond Street as the whites in South Africa are from the blacks.

Her delicate hand gripped the cameo brooch at her breast, so tightly that I could see her knuckles turn white.

'You'd look like a prince, Fergie,' she whispered. 'As you should.'

I considered the consequences of obliging her. My eyes went skelly with apprehension.

'Jock Dempster wad lift it up,' I groaned.

'And if he did you would give him a right good kick on the shin, wouldn't you? Have you got my red hair for nothing?'

Too embarrassed to compare our hair, I studied my boots. As weapons they were formidable, with their tackets. I had the courage too to use them. But it wouldn't do any good. Anybody I kicked for laughing would howl with pain all right, but then everybody else would laugh all the more. Fergie Lamont in a kilt would be funny, Fergie Lamont in a fury would be funnier still.

* * *

My mother's tears frightened me. I had seen women weeping before, but for reasons easily understood; when someone had died, when the rent couldn't be paid, if a husband had been brutal. These tears of my mother's had some cause more terrible than death or poverty or cruelty.

'Whit was it you did?' I whispered, once again. 'Why did you go away? Why is everybody so angry?'

Her scent reminded me of the roses in my grandfather's garden. Other boys' mothers smelled of pipeclay, scrubbing brushes, baby's milk, parozone, and blacklead. She spoke too in a more ladylike way than any of my teachers. I would have liked very much to be able to brag about her to my friends, but I couldn't, there were too many things to be settled first; and I just couldn't see who was going to settle them.

'Oh, something terrible,' she murmured.

'If you go away again,' I said, 'take me with you.'

She considered it for half a minute, a long time.

'We'll see, Fergie. Let's try on the kilt, shall we?'

'Oh, a' right.'

With a groan I took off my breeks. I placed them where they would be quickly available if I lost my nerve.

Eagerly she wrapped the kilt round me.

To my relief it was too long.

'Kneel,' she said.

'Hae I to pray?'

'I doubt if that would help much, Fergie. Soldiers kneel, you see, to find out what's the right length. The edge should just touch the ground.'

When I knelt the kilt lay in folds on the floor.

'That's easy mended.' She tugged the waist up to my neck almost.

'I can hardly breathe.'

She buckled it there.

'Your jersey will cover it. Look. What a pity you've not got a tweed jacket and a sporran and green stockings.'

'I'm glad I havenae.'

'Don't be silly. You look braw.'

I thought I looked a terrible jessie. They were sure to laugh at me.

16. Lanarkshire *c.* 1900

If it was mebbe the heich stiff collar [my faither] wore on the Saubbath that made him sae girnie and crabbit, it was the silly claes I had to weir mysell that made the day a misery for me. An o aa the weary Saubbaths that eir I spent, the warst was whan my minnie dressed me up in a new pair o breeks, wi a jaiket to match, in broon velvet claith, wi a yella blouse and a broun silk tie, wi yella socks like a lassie's, and silly shune wi buttons insteid o laces. For ordinar I wore coorse breeks and a guernsey, and tacketty buits.

The hat, tae, was like a lassie's, a big wide strae affair wi an elastic band that grippit roun the chin. It was ower ticht and hurt me.

'Ye'll hae us late for the kirk. Hurry.'

That was aa [my minnie] said, for I didna think she likit the thocht o the trail to the kirk ony mair nor I did mysell, and whan we came alongside my faither, on oor wey back to the hoose, she pat in a word for me.

'I think he had forgotten what day it was. He was pouin grossets.'

But she took me into the big bedroom up the stair and dressed me in the new claes, for aa that.

Whan we had taen the road, and were walkin through Kirkfieldbank, my faither on ae side o me and my minnie on the ither, on oor wey to the service, I felt like a clippit yowe whan it leaves the fank an stauns hingin its heid in shame fornent its ain lamb, for hauf the laddies o the place were staunin at the brig-end wi naethin to dae but stare, and I kent that whan we walkit past them they wad hae a guid lauch.

And shair eneuch, as sune as we drew forenent them there was a lood snicker. My faither and my minnie walkit on wi their heids in the air, but I turnt mine and gied a guid glower.

It just made them waur. There wasna ane withoot a braid grin on his face, and they grinned aa the mair whan they saw I was nettlet.

Then, juist as we had passed them and were on the middle o the brig, I heard ane o them sayin something aboot my lassie's shune, and there was a lood roar. I had juist time to keek roun and fin that the ane wha had spoken was Will MacPherson, whan my faither gied me a teug and telt me to waulk straucht or he wad clowt my lug.

Will MacPherson was juist my ain size. I vowed I wad hae a bash at him the first time I met him by himsell.

It was a wearie walk up the Lanark brae, and we were sair pecht when we won to the tap, but the easin o the brae brocht nae relief, for whan we won to the fute o the Bloomgait we could hear the kirk bells, and my faither streitched his lang legs in case we wad be late. I had to rin, and my minnie nearly burst her hobble skirt.

We won to the kirk door juist as the bells gied their last clap, and my hairt sunk to my shune, for I kent then that the haill congregation wad be sittin waitin, and wad stare at me mair nor ordinar whan I gaed past the pews to sit heich abune them aa in my ain chair aneth the poupit. For though ither laddies sat wi their families in the body o the kirk, my faither and mither sang in the choir, and I caaed the haunle that pumpit the air into the organ.

To tell the truith, gin it hadna been for Denner-Time Davie, the meenister, there wadna hae been a body in that kirk o ony importance that wasna syb to me through my faither, for my Lanark grandfaither was the precentor, and conductit the choir wi a wee black stick; my aunt Lizzie played the organ, watchin the wee black stick in a lookin-gless hung aside her music; and my uncle Geordie was an elder and gaed roud wi the plate. My Lanark grannie bade at hame in the Gusset Hoose to hae the denner ready, but she had a haund in kirk maitters tae, for it was she wha made the communion wine, wi Linmill rasps.

As I walkit past the pews in front of my faither and my minnie I felt shair that the haill congregation were splitting their sides, but whan I had won to my sait and lookit doon they aa seemed solemn eneuch, though I could see Scott the draper and Lichtbody the lawyer were soukin peppermints.

Then I saw that Finlay o Jerviswuid's laddie was haein a fit o the giggles, and I could hae sunk through the flair wi shame.

Finlay's laddie was twice my size. I couldna bash him. I wad hae to gie Will MacPherson a double doze.

It seemed years afore Denner-Time Davie cam in frae the session-room, like a hungert craw in his black goun, to clim to the poupit abune me and kneel doun to pray, and he couldna hae been very shair o his sermon that mornin, for he bade on his knees langer nor his ordinar, askin nae dout for guidance on the akward bits. I had anither look at the Finlay laddie, and wheneir his een met mine he took anither fit o the giggles.

I could hae grutten then, and I canna say I felt very fond o my minnie, though I worshipped for ordinar the very grun she walkit. What wey did she hae to dress me up like a jessie, thocht I, whan she kent I had to sit for sae lang fornent sae mony folk.

But Denner-Time Davie rase at last, and I rase tae, to tak my place ahint the curtain at the side o the organ; and I was neir sae gled in aa my life to win oot o folk's sicht.

I stertit to caa the organ haunle. There was a wee lump o leid on the end o a string, that drappit as the organ filled wi air, and aye whan it was doun to the bottom mark on the side o the organ ye took a bit rest, and didna pump again till it had risen hauf wey to anither mark at the tap, that showed that the organ was tuim. Weill, I pumpit till the leid was at the bottom mark, and syne sat doun on the organ bench, and insteid o keekin through a wee hole I had in the curtain, as I did for ordinar, to see who werena singin, I fell into a dwam and thocht o Will MacPherson and the Finlay laddie, and what I wad dae to them for lauchin at my silly new clothes.

I forgot the wee lump o leid.

I had Will MacPherson flat on the grun, face doun, and was sittin on his back rubbin his neb in the glaur, when aa at ance the organ gied a keckle like a clockin hen, and stoppit athegither. The singin o the congregation began to dee oot tae, though my grandfaither roared like a bull to encourage the choir, and by the time I had tummlet to what was wrang, and had lowpit for the haunle in a panic, the feck o folk had dried up.

The organ roared oot again, for my aunt Lizzie had kept her fingers gaun, but I kent I was in disgrace.

For the rest o the service, till sermon time, I had my ee on that lump o leid like a craw wi its ee on a gun, but I was in sic dreid o the sermon comin, when I wad hae to sit fornent the congregation again, that I didna fin it easy, and there were whiles whan I was in sic a panic I could haurdly dae richt. I was ower eager, and ance whan the wecht gaed a wee thing ower laich the organ nearly blew through the rufe.

Whan I gaed oot to my chair again to sit through the sermon, I daurtna lift my heid. I prayed to God that Denner-Time Davie wadna tak lang, but there maun hae been sin in my hairt, for my prayer wasna answert, and the sermon gaed on like a Kirkfieldbank kimmer at her kitchen door.

* * *

It wasna juist the man's dreichness that bothert me. He had a big bible forenent him, lyin on a kind o cushion, and he had a habit o thumpin his bible to bring his peynts hame. Ilka thump he gave the bible drave the stour frae the cushion, and it rase in the air and syne settlet, and on its wey to the flair it driftit ower my heid, for I was sittin juist aneath him, and it gat into my een, and up my nose, and whiles gart me sneeze. And I didna like to sneeze sittin up there fornent the congregation, for it gart ilka body wauken up and stare.

As the sermon gaed on, though, he lost his first fire, and thumpit at the bible less and less, and in the end I maun hae drappit aff to sleep, for whan he did feenish I didna notice, and had to be waukent by a shake frae my aunt Lizzie.

I was in sic disgrace by that time that I didna care what happened, and through the haill o the last hymn I pumpit the organ like to ding doun the kirk. The singin could haurdly be heard.

Whan I gaed to the kirk door to wait for my faither and my minnie the folk were aa grinnin at me, and I hung my heid. My minnie, whan she cam forrit, lookit sae disjaskit that I gey nearly saftent, but the crabbit look in my faither's een set my back up again, and I determined to sulk aa day.

17.   Edinburgh 1787–1793

I often think I see myself in my usual High School apparel, which was the common dress of other boys. It consisted of a round black hat; a shirt fashioned at the neck by a black ribbon, and, except on dress days, unruffled; a cloth waistcoat, rather large, with two rows of buttons and of button holes, so that it could be buttoned on either side, which, when one side got dirty, was convenient; a single breasted jacket, which in time got a tail and became a coat; brown corduroy breeches, tied at the knees by a showy knot of brown cotton tape; worsted stockings in winter, blue cotton stockings in summer, and white cotton for dress; clumsy shoes made to be used on either foot and each requiring to be used on alternate feet daily; brass or copper buckles. The coat and waistcoat were always of glaring colours, such as bright blue, grass green, and scarlet. I remember well the pride with which I was once rigged out in a scarlet waistcoat and bright green coat. No such machinery as what are now termed braces or suspenders had then been imagined.

18.   Fife 1877

. . . when the great day at last arrived my trusty trunk was filled to the brim with an outfit which would make a new girl of today [1920s] laugh with derision, and a housemistress of today weep with pity. In these happy times, when a girl's underwear has been aptly described as consisting of three garments, two of which are stockings, picture the following: masses of strong, dark, woollen and cotton stockings; thick woollen combinations (high in the neck and long in the sleeve); solid cotton ditto; stout longcloth nightdresses; sturdy flannel petticoats; substantial linsey woolsey petticoats; starched white petticoats; serge frocks for school wear; cashmere for Sunday; velveteen for every evening; a sort of silky alpaca, known as 'lustre' for parties; lace boots; button boots; a long grey ulster for weekdays; a fawn camel's-hair coat for best; a felt hat with a wing; a velvet hat with an ostrich feather; hair ribbons; thick kid gloves; coloured silk mittens to match party frocks; stiff linen collars and cuffs; and yards of scratchy frilling to sew into necks and wrists, even of gym suits! Everything was strong, everything was long. I too was very long, though only thirteen, and unluckily for me a great-aunt, who was staying with us during the preparation of my outfit, remarked to my mother – 'Don't you think, my dear, that it is high time dear Julia adopted more womanly petticoats?' The consequence of which was that my skirts were well on their way to my ankles, and as I never wore less than two under my heavy dress I carried a mighty load, and now understand why I so often had a backache.

SCHOOLDAYS

❦

taken from

My Mother was a persone of singular vertue and religion, but died in the 25 year of her age, after she had born to my Father 7 children.

I was born on the 8 of feb. 1676, and have reasone to be thankful to God that tho I be not descended of noble parents or from an Antient Family, yet I am the son of those who bore deservedly a very great name for Religion, Vertue, Honour, and Honesty.

I was put to the school of Pennicuik after my Mother died, and found a very careful master in the persone of one Mr Alex. Strauchan, only that, according to the bad custome of these times, he was too severe a disciplinarian. I learnt from this never to suffer any man to use my children and young friends as if born to be slaves. Boys who have a Genius for learning ought to be alured to their books, and those who want this Genius ought to be put to Mechanick occupations, in which they may become far more useful to humane society than if bred schollars.

With this Mr Strauchan I learnt Latine, and afterwards with another master in the same school I was taught Greek.

I spent 7 years at this kind of emploiment, but if in the meantime I had learnt to write a tolerable hand, the Memoirs I am now writeing had been more legible. One thing indeed contributed mainly to make me write ill, which was an exercise about that time common in schools, to write long notes of sermons after the minister. This practise, however, served a little to fix our attention, and keep us from doing worse things.

Here, at school, a very great misfortune befell me about my age of Thirteen, for a country man's Horse standing sadled and brideled in my way, I got upon him, and as Boys used to do, I put him to the Gallop, but he proved to be too headstrong for me. I cou'd not command him, and to be free of a precipice to which he directed his course, I threw myself off, and both broke and disjointed my right leg. I was brought home in a very sad condition, and continued in torture and misery for at least 4 months after. My kind father attended me night and day, and no assistance was wanted that cou'd be procured by either physitians or Chyrurgeons, however, I got no benefite by them till nature perfected the cure, in a word, my leg sweled so sore at first that it could never be set, and the Tibia being not only broken but disjoynted and split, I had several ulcers in my leg, which required a great deal time in the cure. These continued to run for near 6 months, and if it had not been for the extraordinary care of Mr Robt. Clerk, my unckle, and who was a very expert chyrurgeon, I must have lost my leg. I recovered at last, and contented myself with this reflexion, that my misfortune came from the wise hand of providence in order to curb the vast inclinations I had to rambling and such violent exercises as I cou'd never have indured.

After this misfortune I continued near a year with my Greek Master at Pennicuik, and then I was sent to the College of Glasgow [at the age of sixteen].

I studied in that place Logicks and Metaphysics for two winters, and with great application, but never felt any benefit from them that I was sensible of, on the contrary, I found them so hurtful that I many time afterwards repented my having spent so much time upon them, and indeed it cost me as many years to unlairn what I had learnt at Glasgow.

2.   Loch Lomondside *c.* 1730

I was soon after sent to school at a village hard by, of which he [my grandfather] had been dictator time out of mind; but, as he never paid for my board, nor supplied me with clothes, books, and other necessities I required, my position was very ragged and contemptible, and the schoolmaster, who, through fear of my grandfather, taught me *gratis*, gave himself no concern about the progress I made under his instruction.

In spite of all these difficulties and disgraces, I became a good proficient in the Latin tongue; and, as soon as I could write tolerably, pestered my grandfather with letters to such a degree, that he sent for my master, and chid him severely for bestowing such pains on my education, telling him that, if ever I should be brought to the gallows for forgery, which he had taught me to commit, my blood would lie on his head.

The pedant, who dreaded nothing more than the displeasure of his patron, assured his honour that the boy's ability was more owing to his own genius and application than to any instruction or encouragement he received; that, although he could not divest him of the knowledge he had already imbibed, unless he would empower him to disable his fingers, he should endeavour, with God's help, to prevent his future improvement. And, indeed, he punctually performed what he had undertaken; for, on pretence that I had written impertinent letters to my grandfather, he caused a board to be made with five holes in it, through which he thrust the fingers and thumb of my right hand, and fastened it with whipcord to my wrist, in such a manner as effectually debarred me the use of my pen.

But this restraint I was freed from in a few days, by an accident which happened in a quarrel between me and another boy, who, taking upon him to insult my poverty, I was so incensed by this ungenerous reproach, that with one stroke of my machine I cut him to the skull, to the great terror of myself and schoolfellows, who left him bleeding on the ground, and ran to inform the master of what had happened. I was so severely punished for this trespass, that, were I to live to the age of Methusalem, the impression it made on me would not be effaced; no more than the antipathy and horror I conceived for the merciless tyrant who inflicted it.

The contempt which my appearance naturally produced in all who saw me, the continual wants to which I was exposed, and my own haughty disposition, impatient of affronts, involved me in a thousand troublesome adventures, by which I was at length inured to adversity, and emboldened to undertakings far beyond my years. I was often inhumanly scourged for crimes I did not commit, because, having the character of a vagabond in the village, every piece of mischief, whose author lay unknown, was charged upon me. I have been found guilty of robbing orchards I never entered, of killing cats I never hurted, of stealing gingerbread I never touched, and of abusing old women I never saw. Nay, a stammering carpenter had eloquence enough to persuade my master that I had fired a pistol loaded with small shot into his window; though my landlady and the whole family bore witness that I was abed fast asleep at the time when this outrage was committed. I was once flogged for having narrowly escaped drowning, by the sinking of a ferry-boat in which I was passenger. Another time, for having recovered of a bruise occasioned by a horse and cart running over me. A third time, for being bitten by a baker's dog. In short, whether I was guilty or unfortunate, the correction and sympathy of this arbitrary pedagogue were the same.

Far from being subdued by this infernal usage, my indignation triumphed over that slavish awe which had hitherto enforced my obedience; and the more my years and knowledge increased, the more I perceived the injustice and barbarity of his behaviour. By the help of an uncommon genius, and the advice and direction of our usher, who had served my father in his travels, I made a surprising progress in the classics, writing and arithmetic; so that, before I was twelve years old, I was allowed by everybody to be the best scholar in the school. This qualification, together with a boldness of temper, and strength of make, which had subjected almost all my contemporaries, gave me such influence over them, that I began to form cabals against my persecutor; and was in hope of being able to bid him defiance in a very short time.

Being at the head of a faction, consisting of thirty boys, most of them of my own age, I was determined to put their mettle to trial, that I might see how far they were to be depended upon, before I put my grand scheme in execution: with this view we attacked a body of stout apprentices, who had taken possession of a part of the ground allotted to us for the scene of our diversions, and who were then playing at nine-pins on the spot; But I had the mortification to see my adherents routed in an instant, and a leg of one of them broke in his flight by the bowl, which one of our adversaries had detached in pursuit of us.

This discomfiture did not hinder us from engaging them afterward in frequent skirmishes, which we maintained by throwing stones at a distance, wherein I received many wounds, the scars of which still remain. Our enemies were so harassed and interrupted by these alarms, that they at last abandoned their conquest, and left us to the peaceful enjoyment of our own territories.

It would be endless to enumerate the exploits we performed in the course of this confederacy, which became the terror of the whole village; insomuch, that, when different interests divided it, one of the parties commonly courted the assistance of Roderick Random (by which name I was known) to cast the balance, and keep the opposite faction in awe.

Meanwhile I took the advantage of every playday to present myself before my grandfather, to whom I seldom found access, by reason of his being closely besieged by a numerous family of his female grandchildren, who, though they perpetually quarrelled among themselves, never failed to join against me, as the common enemy of all. His heir, who was about the age of eighteen, minded nothing but fox-hunting, and indeed was qualified for nothing else, notwithstanding his grandfather's indulgence, in entertaining a tutor for him at home; who at the same time performed the office of parish-clerk.

This young Acteon, who inherited his grandfather's antipathy to everything in distress, never set eyes on me without uncoupling his beagles, and hunting me into some cottage or other, whither I generally fled for shelter. In this Christian amusement, he was encouraged by his preceptor, who, no doubt, took such opportunities to ingratiate himself with the rising sun, observing that the old gentleman, according to the course of nature, had not long to live, for he was already on the verge of fourscore.

The behaviour of this rascally sycophant incensed me so much, that one day, when I was beleaguered by him and his hounds in a farmer's house, where I had found protection, I took aim at him (being an excellent marksman) with a large pebble, which struck out four of his teeth, and effectually incapacitated him from doing the office of a clerk.

3.   Ayrshire 1750s

. . . from the age of eight to the age of twelve I enjoyed reasonably good health. I had a governor who was not without sentiment and sensibility. He began to form my mind in a manner that delighted me. He set me to reading *The Spectator*; and it was then that I acquired my first notions of taste for the fine arts and of the pleasure there is in considering the variety of human nature. I read the Roman poets, and I felt a classic enthusiasm in the romantic shades of our family's seat in the country. My governor sometimes spoke to me of religion, but in a simple and pleasing way. He told me that if I behaved well during my life, I should be happy in the other world. There I should hear beautiful music. There I should acquire the sublime knowledge that God will grant to the righteous; and there I should meet all the great men of whom I had read, and all the dear friends I had known. At last my governor put me in love with heaven, and some hope entered into my religion.

My father, who is one of the ablest and worthiest men in the world, was very busy and could not take much immediate care of my education. He did as others do and trusted me to teachers. From five to eight I attended a school, where I was very unhappy. From eight to twelve I had my first governor, and during those four years I can say that I was happy except on Sundays, when I was made to remember the terrible Being whom those about me called God. The Scots Presbyterians are excessively rigid with regard to the observance of the Sabbath. I was taken to church, where I was obliged to hear three sermons in the same day, with a great many impromptu prayers and a great many sung psalms, all rendered in a stern and doleful manner. In the evening I was made to say my catechism and to repeat psalms translated into the vilest doggerel. I was obliged by my religion 'not to do my own work, speak my own words, nor think my own thoughts, on God's holy day.' I tried in sincerity of heart to conform to that command; especially not to think my own thoughts. A fine exercise for a child's mind!

When I was twelve years old, my governor was appointed minister of a parish, and I was given another governor, a very honest man but harsh and without knowledge of the human mind. He had gone through the usual course of school and college. He had learned his lessons well, and all he had learned he had made part of himself. He was a dogmatist who never doubted. He felt and acted according to system.

One day when I said I had a friend whom I loved more than my brothers, he called me a blockhead and said, 'Do you not know how affection develops? First you love your parents, then your brothers, then you spread yourself abroad on the rest of the human race.'

He made me read the ancient authors, but without getting any pleasure from them. He had no other idea than to make me perform a task. When I asked him questions about the poets, for instruction or amusement – and why should I not have looked for amusement? – he lost his temper and cried out with a schoolmaster's arrogance, 'Come, come, keep at work, don't interrupt the lesson. Time is flying.' Consequently I got the habit of reading without any profit. It was enough to say that I had read such and such an author.

In my twelfth year I caught a very severe cold. I was given a great many medicines, and my naturally weak stomach became so upset that I could hardly digest anything. I confess that the fear of having to go back to what were called my studies made me hope I could stay ill. The greatest doctors in Scotland were called in. I was naughty enough to take measures to prevent their medicines from having any effect on me. I could somehow or other control the operations of my stomach, and I immediately threw up everything they made me take. I even endured blisters, congratulating myself on not having to *work*. The Faculty decided that I was suffering from an extraordinary nervous illness, and I confess I laughed heartily to myself at their consultations. I was weakened in body and mind, and my natural melancholy increased. I was sent to Moffat, the Spa of Scotland. I was permitted a great deal of amusement. I saw many lively people. I wished to be lively myself, and insensibly regained my health, after having imagined that I should certainly be ill all my life.

At thirteen I was sent to the University. There I had more freedom. The place rather pleased me, and during the three years that I was studying languages, I attained high distinction and my professors said I would be a very great man . . .

4.   Ayrshire 1765

When the boys began to go to school (which they did when Robert was still under six) their musical incapacity proved a real source of affliction. Although two of the youngest in the class – and the school was no more than a class – they won their way to the top in most subjects. In particular they excelled in reading and in all memory-work. But when it came to singing the Psalms of David in metre they were the schoolmaster's despair. He plied the tawse unsparingly, but without results that could be called musical.

So it was settled. Murdoch ['a very genteel young man who had but recently qualified as a schoolmaster . . . eighteen years of age, full of promise and pedantry'] was to come to Alloway where he would be housed in turn with the Burneses and the four other families whose children would attend daily at a room in the village to be instructed. Besides his keep he would be guaranteed a salary of about sixpence a day. Upon this satisfactory result a drink was ordered at the employer's expense, and drunk to the undertaking. Some six weeks later Murdoch walked over, bringing with him some clean shirts, a spelling-book, *Fisher's English Grammar*, Masson's *Collection of Prose and Verse*, a New Testament, and a new seven-thonged leather tawse.

The arrangement lasted for two years and was a success. Incidentally it provided Robert and Gilbert with the longest spell of schooling they were to have. All later periods of formal education, when added together, were scarcely to equal one-third of their time under Murdoch . . . He also tried, according to promise, to make them sing the Sternhold and Hopkins version of the Psalms. But here he failed, especially with Robert, even with the aid of the stinging new tawse. At length he had to admit that Robert had 'an ear remarkably dull, and a voice untuneable'. The Dominie had nothing against thrashing as an aid to learning, and he found himself oftener impelled to thrash Robert than the merrier and more docile Gilbert, who was from the first his favourite . . .

But there was a 'stubborn something' in this thick-set little boy (Robert) with the dangerous dark eyes that gave an adult pause and called for chastisement . . .

None the less, the Burnes boys were Murdoch's pet pupils . . .

5.   1767

'OF BEHAVIOUR AT SCHOOL'

1. Behave to your teachers with humility, and to your schoolfellows with respect.
2. Do not run into the school, but advance decently and slowly to the door.
3. Make your bow or curtsey, when you enter, and walk straight to your seat.
4. Never talk in the school, for it interrupts yourself and others.

6. If you have anything to say to the master, wait till he is at leisure, and then speak with modesty and plainness.
7. Observe nothing at school but your book, and never neglect that.
8. Never quarrel at school, for it shows idleness and a bad temper.
9. When the master speaks to you, rise up to hear him, and look him in the face as he speaks, with modesty and attention.
10. Begin not to answer before he has done speaking, and then bow to him respectfully, and answer with humility.

11. If you have occasion to complain of a schoolfellow, first speak to him softly and desire him to desist.

12. If he will not, then rise up and wait an opportunity; and when the master's or usher's eye is upon you, bow and say softly, and in a few words, what your complaint is.

13. Never speak loud in school; answer a question moderately; repeat your lesson distinctly; and on no other occasion speak at all.

14. When a stranger is in school, do not stare at him.

18. When the school hours are over, go out, as you came in, quietly, softly, and decently.

19. Never run or crowd to get at the door, for it will be free for you in a few minutes waiting.

20. When out of the school, go home without hurry and without delay; do not run, nor do not loiter; but do this, as in all things else, with discretion.

21. Do not speak at home, or elsewhere, of what has been done in school; for nothing that passes there should be told out.

6.   Edinburgh 1787–1793

In October 1787 [at the age of eight] I was sent to the High School. Having never been at a public school before, and this one being notorious for its severity and riotousness, I approached its walls with trembling and felt dizzy when I sat down amidst above 100 new faces. We had been living at Leith, for sea bathing, for some weeks before; and I was taken to school by our tutor. The only thing that relieved my alarm as he hauled me along was the diversion of crossing the arches of the South Bridge, which were then unfinished, on planks.

The person to whose uncontrolled discipline I was now subjected, though a good man, an intense student, and filled, but rather in the memory than in the head, with knowledge, was as bad a schoolmaster as it is possible to fancy. Unacquainted with the nature of youth, ignorant even of the characteristics of his own boys, and with not a conception of the art or of the duty of alluring them, he had nothing of it but to drive them; and this he did by constant and indiscriminate harshness.

The effects of this were very hurtful to all his pupils. Out of the whole four years of my attendance there were probably not ten days in which I was not flogged, at least once. Yet I never entered the class, nor left it, without feeling perfectly qualified, both in ability and preparation, for its whole business; which, being confined to Latin alone, and in necessarily short tasks, since every one of the boys had to rhyme over the very same words, in the very same way, was no great feat. But I was driven stupid. Oh! the bodily and mental wearisomeness of sitting six hours a-day, staring idly at a page, without motion and without thought, and trembling at the gradual approach of the merciless giant. I never got a single prize, and once sat *boobie* at the annual public examination. The beauty of no Roman word, or thought, or action, ever occurred to me; nor did I ever fancy that Latin was of any use except to torture boys.

After four years of this class, I passed on to that of the Rector, Dr Alexander Adam, the author of the work on Roman Antiquities, then in the zenith of his reputation. He had raised himself from the very dust to that high position. Never was a man more fortunate in the choice of a vocation. He was born to teach Latin, some Greek, and all virtue. In doing so he was generally patient, though not, when intolerably provoked, without due fits of gentle wrath; inspiring to his boys, especially the timid and backward; enthusiastically delighted with every appearance of talent or goodness; a warm encourager by praise, play and kindness; and constantly under the strongest sense of duty . . .

He suffered from a prejudice likely to be injurious in those days. He was no politician; insomuch that it may be doubted whether he ever knew one public measure or man from another. But a Latin and Greek schoolmaster naturally speaks about such things as liberty, and the people, and the expulsion of the Tarquins, and republics, and this was quite sufficient for the times; especially as any modern notions that he had were popular, and he was too honest, and too simple, to disguise them. This innocent infusion of classical patriotism into the mind of a man whose fancy dwelt in old Rome, made him be watched and traduced for several years. Boys were encouraged to bring home stories of him, and of course only reported what they saw pleased. Often, and with great agitation, did the worthy man complain of the injustice which tolerated these youthful spies; but his chief sorrow was for the corruption to which the minds of his pupils were exposed. I remained in the Rector's class two years.

7. Edinburgh *c.* 1815

It was not long before we found ourselves at Edinburgh, or rather in the Castle, into which the regiment marched with drums beating, colours flying, and a long train of baggage-wagons behind. The Castle was, as I suppose it is now, a garrison for soldiers. Two other regiments were already there the one an Irish, if I remember right, the other a small Highland corps.

'But now to the point,' (said my father). 'Were it not for the language, which, if the boys were to pick it up, might ruin their prospects for life, – were it not for that, I should very much like to send them to a school there is in this place, which everybody talks about – the High School I think they call it. 'Tis said to be the best school in the whole island; but the idea of one's children speaking Scotch – broad Scotch! I must think the matter over.'

And he did think the matter over; and the result of his deliberation was a determination to send us to the school. Let me call thee up before my mind's eye, High School, to which, every morning, the two English brothers took their way from the proud old Castle through the lofty streets of the Old Town. High School! – called so, I scarcely know why; neither lofty in thyself nor by position, being situated in a flat bottom; oblong structure of tawny stone, with many windows fenced with iron netting – with thy long hall below, and thy five chambers above, for the reception of the five classes, into which the eight hundred urchins, who styled thee instructress, were divided. Thy learned rector and his four subordinate dominies; thy strange old porter of the tall form and grizzled hair . . .

Yes, I remember all about thee, and how at eight of every morn we were all gathered together with one accord in the long hall, from which, after the litanies had been read (for so I will call them, being an Episcopalian), the five classes from the five sets of benches trotted off in long files, one boy after the other, up the five spiral staircases of stone, each class its destination; and well do I remember how we of the third sat hushed and still, watched by the eye of the dux, until the door opened, and in walked that model of a good Scotchman, the shrewd, intelligent, but warm-hearted and kind dominie, the respectable Carson.

* * *

111

I certainly acquired there a considerable insight in the Latin tongue; and, to the scandal of my father and horror of my mother, a thorough proficiency in the Scotch, which, in less than two months, usurped the place of the English, and so obstinately maintained its ground, that I still can occasionally detect its lingering remains. I did not spend my time unpleasantly at this school, though, first of all, I had to pass through an ordeal.

'Scotland is a better country than England,' said an ugly, blear-eyed lad, about a head and shoulders taller than myself, the leader of a gang of varlets who surrounded me in the playground, on the first day, as soon as the morning lesson was over. 'Scotland is a far better country than England, in every respect.'

'Is it?' said I. 'Then you ought to be very thankful for not having been born in England.'

'That's just what I am, ye loon; and every morning when I say my prayers, I thank God for not being an Englishman. The Scotch are a much better and braver people than the English.'

'It may be so,' said I, 'for what I know – indeed, till I came here, I never heard a word either about the Scotch or their country.'

'Are ye making fun of us, ye English puppy?' said the blear-eyed lad; 'take that!' and I was presently beaten black and blue. And thus did I first become aware of the differences of races and their antipathy to each other.

. . . The Scotch are certainly a most pugnacious people; their whole history proves it. Witness their incessant wars with the English in the olden time, and their internal feuds, highland with lowland, clan with clan, family with family, Saxon with Gael. In my time, the schoolboys, for want, perhaps, of English urchins to contend with, were continually fighting with each other; every noon there was at least one pugilistic encounter, and sometimes three. In one month I witnessed more of these encounters than I had ever previously seen under similar circumstances in England. After all there was not much harm done. Harm! what harm could result from short chopping blows, a hug, and a tumble? I was witness to many a sounding whack, some blood shed, 'a blue ee' now and then, but nothing more. In England, on the contrary, where the lads were comparatively mild, gentle, and pacific, I had been present at more than one death caused by blows in boyish combats, in which the oldest of the victors had scarcely reached thirteen years; but these blows were in the jugular, given with the full force of the arm shot out horizontally from the shoulder.

But the Scotch – though by no means proficient in boxing (and how should they box, seeing that they have never had a teacher?) – are, I repeat, a most pugnacious people; at least they were in my time. Anything served them, that is, the urchins, as a pretence for a fray, or, Dorically speaking, a *bicker*; every street and close was at feud with its neighbour; the lads of the school were at feud with the young men of the college, whom they pelted in winter with snow, and in summer with stones; and then the feud between the Old and New Town!

8.   Edinburgh 1846

The Rector and Masters feel it to be their duty to remind the ingenuous Youth educated in this venerable Institution, that the moral well-being of man is paramount even to his intellectual advancement. You are, accordingly, affectionately admonished to seek that fear of the Lord, which is the beginning of wisdom; and while you are not slothful in business, in the days of your youth to remember your Creator . . .

. . . the following rules comprehend the duties mainly to be enforced; and other violations of the great principles of right, while you are earnestly warned against them, will be dealt with as each case may require:

I. All flagrant violations of the moral law, lying, dishonesty, swearing, obscenity, immodesty of every kind, are forbidden under the severest penalties, as most displeasing to God, degrading to your own nature, and hateful in the eyes of men.

VI. You are enjoined to behave courteously to your schoolfellows, loving your neighbours as yourselves, in honour preferring one another. The seniors are enjoined to comport themselves in a kindly manner to those who are younger and weaker, and any attempt at oppression will be regarded as a proof of unmanly spirit, and energetically repressed.

* * *

IX. Disturbing any of the Classes in the course of your games, by shouting, staring in at the windows, or in any other way, is peremptorily forbidden.

XVI. Missiles of every description, whether stones, gravel or snowballs, are absolutely forbidden.

XVII. No gunpowder, fireworks, or firearms of any description, are permitted to be brought within the grounds, under penalty of confiscation, and such punishment as may be necessary.

XVIII. In addition to the spacious playground provided by the Patrons for your recreation, you have the free range of the [nearby] Hill, at fit opportunities . . .

XIX. In your enjoyment of this, and of all your privileges, you are warned against molesting or injuring others in any way. You are especially forbidden to come into hostile contact by throwing stones, or otherwise, with any other boys, or assemblages of boys, and this, notwithstanding any pretext whatsoever.

XXI. Nothing can be more improper or hurtful to the character of the school, than that, congregated on the edge of a great thoroughfare, you should abuse your position, to annoy or injure the public, by shouting or throwing missiles, or by any other means. This will be prevented by severe penalties. And, more especially, you are warned against yielding to the childish excitement produced by the appearance of the military, as complaints have been made of violations of this necessary rule.

9.   Cromarty *c.* 1810–1815

. . . As the school windows fronted the opening of the firth, not a vessel could enter the harbour that we did not see; and, improving through our opportunites, there was perhaps no educational institution in the kingdom in which all sorts of barques and carvels, from the fishing yawl to the frigate, could be more correctly drawn on the slate, or where any defect in hulk or rigging, in some faulty delineation, was surer of being more justly and unsparingly criticised.

Further, the town, which drove a great trade in salted pork at the time, had a killing-place not thirty yards from the school-door, where from eighty to a hundred pigs used to die for the general good in a single day; and it was a great matter to hear, at occasional intervals, the roar of death outside rising high over the general murmur within, or to be told by some comrade, returning from his five minutes leave of absence, that a hero of a pig had taken three blows of the hatchet ere it fell, and that even after its subjection to the sticking process, it had got hold of Jock Keddie's hand in its mouth, and almost smashed his thumb. We learned, too, to know, from our signal opportunities of observation, not only a good deal about pig-anatomy, – especially about the detached edible parts of the animal, such as the spleen and the pancreas, and at least one other very palatable viscus besides, – but became knowing also about the take and curing of herrings.

All the herring boats during the fishing season passed our windows on their homeward way to the harbour; and, from their depth in the water, we became skilful enough to predicate the number of crans aboard of each with wonderful judgment and correctness. In days of good general fishings, too, when the curing yards proved too small to accommodate the quantities brought ashore, the fish used to be laid in glittering heaps opposite the school-house door; and an exciting scene, that combined the bustle of the workshop with the confusion of the crowded fair, would straightaway spring up within twenty yards of the forms at which we sat, greatly to our enjoyment, and, of course, not a little to our instruction.

We could see, simply by peering over book or slate, the curers going about rousing their fish with salt, to counteract the effects of the dog-day sun; bevies of young women employed as gutters, and horridly incarnadined with blood and viscera, squatting around the heaps, knife in hand, and plying with busy fingers their well-paid labours, at the rate of sixpence per hour; relays of heavily-laden fish-wives bringing ever and anon fresh heaps of herring in their creels; and outside of all, the coopers hammering as if for life and death, – now tightening hoops, and now slackening them, and anon caulking with bulrush the leaky seams.

It is not every grammar school in which such lessons are taught as those in which we were all initiated, and in which all became in some degree accomplished, in the grammar school of Cromarty!

* * *

The school, like almost all the other grammar-schools of the period in Scotland, had its yearly cockfight, preceded by two holidays and a half, during which the boys occupied themselves in collecting and bringing up their cocks. And such always was the array of fighting birds mustered on the occasion, that the day of the festival, from morning till night, used to be spent in fighting out the battle. For weeks after it had passed, the school floor would continue to retain its deeply-stained blotches of blood, and the boys would be full of exciting narratives regarding the glories of gallant birds, who had continued to fight until both their eyes had been picked out, or who, in the moment of victory, had dropped dead in the middle of the cock-pit.

The yearly fight was the relic of a barbarous age; and, in at least one of its provisions, there seemed evidence that it was of an intolerant age also: every pupil at school, without exemption, had his name entered on the subscription-list, as a cock-fighter, and was obliged to pay the master at the rate of twopence per head, ostensibly for leave to bring his birds to the pit; but, amid the growing humanities of a better time, though the twopences continued to be exacted, it was no longer imperative to bring the birds; and availing myself of the liberty I never brought any. Nor, save for a few minutes, on two several occasions, did I ever attend the fight. Had the combat been one among the boys themselves, I would readily enough have done my part, by meeting with any opponent of my years and standing; but I could not bear to look at the bleeding birds. And so I continued to pay my yearly sixpence, as a holder of three cocks, – the lowest sum deemed in any degree genteel, – but remained simply a fictitious or paper cock-fighter . . .

Neither, I must add, did I learn to take an interest in the sacrificial orgies of the adjoining slaughterhouse. A few of the chosen schoolboys were permitted by the killers to exercise at times the privilege of knocking down a pig, and even, on rare occasions, to essay the sticking; but I turned with horror from both processes; and if I drew near at all, it was only when some animal, scraped and cleaned, and suspended from the beam, was in the course of being laid open by the butcher's knife, that I might mark the forms of the viscera, and the positions which they occupied.

My sister went no more to the school than that quarter, having to go to the fields to help to work for the family bread. When the summer of 1819 came, I [at the age of eight] left school also, to herd the farmer's cows. In the winter of 1819 I again went to school, and got into severe trouble with the teacher on one occasion . . .

. . . The term 'ragged radicals' was a common one in the news-papers of that time, and the boys who heard their fathers read the newspapers or talk of the news, brought this name of reproach to the school. It was suggested one day by some of them, that an excellent play might be got up in the Eel Yards, a meadow with some large trees in it, if the scholars divided themselves into soldiers and radicals. As the soldiers were the most respectable in the eyes of the better dressed sons of farmers and tradesmen, and as they took the lead in everything, they made themselves soldiers; and, in addition to that, took upon themselves to pick out those who were to be radicals. This was done according to the quality of the clothes worn, and I, consequently, found myself declared to be a radical.

The first day's play passed with no greater disasters to me than the brim torn from an infirm hat which I wore, my trousers split up, all the buttons torn from my waistcoat, and my neck stretched considerably on the way to strangulation. For being a radical who seemed inclined to look upon the treatment I received as too serious for play, I was condemned to be hanged.

It happened that the clothes I wore were not of the usual corduroy worn by the sons of farm labourers and always worn by me, save in that year. Mine had been remade the year before from some cast-off clothes given a year or two before that to the brother next in age to me by his master. There was a brown coat which had been reduced in size, but it was still too large for me; trousers which had once been of a very light blue or grey; and the infirm hat already named, which came to our family I do not precisely remember how; but it had so broad a brim at first, that my mother cut part of it to let me see from below it, and still it was so broad that some of the boys nicknamed me after some people whom I had never seen nor heard of, but who were said to wear broad-brimmed hats. These clothes having been old when I got them, and having been worn by me all the summer in the woods

herding the cows, and all the autumn, they were not in sound
condition. But my poor mother always kept them patched up; and
I never once went out then or any time, with an open rent or a worn
hole in my clothes. As she spun wool for stockings, and lint for shirts,
herself, and my father knitted stockings at night, and my sisters made
shirts, I was equal in those articles to any one in the school . . .

So I went [back] to the school, my mother begging of me, with tears
in her eyes, not to get my clothes torn again, or else it would kill her to
see me in such rags, and to have to sit up every night to mend them.
But 'soldiers and radicals' was again the play, and again I was the
radical upon whom the greatest numbers of soldiers concentrated their
warfare. They had seen me thrashed by the schoolmaster until I was
blistered, without crying or shedding a tear, which made them think I
could stand any amount of punishment or torment, without feeling it;
in short I was believed to be a great stubborn lad, who had no feeling
in him. Had they seen me after leaving my mother that morning, and
carrying her injunctions with me, in a heart that was bursting with her
words, they would have seen whether I had tears in me or not, and
whether they would not come out.

As soon as I made my appearance, the cry of the 'ragged radical'
was raised; the soldiers charged on me, and knocked my infirm hat
over my eyes with my head through the crown of it. Some laid hold of
me by the feet to carry me off to be hanged and beheaded, *as the real
law upon the real radicals had taught them to imitate in play.* I made a
violent effort to free myself, and the rents of yesterday, which my
mother had so carefully sewed, broke open afresh. The hat I raised
from where it had sunk over my face, and saw part of the brim in the
hands of a lad who was a kind of king of the school, or cock of the
walk, with some of my poor mother's threads hanging from it. He was
older than I, and was a fighter.

I had never fought, nor had heard of two human creatures going
together to fight, until I came to that school. Yet neither had I heard of
the divine principle of forbearance and forgiveness, as regards blows
upon the body, and the laceration of feelings worse than blows upon
the body – my father, who gave me many good precepts, never having
contemplated the possibility of my being a fighting boy. (My child,
you will be brought up where there are policemen and law, lawyers
and magistrates to take your part if you are injured; never raise your

own hand against any one.) But I was a strong boy for my age, and I had received very bad treatment. My honour and the remembrance of my affectionate mother's toils made me feel like a giant. I amazed the king of the school by giving him a blow in the face that laid him flat on his back, and amazed the onlookers by giving several of them as much with same results. Not that I escaped without blows myself. I got many, but they were returned with principle and interest.

Someone ran to the schoolmaster and told that I was thrashing 'Master' Somebody, for he being a gentleman's son was called 'Master', while I had to submit to a nick-name, derived from the state of my clothes. The school was summoned in at once, it being near the schoolhour in the morning. Some of those whose noses were bleeding ran to school with them in that state to let their disasters be seen. Another one and myself tried to get water to wash our faces, for mine was in as bad a condition as the worst of theirs; but the frost was so hard, that we could not break the ice to get water, and at last were compelled to obey the repeated summons to school in the dreadful guise we were then in; my clothes being torn half off me in addition to the hideousness of the blood streaming from my face.

The schoolmaster stood with the *taws* ready to flagellate the moment I entered the school. He inquired who began the fight, and everyone named me. He at once ordered me to hold up my right hand, which I did, and received a violent cut on the edge of it, given with his whole strength. He ordered my left hand up, and up it went and received a cut of the same kind; then my right, which got what it got before; and so on he went until I had got six cuts (skults we called them) on each hand. He had a way of raising himself upon his toes when he swung the heavy *taws* round his head, and came down upon his feet with a swing, giving the cuts slantingly on the hand.

He saw me resolved to take all he could give without a tear, whereupon he began to cut at the back of my hands. I drew them behind me to save them, which seeing, cut at the open places of my torn clothes, where my skin was visible; and always as I wriggled to one side to save those bare places, I exposed other bare places on the other side, which he aimed at with terrible certainty. After a time he pushed me before him, still thrashing me on the bare places, and on the head, until he got me to the further end of the school, where the coals lay in a corner. He thrashed me until I got on top of the coals.

Here he ordered me to sit down and remain until he gave me liberty to leave that place, which he did not do until evening.

The day was piercing cold. The house was an old place, with no furniture nor partition in it. I sat at the end farthest from the fireplace, and near to the door, which was an old door that did not fit its place, and which allowed the wind to blow freely through. It blew through and about me as if it had been another schoolmaster, and was as partial to the farmer's sons, and as cruel to the ragged boys of farm labourers, as he was.

11. Fife 1840s

. . . My father's four or five looms occupied the lower story; we resided in the upper, which was reached, after a fashion common in the older Scottish houses, by outside stairs from the pavement. It is here that my earliest recollections begin, and, strangely enough, the first trace of memory takes me back to a day when I saw a small map of America. It was upon rollers and about two feet square. Upon this my father, mother, Uncle William, and Aunt Aitken were looking for Pittsburgh and pointing out Lake Erie and Niagara. Soon after my uncle and Aunt Aitken sailed for the land of promise.

At this time I remember my cousin-brother, George Lauder ('Dod'), and myself were deeply impressed with the great danger overhanging us because a lawless flag was secreted in the garret. It had been painted to be carried, and I believe was carried by my father, or uncle, or some other good radical of our family, in a procession during the Corn Law agitation. There had been riots in the town and a troop of cavalry was quartered in the Guildhall. My grandfathers and uncles on both sides, and my father, had been foremost in addressing meetings, and the whole family circle was in a ferment.

I remember as if it were yesterday being awakened during the night by a tap at the back window by men who had come to inform my parents that my uncle, Bailie Morrison, had been thrown into jail because he had dared to hold a meeting which had been forbidden. The sheriff with the aid of the soldiers had arrested him a few miles from the town where the meeting had been held, and brought him into the town during the night, followed by an immense throng of people. Serious trouble was feared, for the populace threatened to rescue him, and, as we learned afterwards, he had been induced by the provost of the town to step forward to a window overlooking the High Street and beg the people to retire. This he did, saying: 'If there be a friend of the good cause here tonight, let him fold his arms.' They did so. And then, after a pause, he said, 'Now, depart in peace!' My uncle, like all our family, was a moral-force man and strong for obedience to law, but radical to the core and an intense admirer of the American Republic.

One may imagine when all this was going on in public how bitter were the words that passed from one to the other in private. The denunciations of monarchical and aristocratic government, of privilege in all its forms, the grandeur of the republican system, the superiority of America, a land peopled by our own race, a home for freemen in which every citizen's privilege was every man's right – these were the exciting themes upon which I was nurtured. As a child I could have slain king, duke, or lord, and considered their deaths a service to the state and hence an heroic act.

Such is the influence of childhood's earliest associations that it was long before I could trust myself to speak respectfully of any privileged class or person who had not distinguished himself in some good way and therefore earned the right to public respect . . . I wondered that intelligent men could live where another human being was born to a privilege which was not also their birthright.

12.   North-East *c.* 1830

. . . my father was the clergyman of a country parish in the north of Scotland – a humble position, involving plain living and plain ways altogether.

[My mother] is very beautiful in my memory, but during the last months of her life we seldom saw her, and the desire to keep the house quiet for her sake must have been the beginning of that freedom which we [four boys] enjoyed during the whole of our boyhood.

I began life, and that after no pleasant fashion, as near as I can guess, about the age of six years. One glorious morning in early summer I found myself led by the ungentle hand of Mrs Mitchell [the housekeeper] towards a little school on the outside of the village, kept by an old woman called Mrs Shand . . .

Mrs Mitchell opened the door, and led me in. It was an awful experience. Dame Shand stood at her table ironing. She was as tall as Mrs Mitchell, and that was enough to prejudice me against her at once. She wore a close-fitting widow's cap, with a black ribbon round it. Her hair was grey, and her face was as grey as her hair, and her skin was gathered in wrinkles about her mouth, where they twitched and twitched, as if she were constantly meditating something unpleasant. She looked up inquiringly.

'I've brought you a new scholar,' said Mrs Mitchell.

'Well. Very well,' said the dame in a dubious tone. 'I hope he's a good boy, for he must be good if he comes here.'

'Well, he's just middling. His father spares the rod, Mrs Shand, and we know what comes of that.'

They went on with their talk, which, as far as I can recall it, was complimentary to none but the two women themselves. Meantime I was making what observations my terror would allow. About a dozen children were seated on forms along the walls, looking over the tops of their spelling-books at the newcomer. In the farther corner two were kicking at each other as opportunity offered, looking very angry, but not daring to cry. My next discovery was terribly disconcerting. Some movement drew my eyes to the floor; there I saw a boy of my own age on all-fours, fastened by a string to a leg of the table at which the dame was ironing, while – horrible to relate! – a dog, not very big but very ugly, and big enough to be frightened at, lay under the table watching him. I gazed in utter dismay.

'Ah, you may look!' said the dame. 'If you're not a good boy, that is how you shall be served. The dog shall have you to look after.'

I trembled and was speechless. After some further confabulation, Mrs Mitchell took her leave, saying –

'I'll come back for him at one o'clock, and if I don't come, just keep him till I do come.'

The dame accompanied her to the door, and then I discovered that she was lame and hobbled very much. A resolution arose full-formed in my brain.

I sat down on the form near the door, and kept very quiet. Had it not been for the intention I cherished, I am sure I should have cried.

When the dame returned, she resumed her box-iron, in which the heater went rattling about, as, standing on one leg – the other was so much shorter – she moved it to and fro over the garment on the table . . .

The ironing of course required a fire to make the irons hot, and as the morning went on, the sunshine on the walls, conspiring with the fire on the hearth, made the place too hot for the comfort of the old dame. She went and set the door wide open. I was instantly on the alert, watching for an opportunity. One soon occurred.

A class of some five or six was reading, if reading it could be called, out of the Bible. At length it came the turn of one who blundered dreadfully. It was the same boy who had been tied under the table, but he had been released for his lesson. The dame hobbled to him, and found he had his book upside down; whereupon she turned in wrath to the table, and took from the drawer a long leather strap, with which she proceeded to chastise him. As his first cry reached my ears I was halfway to the door. On the threshold I stumbled and fell.

'The new boy's running away!' shrieked some little sycophant inside.

I heard with horror, but I was up and off in a moment. I had not, however, got many yards from the cottage before I heard the voice of the dame screaming after me to return. I took no heed – only sped the faster. But what was my horror to find her command enforced by the pursuing bark of her prime minister. This paralysed me. I turned, and there was the fiendish-looking dog close on my heels. I could run no longer. For one moment I felt as if I should sink to the earth for sheer terror. The next moment a wholesome rage sent the blood to my brain. From abject cowardice to wild attack – I cannot call it courage – was the change of an instant. I rushed towards the little wretch. I did not know how to fight him but in desperation I threw myself upon him, and dug my nails into him. They had fortunately found their way to his eyes. He was the veriest coward of his species. He yelped and howled, and struggling from my grasp ran with his tail merged in his person back to his mistress, who was hobbling after me. But with the renewed strength of triumph I turned again for home, and ran as I had never run before. When or where the dame gave in, I do not know; I never turned my head until I had laid it on Kirsty's bosom, and there I burst out sobbing and crying. It was all the utterance I had left.

(Kirsty was a Highland woman who had the charge of the house in which the farm servants lived. She was a cheerful, gracious, kind woman – a woman of God's making, one would say, were it not that, however mysterious it may look, we cannot deny that He made Mrs Mitchell too.)

As soon as Kirsty had succeeded in calming me, I told her the whole story. She said very little, but I could see she was very angry. No doubt she was pondering what could be done. She got me some milk – half cream I do believe, it was so nice – and some oatcake, and went on with her work.

While I ate I reflected that any moment Mrs Mitchell might appear to drag me back in disgrace to that horrible den. I knew that Kirsty's authority was not equal to hers, and that she would be compelled to give me up. So I watched an opportunity to escape once more and hide myself, so that Kirsty might be able to say she did not know where I was.

When I had finished, and Kirsty had left the kitchen for a moment, I sped noiselessly to the door, and looked out into the farmyard. There was no one to be seen. Dark and brown and cool the door of the barn stood open, as if inviting me to shelter and safety; for I knew that in the darkest end of it lay a great heap of oat-straw. I sped across the intervening sunshine into the darkness, and began burrowing in the straw like a wild animal, drawing out handfuls and laying them carefully aside, so that no disorder should betray my retreat. When I had made a hole large enough to hold me, I got in, but kept drawing out the straw behind me and filling the hole in front. This I continued until I had not only stopped up the entrance, but placed a good thickness of straw between me and the outside. By the time I had burrowed as far as I thought necessary, I was tired, and lay down at full length in my hole, delighting in such a sense of safety as I had never before experienced. I was soon fast asleep.

And as I slept I dreamed my dream. The sun was looking very grave, and the moon reflected his concern. They were not satisfied with me. At length the sun shook his head; that is, his whole self oscillated on an axis, and the moon then shook herself in response. Then they nodded to each other as if to say, 'That is entirely my own opinion.' At last they began to talk; not as men converse, but both at once, yet each listening while each spoke. I heard no word, but their lips moved most busily; their eyebrows went up and down; their eyelids winked and winked, and their cheeks puckered and relaxed incessantly. There was an absolute storm of expression on their faces; their very noses twisted and curled. It seemed as if, in the agony of their talk, their countenances would go to pieces. For the stars, they darted about hither and thither, gathered into groups, dispersed, and formed new groups, and having no faces yet, but being a sort of celestial tadpoles, indicated by their motions alone that they took an active interest in the questions agitating their parents. Some of them kept darting up and down the ladder of rays, like phosphorescent sparks in the sea foam.

I could bear it no longer, and awoke. I was in darkness, but not in my own bed. When I proceeded to turn, I found myself hemmed in on all sides. I could not stretch my arms, and there was hardly room for my body between my feet and my head. I was dreadfully frightened at first, and felt as if I were being slowly stifled. As my brain awoke, I recalled the horrible school, the horrible schoolmistress, and the most horrible dog, over whose defeat, however, I rejoiced with the pride of a dragon-slayer.

Next I thought it would be well to look abroad and reconnoitre once more. I drew away the straw from the entrance to my lair; but what was my dismay to find that even when my hand went out into space no light came through the opening. What could it mean? Surely I had not grown blind while I lay asleep. Hurriedly I shot out the remainder of the stopper of straw and crept from the hole. In the great barn there was but the dullest glimmer of light; I had almost said the clumsiest reduction of darkness. I tumbled at one of the doors rather than ran to it . . .

I stepped out into the night with grass of the corn-yard under my feet, the awful vault of heaven over my head, and those shadowy ricks around me. It was a relief to lay my hand on one of them, and feel that it was solid . . . Away in the north was the Great Bear. I knew that constellation, for by it one of the men had taught me to find the pole-star. Nearly under it was the light of the sun, creeping round by the north towards the spot in the east where he would rise again. But I learned only afterwards to understand this.

I gazed at that pale faded light, and all at once I remembered that God was near me. But I did not know what God is then as I know now, and when I thought about him then, which was neither much nor often, my idea of him was not like him; it was merely a confused mixture of other people's fancies about him and my own. I had not learned how beautiful God is; I had only learned that he is strong. I had been told that he was angry with those that did wrong; I had not learned that he loved them all the time, although he was displeased with them, and must punish them to make them good. When I thought of him now in the silent starry night, a yet greater terror seized me, and I ran stumbling over the uneven field.

Does my reader wonder whither I fled? Whither should I fly but home? True, Mrs Mitchell was there, but there was another there as well. Even Kirsty would not do in this terror. Home was the only refuge, for my father was there. I sped for the manse.

But as I approached it a new apprehension laid hold of my trembling heart. I was not sure, but I thought the door was always locked at night. I drew nearer. The place of possible refuge rose before me. I stood on the grass-plot in front of it. There was no light in its eyes. Its mouth was closed. It was silent as one of the ricks. Above shone the speechless stars. Nothing was alive. Nothing would speak. I went up the few rough-hewn granite steps that led to the door. I laid my hand on the handle, and gently turned it. Joy of joys! the door opened. I entered the hall. Ah! it was more silent than the night. No footsteps echoed; no voices were there. I closed the door behind me, and, almost sick with the misery of a being where no other being was to comfort it, I groped my way to my father's room. When I once had my hand on his door, the warm tide of courage began again to flow from my heart. I opened this door too very quietly, for was not the dragon asleep down below?

'Papa! Papa!' I cried, in an eager whisper. 'Are you awake, Papa?'

No voice came in reply, and the place was yet more silent than the night or the hall. He must be asleep. I was afraid to call louder. I crept nearer to the bed. I stretched out my hands to feel for him. He must be at the farther side. I climbed up on the bed. I felt all across it. Utter desolation seized my soul – my father was not there! Was it a horrible dream? Should I ever awake? My heart sank totally within me. I could bear no more. I fell down on the bed weeping bitterly, and wept myself asleep.

Once more I awoke to a sense of misery, and stretched out my arms, crying, 'Papa! Papa!' The same moment I found my father's arms around me; he folded me close to him, and said –

'Hush, Ranald, my boy! Here I am! You are quite safe.'
I nestled as close to him as I could go, and wept for blessedness.
'Oh, Papa!' I sobbed, 'I thought I had lost you.'
'And I thought I had lost you, my boy. Tell me all about it.'

13.   Fife 1860s/1870s

My earliest recollection of my schooldays is of a lady teacher who
punished us by striking our little outstretched hands with a hardwood
stick about the thickness of a golf club shaft. She struck with such
force that the little hands showed the welts for hours afterwards. But I
have no recollection of objecting parents! In fact 'cruel and unusual
punishments' now forbidden by law were not unknown in my
schooldays. For example, another boy and I (when about fourteen)
got into a fight which had scarcely started when the janitor came along,
stopped the engagement and haled us before the teacher who was
'Convenor for the week' and in charge of the discipline. He asked us
for what crime we had been sent up and we replied 'for fighting'.

'Well, and who beat?' he demanded.

We told him that we had been interrupted by the janitor before we
had found out.

'Too bad, too bad,' he replied, then turning to the assembled class
he announced, with a smile, 'These boys have been fighting but did
not have time to find out who beat. Now we will find out who beat. I
will give them the "Tawse" until one or the other cries, and the first to
cry will be the one who was beaten.'

Having thus put two Scotch laddies on their mettle he got out his
thick leather belt and ordered us to hold out our hands time about. He
then struck our hands right and left alternately with all his force, and kept
at it until the perspiration streamed down his face. Of course neither of
us cried. Finally he gave up with the remark, 'Well, I am beat.'

That night our hands were so paralysed that we could not feed
ourselves, and it was several days before either of us could hold a pen.
Such punishment for an offense involving no moral turpitude was
disgrace to the school and to the teacher, but I have no recollection of
objecting parents. Parents now-a-days would have such a teacher
arrested – and rightly so.

* * *

127

I left [the Madras College] in my sixteenth year. I was not further advanced than other boys of my age, but I was sent into commercial life able to write a legible hand, to do almost any problems in arithmetic – many of them mentally, that is, not putting down any figures but the answer – and to write simple English clearly and grammatically. In addition to these solid accomplishments, I had had Latin as far as Caesar, Euclid and Algebra in moderation, and I could read a French or German book rapidly enough to enjoy the story. Nor was Art neglected. We had an excellent drawing teacher and all kinds of drawing and painting were taught – engineering, mechanical, landscape, in water colors, oils, etc. I still have hanging on the walls of my home the large French Crayon drawings of dogs and horses, after Landseer, which won me first prize in that department. No one notices them because they look just like engravings. So far as I have been able to judge, the average American boy of fifteen would have difficulty in showing a better educational foundation.

14.   Glasgow *c.* 1885

. . . That was the only time I got six. But though my hands were numb he [the headmaster of Hillhead School] did not break my spirit. Towards the last I was feeling distinctly murderous. It was not so much what he did to me as the gusto with which he did it. I found myself eyeing a heavy ink-well on his desk and wondering what would happen if I hurled it at his head. It was red ink too. I believe another lash would have made me do it.

One does not forgive and forget punishment that is severe and unjust. Years after, when I heard that he had been drowned while bathing, I laughed for joy. Yet I have no doubt he gave no further thought to the matter and would have been profoundly surprised at my lasting resentment.

15.   Orkney 1890s

Yet there were times when I enjoyed going to school; it all depended on who was teaching me. I passed under a whole regiment of teachers there, male and female; teachers who shouted at me, who hit me over the head with the pointer, who strapped me (for the tawse was used vigorously), who took an interest in me, who sneered at me (and they were the worst); teachers whose personal habits I came to know as I grew older; who drank, or were infatuated with the pretty girls in their class, or had a curious walk or some curious habit. We studied them with the inquisitiveness of visitors to a zoo; for to us they were really animals behind bars. There were teachers who terrified us, and whose eyes, fixed on us, could assume the hypnotic stare of an animal trainer. I knew the appearance of all the straps in all the classrooms: there were thick voluptuous ones, and thin, mean, venomous ones; laid down on the desk after execution, they folded up with ruthless grace like sleepy cats. In some of them the tails had been burned over a fire to make them sting more sharply. Certain boys were punished day after day as part of the routine: a brutal ceremony which we watched in a silent fascination and dread which might easily have implanted in us a taste for sadism and insidiously corrupted us. The punishment varied from three strokes on the hand to twelve. There were teachers who did not use the strap more than three or four times a year, and others who flogged on monotonously day after day, as if they were pounding some recalcitrant substance, not the hands of living boys. I avoided the strap as well as I could; in some classes I could completely forget it, and then I liked school, for the teachers were invariably good at their work. One teacher, Miss Annan, did not use the strap at all. She had a cheerful, impudent, devoted class who only needed her presence to become inspired. She taught us English, and but for her we might never have realized what the subject meant beyond the drudgery of parsing and analysis. She opened our eyes; we felt we were a sort of aristocracy, for what we did for her we did freely. She must have been a remarkable woman; she seemed to have endless charm, vitality, and patience. She filled us with confidence and a kind of goodness which was quite unlike the goodness asked from us by the other teachers. Yet she never put us on our honour; she simply took us as we were and by some power changed us.

16.   Fife 1920s/1930s

. . . a retiral further up the school brought a new teacher to the village, and Miss Balsilbie came like a daughter of Zion to give us glimpses of the promised land.

When she swept through the pale green door of Room Five at the start of the new session, I felt my toes tingle and my tongue cleave to the roof of my mouth . . . She was all sweet in my nostrils, Miss Balsilbie, carrying continents in the palm of her hand. The perfumes of the east were flung from her black hair, scattered by the corn-sowing wave of her arm as she welcomed us to her new kingdom, the garden of delights, and we her open-mouthed subjects, too tattered and untaught to say a word.

Roses are what I remember.

White ones.

Miss Balsilbie's blouses were white roses that fluffed and fell as she breathed, and the merest puff from an ungallant infant might have blown them clean off her back. What would happen should all those soft and snow-crimped petals fall fluttering to the floor of the classroom?

But Miss Balsilbie carried her white roses all round the room, visiting each desk in turn. When she came to me I was beating my head against the blind brutal wall of my sums, which I could never do easily or well. My jotter was a mass of erasions and errors, filthy with ignorance. She leaned over me, reaching for the page. I hid my inky, nail-bitten fingers between my knees. The rose petals brushed my cheek, whispered against the scarred lid of my ugly, lumpish desk. I held my breath as tightly as I could. Miss Balsilbie reached out her white, swansnecked, swansdowned arm, and her hand touched my exercise book. She held a long, beautifully sharpened pencil between her fingers, a red pencil. Her nails were polished a vivid scarlet, like strawberries, like blushing blood-red moons. No scars from the gutting-troughs warred with those milk-washed hands of hers.

> *How should I your true-love know*
> *From another one?*

Her pale-blue veins ran like dim rivers in an undiscovered country, the land of lost content, the land of milk and honey . . . My head swam.

'No, no dear,' she drawled, 'you don't know how to divide, do you? Here, let me show you.'

She squeezed herself into the desk beside me, tucking in her shimmering silk skirt. It rustled mysteriously like the quiet turn of the tide, fell over my knees in cool waves. It made me shiver.

'Goodness me, you are shaking, my poor boy. What in the world is the matter with you?'

She put her pencil on my desk and placed her arm around me.

'You don't have to be frightened of me now, dear, do you? Even though you can't divide.'

She gave a tinkling little laugh and hugged me close, drew me towards the dazzling white world of the snowdrift. I sank into it, through the fluttering flakes and into the heart of the rose. When I came out of it, the day had changed irrevocably; another terrible beauty was born; my heart was cold as ice. It belonged to Miss Balsilbie, Miss Balsilbie now my Snow Queen, queen of my crystal heart, why was your reign so short? Too short to let me understand the heart of the rose, you froze me until the day I could divide.

But by then it was too late.

And so, Miss Balsilbie, you ravished my heart with one of your eyes, with one chain of your neck. Honey and milk were under your tongue, and the smell of your clothes was like the smell of Lebanon.

You were too good to last.

A garden enclosed, a spring shut up, a fountain concealed.

She had given us the apples of the trees of the wood, Miss Balsilbie, when our understanding was not yet ripe. So the headmaster banished her from the garden of delights, and the flaming sword of Miss Sangster's vengeance guarded the school gates. We never saw her again.

But Miss Sangster was waiting for us.

She was a long frozen leek of a woman, Miss Sangster, standing straight and hard as an undriven nail. From her coat-hanger shoulders her smock hung like a faded flag, covering her bony, crepe-stockinged shanks almost down to her ankle boots.

Even on her own head she had no mercy. The thin grey hair lay like ash on the pink skull. She parted it simply, without a shred of pity for her womanhood, shearing it just below her ears on either side, and leaving bare the reptilian nape of her neck. Her eyes were glittering pinpricks under her glasses, her lips were pursed prunes. Vinegar ran in her veins and chalk in her arteries. She blew on the embers of dead days with her dusty breath, warming her cold fingers before the tired fires of life. Those fingers of hers were always ringed with warts and plasters and little bandages. They were the broken hands of a loveless lady, the sex within her denied and defeated long ago. But with these hands Miss Sangster beat us into daily submission.

17.   1920s

Andy tries to copy the figure 7 from the blackboard on to the clean new page of his jotter. It is Friday, so it is jotters instead of slates, and he has to be specially careful, Miss Wood says. His pencil wobbles and the 7 looks like a worm. He tries again and it looks like a worm that someone had almost bitten in half.

Andy looks to his left. Fiona, at the next oak-and-iron desk, has drawn a whole line of beautiful 7s, almost as good as Miss Wood's on the blackboard. Miss Wood isn't looking, she is bending over someone at the front of the class, so Andy finishes his line of 7s in a rush. They look like a fence that is falling down.

He glances to his left again. Fiona is sitting up 'properly', holding her pen 'properly' in her plump fingers. She is half-way through her second line of 7s, all of them perfect.

He looks to his right. Geordie, who shares his desk, is working hard. His short legs are twisted together and his head is almost on the desk and his tongue is sticking out. He has drawn two careful 7s, almost as perfect as Fiona's. He untwists his legs, twists them again the other way round, licks his pencil, and starts on his third 7. MacMillan is slow but sure, Miss Wood says, but she'll be cross if she sees him licking his pencil.

My big brother, Andy thinks, writes his figures *very very* fast and they come out like Miss Wood's, so he does his second line *very very* fast. They come out like a line of telegraph poles getting bigger and bigger and more and more uneven. He looks up and Miss Wood is arriving at his desk, smelling of peppermints and leather shoes. Her black gown is dusty with chalk. She has a 'lady' smell too, so Andy tries to hold his breath.

'You must be more careful, Robb,' she says, bending down from her great height and putting his fingers round his pencil 'properly'. She guides his hand to make the first 7 of his third row. It is, of course, nearly perfect.

'Now, try that yourself,' says Miss Wood. Andy tries, still holding his breath. He breaks the point of his pencil. He is too frightened to look up, and tries to breathe without breathing.

'Careless, boy!' he hears Miss Wood saying crossly. She is not really angry, though. She reaches into the deep flying pocket of her gown for her shiny pen-knife, sharpens Andy's pencil, and moves away to someone else, after pleased glances at Fiona and Geordie. Andy takes several deep breaths, as quietly as he can. His big brother can sharpen a pencil, but he can't.

Andy needs to go to the bathroom, but he doesn't want to ask Miss Wood if he may leave the room. She will be cross with him, after the broken pencil. He presses his legs together and hopes for the best. He tries another 7 and it looks like a squashed worm. The next he tries is better, but much too big. The next is almost perfect, but even bigger.

Fiona, Andy can see, had finished a whole neat page of proper 7s, all the same height. Her finger-nails are round at the top, a much nicer shape that his blunt ones. They are spotless underneath too, while his are black. His big sister says, 'Your nails are going to a funeral'. Andy wishes he could hide them. The pleats in Fiona's kilt are perfect.

The playtime bell, it must ring soon. Andy breaks his pencil again, but pretends to go on writing. Fiona turns to him, half closes her eyes and puts out the tip of her pink tongue. Then she looks at the mess in his jotter, opens her eyes wide, and makes an O of her mouth. She has noticed! She *always* notices. Why does he have to sit in the row next the girls? None of the boys want to sit there. It was Miss Wood who made him. Andy wishes with all his heart that he was right at the other end of the room. Not that he wants to leave Geordie, who is his friend.

His friend is sighing and straightening out his legs. He is wearing a khaki jersey several sizes too large for him which would fit a very wee soldier, ragged tweed shorts, odd stockings with holes in them which are draped right down round his ankles, and gym shoes without laces, but he doesn't care. He doesn't care a bit. His legs are short and thick and dirty and sun-burned. Andy glances down at his own scrawny, warty, clean, pale knees sticking out between his clean flannel shorts and his clean grey carefully-darned stockings. His tackety boots are shiny. Father cleans them, laughing about Lloyd George and Mother getting the vote. Grown-ups have boring secrets. Andy can't run as fast as Geordie, or kick a ball as cleverly and fiercely, and he never gets sunburned. He wants to go to the bathroom – it is called the 'lavvy' at school.

The playtime bell goes at last, but Miss Wood is slow about letting the class out. Andy thinks he is going to wet his pants, but she goes on fussing about passing forward the pencils, then spends for ever counting them. Pencils are precious, because of the War to End War. So are jotters. Then everybody has to sit up straight enough to please Miss Wood, which is very straight indeed. After she is satisfied that everyone is like a poker, she gives the magic signal and Andy marches out with the others.

18. Angus *c.* 1930

On Monday morning it was back to school for Lexy and me. (Little Nancy was only three.)

I hated it, especially as there were no other traveller children at it for us to play with. The other children avoided us and taunted us continually and we were not allowed to sit on the same seat as a 'country' child. Of course we were behind with our lessons, but most teachers more or less just suffered us in their classes. I was in the Qualifying class now, and the teacher was a man.

One day he asked me, and another girl who sat in the seat at my back, to come out. 'Look at these exercise books,' he said. 'This is the third time this has happened, and it is too often to be coincidental. Both these sums are wrong, and both identical. One of you must be copying.'

This girl piped up. 'It is Betsy, sir. She is always looking round copying off me.' I was stunned. Apart from not having enough interest to be bothered copying, I would have needed a neck like a swan to manage it. Yet her word was accepted without question.

'I will have to strap you, Betsy.' I said nothing. I never did at school, having long before found out that it was useless. The schoolmaster took his strap out of a drawer and said 'Hold out your hand.'

As I held out my hand I heard the girl who had accused me, and some of the others, tittering. At this I felt all the suppressed venom welling up and the rebellious pride, which I had inherited from my mother, rose in me. I withdrew my hand just as the strap descended. It caught the teacher with some force just below his knee. Then I gave him two sharp kicks on the shin bone and fled out of the room.

Unfortunately the headmaster was just making his way to our room and he caught me in the corridor. I was shaking from head to foot and unable to answer him. I suppose I was really in a state of terror.

He led me by the arm back to the class where the young teacher, his face fiery red, was just trying to overcome his astonishment at my behaviour. 'What has happened?' the headmaster asked. 'That . . . that . . . girl!' the teacher replied, suppressing what he really meant to call me. 'She refused to take the strap and actually kicked me on the shins.'

I felt more composed now, somehow feeling a comfort in the headmaster's presence. 'Is this true, Betsy?' 'Yes, sir,' I replied. 'You know this is a very serious affair. I will have to deal with you myself. Come with me down to my room.' I followed him quite meekly. I couldn't care less if he strapped me a hundred times – as long as it was out of sight of those sniggering children.

On reaching his room the headmaster seated himself on his chair and looked up at me. 'Now then, Betsy, tell me all about it.' 'The girl behind me blamed me for copying, sir. I've never copied in my life. Then her and the others started making a fool of me when I was about to be strapped.' 'You didn't care much for that, did you?' he asked – then surprised me by saying, before I could answer, 'Neither would I.'

He then reached into a drawer. For his strap, I supposed. But instead it was an exercise book that he took out. 'Sit down, child,' he said, handing me the book. He then started to ask me a lot of questions about sums, spelling, and asked me to write down what I thought were the answers. He then gave me mental arithmetic.

'Well, Betsy, I think you could prove to Mr Arbuckle that you don't need to copy – if you would just try.' Not quite understanding his meaning, I asked 'How, Sir?' 'By doing as I tell you. Come back to my room when school is finished and I'll give you some books. Now off with you back to your room, and tell no one that you didn't get a walloping. I'll come down with you and talk to Mr Arbuckle. But remember, if you ever kick a teacher again you won't get off so easily.'

After school the headmaster gave me books which explained how all the sums we were getting were done, and one which explained grammar. 'Study these at home,' he said.

This headmaster was the best thing that ever happened to me. He taught me how much one can learn from books, and I became very interested in them. I would lie down and read to my mother and father at night. They would listen enraptured. Mother used to buy the twopenny weeklies we used to get, and waited impatiently for the next instalment of *The Red Barn Mystery* and other favourites of the time.

One day I found an old book in a dump. *Three Men in a Boat* it was called. If you had been passing at the time I was reading it aloud you would have wondered what in the world we all found to laugh so much at. (Of course there were libraries, but we never thought they could be for the likes of us and we wouldn't dare go into one.)

I really did improve at school too – much to the delight of the headmaster, who really took an interest in me and gave me confidence and encouragement. He implored my parents to stay in the town until after the Qualifying Examination for secondary school. I didn't let him down either, being one of the three in my class who won bursaries. He told my parents that he would pay what else was needed for me to go to High School, as this bursary only paid for books or something. I didn't quite understand it.

Poor headmaster! He was pestered and bullyragged by irate parents who were convinced that my getting a bursary had been his doing. As it had in a way, but not in the way that they meant. How was it possible for a tinker child to pass and not their child? They wouldn't believe the poor man that the examination papers went to Forfar and that he wasn't responsible.

But it was the middle of June by this time and the yellow would soon be falling off the broom.

So Daddy wasted no time getting out of the town.

19.   Oban 1950s

If my mother was worried about me getting a man in Primary Five she needn't have bothered.

> *He mo leannan ho mo leannan*
> *Se mo leannan am fear ur*
> *He mo leannan ho mo leannan*

He is a Gaelic-speaker from south Argyll. He teaches us Gaelic songs. And my love's an arbutus by the waters of Lene: his eyes have a soft sapphire sheen too.

His name is Hector, name of heroes; a sailor returned from the sea is he. When his backside itches he scratches it.

He talks to us all the time. As if we were really worth talking to. He lets us talk in class. But we are well-behaved; the boys can smell his authority and respect his casual stocky strength. In return he makes no distinctions between us: no good ones and bad ones, no clever and stupid ones. Walter MacIntyre's story about the spider that came down his mother's plug-hole is as precious to Hector as my careful sentences. My sentences become less careful . . .

Hector is a great drawer. He draws us, we draw him. We draw everything. He shows us how things look smaller in the distance and how shadows always go in the same direction and how you can't see all four sides of a house at once even though you know they're there.

He likes poetry, and lets us choose the poems we like best. It's no bother learning them when you like them yourself. Him and me like the Scottish ones best: Come in ahint ye wannerin tyke, did ever buddy see the like, and Wee sleekit cooerin timorous beastie, o what a panic's in thy breastie, and The Laird o Cockpen he's prood and he's great, his mind's taen up wi the things o the state.

He reads to us, one cheek perched on the lid of someone's desk, acting it out with his voice: exciting stories, making it sound as if he's been there . . .

Hector has just one rule in the week: Friday morning, a Test and Strictly No Talking – while he checks and signs the registers. Well, he's the Headmaster, don't forget. He has to do all that too you see. We help him. I am the class messenger this week, have been all round the school collecting up the registers. I come back into the class feeling all important and self-satisfied and mature. I smile at Hector and go and sit down, wondering why it's so quiet.

'What are we meant to be doing?' I ask Anne. She frowns at me warningly.

'Come out here Anne Gillies. You know you are not allowed to talk during the Arithmetic Test.'

I walk towards him, disbelievingly, as he opens his desk and takes out the heavy leather strap. His eyes are on me, bulbous, beseeching.

He turns me round to face the class then puts himself in between me and them so they can't see. He raises the belt sharply over his right shoulder. I hear it whack against his shiny jacket. 'I'm so sorry. I'm so sorry. You know I have to do this,' he mutters, head down.

'Yes sir,' I sigh, as pain and betrayal snake upwards from my palm to wrist to heart. Holding breath I go back to my seat. Watching fat tears roll down my nose, staining the desk, I sit very still all morning, cradling my hand in the folds of my skirt, making no attempt to work. At play-time he silently gives me a huge white hankie, but says nothing about my going out to play. The others walk out and come back in again very quietly, finding I have not moved. At dinner-time I walk slowly home and bury my face in my mother's lap. My brother has told them what happened. They know. No-one tells me to buck up or suggests I should go back to school that afternoon.

At half-past five Hector comes up our road, flying over the bumps in his wee grey car, sitting incongruous in Grampop's chair with the wings. My mother gives him tea, my father gives him a dram, and they talk quietly while I sit listlessly in the swing outside feeling my face tight with crying.

Poor Hector. He's very upset.

'It's all right. I understand. Yes of course – I'll come back to school on Monday.'

WORK

❧

taken from

THE annals of Aberdeen about this time reveal the existence of a system of kidnapping young persons of both sexes, which, for heartless cruelty and greed of gain, will bear comparison with the descriptions that have been given of the horrors of the African slave trade . . . some of the Magistrates of the city, in their private capacity as merchants, along with the Town Clerk Depute, . . . not content with the profits derived from legitimate articles of trade, . . . endeavoured to augment their gains by means of a traffic which was a disgrace to humanity.

The plan adopted was this: – Some time prior to the date at which it was expected that one of their vessels would leave the port for America, men were sent out for the express purpose of waylaying young persons by any device likely to attact their attention, and having once got hold of them, they were forcibly seized and kept in confinement until the vessel was ready to sail, when they were secretly conveyed on board and shipped off in batches to the plantations. On their arrival in America they were sold as slaves for a period of years, but the treatment they had to endure in their bondage was such that few of them ever came back to their native land . . .

The trade was carried on for five or six years: in the year 1743 alone, sixty-nine young persons are known to have disappeared from Aberdeen as the victims of this infamous traffic, and it is supposed that, between 1740 and 1745, as many as six hundred youths were captured and sold in this inhuman manner . . .

Among the youths who were carried off in the way described was one Peter Williamson . . . One day, apparently about the year 1741, as he was amusing himself on the quay, after the manner of boys of his age, he was enticed on board a vessel by two fellows who belonged to the ship, and as it was on the point of sailing, he was kept in confinement between decks, where he found a number of other youths who were in the same unfortunate position . . . Arriving in America they were sold, and it was Williamson's lot to fall into the hands of a planter in Pensylvania, under whose power he remained for a year or two, but after a number of vicissitudes and romantic adventures, he finally effected his escape . . .

2.   Scotland 1799

. . . there are few people who now know that so recently as 1799 there were slaves in this country. Twenty-five years before, that is, in 1775, there must have been thousands of them; for this was then the condition of all our colliers and salters. They were literally slaves. They could not be killed or directly tortured; but they belonged, like the serfs of an older time, to their respective works, with which they were sold as part of the gearing. With a few very rigid exceptions, the condition of the head of the family was the condition of the whole house. For though a child, *if never entered* with the work, was free, yet entering was its natural and almost certain destination; for its doing so was valuable to its father, and its getting into any other employment in the neighbourhood was resisted by the owner. So that wives, daughters, and sons went on from generation to generation under the system which was the family doom.

3.   Cromarty *c.* 1780

Rather more than eighty years ago, a stout little boy, in his sixth or seventh year, was despatched from an old-fashioned farm-house in the upper part of the parish of Cromarty, to drown a litter of puppies in an adjacent pond. The commission seemed to be not in the least congenial. He sat down beside the pool, and began to cry over his charge; and finally, after wasting much time in a paroxysm of indecision and sorrow, instead of committing the puppies to the water, he tucked them up in his little kilt, and set out by a blind pathway which went winding through the stunted heath of the dreary Maolbhoy Common, in a direction opposite to that of the farm-house – his home for the two previous twelvemonths.

After some doubtful wandering in the waste, he succeeded in reaching, before nightfall, the neighbouring seaport town, and presented himself, laden with his charge, at his mother's door. The poor woman – a sailor's widow, in very humble circumstances – raised her hands in astonishment: 'Oh, my unlucky boy,' she exclaimed, 'what's this? – what brings you here?' 'The little doggies, mither,' said the boy; 'I couldnae drown the little doggies; and I took them to you.'

What afterwards befell the 'little doggies', I know not; but trivial as the incident may seem, it exercised a marked influence on the circumstances and destiny of at least two generations of creatures higher in the scale than themselves. The boy, as he stubbornly refused to return to the farm-house, had to be sent on shipboard, agreeably to his wish, as a cabin-boy; and the writer of these chapters was born, in consequence, a sailor's son, and was rendered, as early as his fifth year, mainly dependent for his support on the sedulously plied but indifferently remunerated labours of his only surviving parent, at the time a sailor's widow.

4.   Ayrshire *c.* 1800

When I had perfited my edication, which was afore Beltane of the next year – I being then weel through my eighth year – it behoved me to think of some gaet of going to the world to seek a living; for it was not thought I was of a proper habit of body for a trade, as I was short-sighted, and very ready to take the cold, which shewed that herding would never do for me. Some calling of a sheltered nature was, therefore, to be thought of. The neighbours of aunty considered, however, I was still young enough; but there was confabble among them anent me, which made it manifest that there would soon be an outcoming.

In the May after, the laddie who kirned James Junor's, the druggist, medicaments, took the kingcost; and being of a weakly constitution, paid the debt of nature in no time. Thus there came to be a vacuity in the druggist's shop, and I was elected, by James, to that office. It was, indeed, as aunty said, a blithe upcast to meet with; and I thought so, too, and often thought so, when dunting the pestle on the bottom of the brass mortar; for I hope ye have gotten a sufficiency of learning to understand that kirning drugs is braying in a mortar with a pestle, similar to the utensil which, as I have heard the one called, that stood above our door, gilded, the effigy of a doctor.

With Mr Junor, I was the best of three years; and it cannot be said, at the end of the term, that I was even then owre old to take my foot in my hand, to see what the world was like ayont the dyke. But it was a pleasant, sober time – the remembrance of it is lowne in my bosom, like a bonny April morning, when the buds biggen, and the birds begin to sing. Nor was my being in that odoriferous shop (as I heard the schoolmistress one day call it) without profit, in a sense; for, at my work, I thought but of such a nice thing it must be to be rich, and used to lilt, in a cutty-crumb voice, keeping time with the pestle –

> The king sits in his parlour,
> Counting o'er his money;
> The queen sits in her garden,
> Eating bread and honey –

thinking his Majesty's duty was the pleasantest vocation of the two.

When I had been two years and a half with that gospel-hearted saint, Mr Junor, tholing as well's I could with his Jobish conjugality, and being nearing on the time to do for myself, I had some wiselike confabble with my aunty.

It was agreed between us, that, as I had no prospect of being a robustious man, I should spouse my fortune as an errander in Glasgow. But the easiest trades are no without their craft . . . so I could not set up as an errander, till I had learnt the outs and ins of that royal city. But, in this, Providence, as in all cases, was large; and the willing-to-do-well will never want a friend as long as there's a God in the heavens.

It happened that aunty had a far-off cousin by her guidman's side – a well-doing weaver in the Gorbals; and he had a wife that was spoken of for that couthy kind of eidency which foretokens thriving; indeed, the truth of the saying had kythed on them, for, in the fulness of time, he was gathered to his fathers, in a bien way, and a bailie.

. . . Thus, it came to pass that, on my eleventh birthday, I went with the carrier to begin the world as an errander in Glasgow.

I weel mind the welcoming I got from John Douce and his wife. It couldna be said he was unjustly a narrow man; but he was, maybe, a thought hard. His wife, however, was a hand-waled woman, and had from the womb been ordained to bless the man she was made for.

* * *

The next morning I rose betimes; and having covenanted with the carrier lad on the road, to shew me some of the town, we went hither and yon together till eight o'clock, in a very satisfactory manner. John Douce, after breakfast, having gone to his looms, his wife said that, as she was not very throng, she would go about with me, adding, it was aye to her a pleasaunce to help them that were so willing to do well. She was, indeed, a prudent woman, and very wisely thought that to make money was the true substantial way to do weel in this world.

When I had learned myself well in the wynds and turns of Glasgow, I took my station aneath the pillars forenent the Tolbooth; but when I gaed home at breakfast time, a thought dowie because I had come to no speed, Mrs Douce said it was not the right side of the street.

'One,' quoth she, 'should aye endeavour to begin the world on the right side of the causeway. It's no doubt a very creditable stance ye have taken; but it's no so good by a degree as the plainstones on the other side where the gentlemen congregate; – and, besides, ye must change that Kilmarnock bonnet. It gars ye look of a country complexion. Do in Rome as they do in Rome; and mind never to make yourself kenspeckle unless it's in snodness; for maist folk, though they cannot tell why, have no broo of them that has onything out-o'-the-way about them.'

In consequence of this advice, I niffered after breakfast with another laddie for his hat with my bonnet and twopence, and took up my stance at a closs mouth wester the Tontine, which was then bigging; the gentlemen, provost, and magistrates making then their howff at where the cross used to be, as I was told.

Good luck was in the change; for an Englisher soon after hired me to take a letter as far west as Madeira Court, and I made such nimble speed with the errand that he gave me a whole sixpence, the first white money I ever had received; in short, before the day was done, I had made a rough ninepence – that is, a bawbee over; and Mrs Douce, when I offered the half to John, would not let him touch it, saying that all I made the first day ought to be my own; for it was the luck arle of a fortune. It could not, therefore, but be said that I had a prospect in the very beginning.

The second day of my erranding, I mind weel, was not splendid; saving a twalpenny job to the Broomielaw, for a scrimping shopkeeper, to a Greenock gabbart, with the bundle of a Highland tartan plaid, belonging to a nauby that was going to Tobermory, I had but a scrimpit measure of luck. To be sure, towards the heel of the evening, a bailie, with a red north-west countenance, being vogie from his punchbowl and the funny stories of his cronies, hired me to go to Ruglen with a letter, on some 'lection ploy; for there was a great sough at that time of a Parlimenting, as it was called, which I have since learnt meant a general election. This achievement caused me to be in the gloaming before I got to John Douce's; and a weary wean I was, both with the length of the road and its sliddiness, caused by the forepart of the day being showery. Mrs Douce, seeing me so scomfished, took pains to hearten me, when I had rested myself, saying that there was no profit in running lang errands, and, therefore, I ought to eschew them.

kingcost: whooping cough; *arle*: earnest, pledge; *gabbart*: lighter, barge

5. Dundee *c.* 1815

When I went to a spinning mill I was about seven years of age. I had to get out of bed every morning at five o'clock, commence work at half-past five, drop at nine for breakfast, begin again at half-past nine, work until two, which was the dinner hour, start again at half-past two, and continue until half-past seven at night. Such were the nominal hours; but in reality there were no regular hours, masters and managers did with us as they liked. The clocks at the factories were often put forward in the morning and back at night, and instead of being instruments for the measurement of time, they were used as *cloaks* for cheatery and oppression . . .

In country mills, a more horrific despotism reigned than in Dundee. There, masters frequently bound the young by a regular contract which gave them a more complete control over their labour and liberties than taking them from week to week. In one establishment in the vicinity of Dundee, the proprietor, a coarse-minded man . . . practised the contract system, and had bothies where he lodged all his male and female workers. They were allowed to cook, sleep, and live in any dog and cat manner they pleased, no moral superintendence whatever being exercised over them. His mill was kept going 17 and frequently 19 hours per day. To accomplish this all meal hours were almost dispensed with, and women were employed to boil potatoes and carry them in baskets to the different flats; and the children had to swallow a potato hastily in the interval of putting up 'ends'. On dinners cooked and eaten as I have described, they had to subsist till half-past nine, and frequently ten at night. When they returned to their bothies, brose, as it is a dish that can be quickly made, constituted their suppers, for they had no time to wait the preparation of a different meal. They then tumbled into bed: but balmy sleep had scarcely closed their urchin eyelids, and steeped their infant souls in blessed forgetfulness, when the thumping of the watchman's staff on the door would rouse them from repose and the words 'Get up: it's four o'clock' reminded them they were factory children, the unprotected victims of monotonous slavery.

At this mill and indeed all mills, boys and girls were often found sleeping in stairs and private places, and they have been seen walking about the flats in a deep sleep, with cans of 'sliver' in their hands. When found in this state, they were caned or kicked according to the mood of their superiors. One poor boy . . . sat down to rest himself, as his legs were sore and swollen by incessant standing. In a few moments he was fast asleep. Whilst enjoying this stolen repose, the master happened to pass. Without the least warning he gave him a violent slap on the side of the head, which stunned and stupefied him. In a half-sleeping state of stupefaction he ran to the roving frame, which he sometimes attended and five minutes had barely elapsed when his left hand got entangled with the machinery, and two of his fingers were crushed to a jelly, and had to be immediately amputated. His unfeeling master gave him no recompense – in fact never asked after him: he was left to starve or die, as Providence might direct.

sliver: semi-liquid, unpalatable mixture of food

6.   East Lothian 1826

I had reached my fourteenth year, when the question arose, what was I to be? We were a large and growing family, and every one of us must do something, and eventually work for a living.

. . . when my mother asked me, 'What would you like to be, Sam?'
I answered, 'I would like to be a painter' – I meant an artist. I had a
taste for drawing and colour, and many years after illustrated one of
my own books . . . But my mother thought that I wished to be a *house-
painter*. 'Oh no!' said she, 'that is a dirty business.' I did not answer,
and the matter slept for a time.

On a future day, she again asked me, 'Would you no like to be a
minister?'

'Oh no!' I said decidedly, 'I'll no be a minister.'

'What for no?'

I could not very well explain then, but I can now. We children were
surfeited with preaching and ministering . . . Our minister was a good
and hard-working man. He, no doubt, gave us all that he had to give;
but he was wearisome and unsympathetic; and his doctrines, though
intended to frighten us into goodness, had perhaps the very reverse
effect. There was no wonder, therefore, that I should not wish to be a
minister.

The next question put to me by mother was this: 'Would you no
like to be a doctor?'

The question was rather startling at first. There were many
prejudices against doctors in my younger days. Our servants used
to tell the trembling children about the 'black doctors' that were ready
to clap a plaster over our mouths, and carry us away no one knew
whither. Then, a regular watch and ward was held over the parish
burying-ground, to prevent the 'doctors' rifling the graves, for the
purposes of the dissecting-rooms at Edinburgh. I remember going
with my father, when he was on the watch, to take the first turn with
him round the churchyard. There were three or four men, I think, one
of whom was elected the foreman. They were supplied with some old
muskets, mounted with bayonets, to give the resurrectionists a warm
welcome. This frightful state of things culminated a few years later, in
the murders by Burke and Hare of living 'subjects' for Dr Knox's
anatomy class at Edinburgh.

But doctors were necessary for many reasons. It so happened that I
fell down a hatchway, and tore open my groin, very near the femoral
artery. The doctor was sent for and put in two stitches, and I was soon
well again. This doctor was Robert Lewins, a very pleasant, kindly
man, full of anecdote. His partner was Dr Robert Lorimer, eldest son
of the minister of the Parish Church, also an excellent person. When I

was recovering from my wound, my mother asked Dr Lewins if he could take me as an apprentice. 'Yes,' he answered, 'my apprentice, James Dorward, is just leaving me for Edinburgh, to attend the classes there; so that I have an opening for your son.' It was arranged accordingly; and on the 6th November 1826, [six weeks before my fourteenth birthday] I was bound apprentice to Drs Lewins and Lorimer for five years.

There was not much to be done in my new vocation. I had to learn the nature and the qualities of drugs, and how to make up prescriptions, pills, mixtures, potions, ointments, blisters, infusions, tinctures, and such like. In course of time, I learnt the arts of bleeding and bandaging.

7.   North-East *c.* 1841

My first job I was $8\frac{1}{2}$ as skiffie to Mrs Lawson, the Banker's wife. It was three months of drudgery and half starvation. I resented being called all the time by my surname. Everything in the kitchen was done – I had to do the washing, the scrubbing brush had about three bristles left in it, 'a board to a board will never wash clothes'. The public rooms were beautiful. I slept in a closet under the stairs. I was glad when I left and was given my first fee of three shillings. I had to start raking out fires at 5 in the morning, and I always slept sound as I fell into my bed over the Bank, at three Frithside Street. It had a beautiful view over Fraserburgh Bay: that was the one thing I liked, when I could get a second to admire it.

I had learned to gut when I was 10; curing had started in a big way. In 1844 during the summer, most Broadsea fishers went to the west coast and the Hebrides. We as lassies went to cook for the men. We lived in sodbuilt bothies on the shore, I shared one with Annie Rogie and Suffie Noble, at Loch Eishort in Skye.

The work was hard for children, but we had a lot of fun. I enjoyed the long sail round the north of Scotland hugging the coast, I was with my father, and had faith in his skeelie seamanship. The scenery was really bonnie. For some reason the Highland folk didn't trust us. You could not make friends with them easily, but a few I did, those who could speak a little English. Kate McLeod, a quinie who brought the milk from Susnish, gave us all the clake. We gutted the herring, and packed them in barrels and ships from Glasgow took them away.

8.   St Kilda 1887

Boys on St Kilda were taught to climb cliffs as soon as they were able. 'The first thing to attract our notice', wrote John Ross the schoolmaster of an August day [in 1887] he spent in a boat at the foot of the cliffs of Conachair, 'was one of the men and his little boy on a rugged but fairly level piece of ground rather down near the sea. One end of the rope was tied round the father's waist while the other was tied round the boy's waist. Most probably, lest he being young, rash and inexperienced, might slip into the sea. There they were all alone then, killing away at a terrible rate, for the boy was collecting while the father kept shaking and twisting.

'The man removing himself from the rope shouldered a burden of dead fulmars and made for a cutting in the rock, too narrow one would think for a dog, and too slippery for a goat. Along this he crawled on hands and knees. A single slip in the middle would have hurled him at least eighty feet sheer down into the sea. But he landed his burden safely and returned for the boy. The rope was tied as before, but only about a yard was left between them this time and that brave little fellow of only ten summers fearlessly followed his father and reached safety without a hitch. This is how the St Kildan's train their young to the rocks and what a dangerous life it is.'

9.   Aberdeenshire *c.* 1910

When I was fifteen I started work on a big estate near Aberdeen. I started as a still-room maid making teas, coffees and toast – no cooking for that was all done in the kitchen. There were always lots of oranges and lemons and we had to make gallons of lemonade and orangeade. You made it as a kind of syrup with sugar and the fruit juice. You had no fridge then, things were kept cool in an icebox. There was a whole row of copper pans and it was our job to clean them. We used a mixture of soft sand and vinegar – real hard on the hands but you didn't just have to think about that. We didn't have to clean the silver or the cutlery as that was the butler's job but we did wash the dinner dishes, washing them just as they came through from the dining room. We never saw the food itself. It went right through to the dining room from the kitchen and we wouldn't have dared to set foot in there – all we saw was what came back on the plates, lobster shells and things like that. The lady would go down to the kitchen every morning to give the staff their instructions for the day. There were four women to do the cooking and preparation. The woman in charge of us didn't like me much though and I changed to working as a housemaid.

We were provided with our uniforms – yellow dresses for the morning and grey or black for afternoon. The kitchen staff wore red and the butlers wore yellow waistcoats and black tail coats. There would have been about forty of a staff including a butler, an under-butler and footmen. Some of them always answered the door – we never got near that part of the house. All sorts of staff they had – even an engineer and most travelled back and fore to the other estate in Sussex. A few housemaids stayed behind to look after the house.

There would have been nine or ten housemaids – we made the beds and tidied the rooms. While the family was at dinner from about eight to ten o'clock we would plump up the cushions in the drawing room and make up the fires. There was always plenty to keep us busy. We worked from six in the morning to ten at night with a half day off each week and a half day every second Sunday. We had to be back in at nine o'clock. The door was locked then and you had to get the night watchman to open up for you if you were late.

There was a private chapel within the house. It was really beautiful with red velvet seats. This was the church I had attended since I was little for I was brought up on the estate. All the staff had to go to the Sunday service. The family brought their own minister, a Mr Anson, from the Sussex estate.

We were down South for nine months of the year, then up to Aberdeenshire for August, September and October.

We lived quite well really. The food was good – always huge roasts of meat, you'd never see anything that size today . . . I remember I got

£1.19/– a month when I started and didn't rise much from that. I stayed with them for five years.

10.   North-East Highlands *c.* 1918

As this story deals with things that happened when I was between eight and nine years old, and the happenings are told as I saw them and understood them, I may as well tell you now that I was no infant prodigy. You will not find in this chronicle any startling revelations of an unusually brilliant child mind surveying its world, or anything of that sort. No. In sober fact, I think I was rather a slow-witted child although what was known as 'clever at the school'. This may be because I did not have any of the kindergarten play-therapy practised on me which is so common nowadays, for in my family there was no money to spare for 'toys and such-like capers'. I do not mean that we lived in dire poverty – far from it – but the view taken was that a normal child would play, anyhow, and that it was no more necessary to provide things for it to play with than it was to provide special equipment to make the lambs, calves and foals skip about the fields. The way to deal with a child, my family thought, was to stop it playing to excess and try to turn its energies into sensible, useful channels. My family found this quite difficult enough, without providing any special playing equipment. I cut a piece of the plough reins to make a skipping-rope and skipped when I was supposed to be cleaning the hen-house; and I dressed Chickabird, my pet hen, in my grand-mother's sun-bonnet and let her walk about the yard in it, so that my uncle said: 'It made a fair ruination of the Ould Leddy's bonnet but you couldna help but laugh when she wasna looking.'

The women of the tight little community of the village down on the shore of Firth used to ask periodically if I 'never thought long up on that hill with no other bairns to play with', and when they asked me such questions I used to think to myself that the village people in general must be weak-minded. I had never 'thought long', wearied or felt bored in my life. I am now of the opinion, in my maturity, that there was indeed a weakness in the reasoning of the village women when they said there were no other 'bairns' at Reachfar, for youth of mind has little relation to years of age, and I had two companions at home, then, in Tom and George – the former our handyman and the latter my uncle who did not like the title of 'uncle' – who had never lost their youth of mind, and now, forty years later, have still not lost it.

Instead of being given toys, then, I was given animals, which carried with them a responsibility from me to them. My nursemaid was my dog Fly, and as soon as I could carry her dish I had to feed her myself every dinner-time. I had Chickabird, my hen (really a series of hens), who hatched a flock of chickens each spring – I had to attend to their going out, their coming in and their feeding. I had a pet lamb every year – I had to see that he was fed and kept out of mischief and see that he was safely in the Little Fieldie with his triangular wooden collar on before I left for school. Someone once gave me an albino rabbit in a hutch which I did not like very much – although white, it was part of the family of vermin which Fly, Angus my ferret and I killed all the time. I neglected to keep it clean, and my father took it up to the moor and set it free. If a thing was mine I had to look after it or it was mine no longer.

I had, too, opportunities to earn pennies to put in Mr Foster's bank in the village that they might save and multiply in case I did well enough at school to be able to 'go on to the Higher Eddication'. My grandfather would pay a half-penny per half-dozen for rabbits, a penny a tail for rats and twopence a tail for moles (he had a particular hatred for moles) if Fly, Angus and I would catch them. I would be given a setting of duck or turkey eggs and a mother hen in the spring and be allowed to sell the production in the village at Christmas if I looked after them and got them good and fat – the food for them was free. But if I neglected them, even for a day, they were put with the general flock and I had lost the trouble and work I had put into them as well as all prospect of the money for them. My father, my uncle and Tom would pay twopence a week each to have their working boots cleaned for six days of the week – cleaning materials were free. But that was sixpence for eighteen pairs of boots, which would be turned back to me if the job was not up to standard with the words: 'Do it right or don't do it at all!'

Although there was no money to spare for 'toys and nonsense', there was always enough for plenty of books and writing materials, wool for knitting and cloth and thread for sewing, and my young aunt, in secret, would pay a farthing-for-small and a halfpenny-for-big for darning the holes in the heavy woollen socks that our men-folk wore . . . The reading and writing had the approval of one and all as a pastime and every one of my family took an interest in it . . .

11.   Glasgow *c.* 1930

It was at the beginning of that summer I got my first job. I was passing Mrs Foley's newspaper shop in Byres Road when I saw the notice in the window: 'Boy Wanted'. I walked in and got the job of delivering newspapers early morning and in the late afternoon – five shillings a week plus threepence if I swept the shop out plus threepence if I washed the windows.

The shop was like Mrs Foley herself – dirty and small. It smelled of old paste, sour milk and cats, and everything seemed a jumble of newspapers, magazines, bottles of ink, school jotters, curled-up writing pads, sun-faded postcards, matches, old-fashioned pens, tatty envelopes, mousetraps, cheap paintbrushes, and worn-out books on shelves that were loaned out for twopence.

. . . The two delivery boys – Alf Sweeney and I – sorted out the newspapers with Mrs Foley every morning at five-thirty and we were off on our rounds with them in a big canvas bag by six-fifteen. Alf did the streets and roads on the north side of Byres Road; I did the terraces and crescents and drives on the west. Alf had the apartment-house stairs to climb. I had the surface mileage.

It is hard for me today not to be cynical or bitter about those days in the West End of Glasgow. That job with the Foleys taught me some first lessons about human beings – and they were unpleasant ones.

Every other day there would a complaint from Mrs Foley or her son that a customer's paper was not delivered on time. Whether these complaints were valid or whether it was a trick to get me to deliver more of them I'll never know. All I *do* know is that I walked – sometimes ran – for miles from six-fifteen every morning and got back gasping at seven forty-five, washed the shop window, swept the shop, ran home, got my breakfast, grabbed my schoolbooks, then ran to school two miles away. And I was still failing.

One complaint *was* valid. It came from a big, tall, distinguished-looking man with dark grey hair who caught me on the landing of an apartment building in Richmond Street. He threw open the door of his flat and grabbed his copy of the *Glasgow Herald* before I could put it in his letter-box.

'You're late!'

I mumbled, 'I'm sorry –'

'This paper should be here at seven. I've complained twice about it.'

'I got – held up, sir.'

'I want it here at *seven*.' He slammed the door. The time was fifteen minutes past seven.

The gentleman was Glasgow's leading churchman – minister of Glasgow Cathedral.

I knew something was wrong when I came into the kitchen and saw the tableau of my father standing at the table with a worried frown on his face, my mother standing at the other side nervously fingering her apron. And, sitting at the table, was a small, bald-headed man wearing a navy-blue raincoat and writing down something on a paper.

I said nothing and waited. After a while the man spoke to my father.

'Only the one child?'

'Yes.'

He looked at me. 'You're Roddy?'

I nodded. 'Yes –' I paused: 'sir.'

He beckoned me to come nearer. 'Come over here, son.'

I took a few steps to the table. My mother said, 'Just tell the man what he wants to know, son.'

The man smiled. 'Nothing to worry about, son. You're working? I mean – at the papers?'

I nodded.

'In – where is it? Mrs Foley's shop? Is that the place?'

I nodded.

'What are you paid, Roddy?'

'Five shillings a week.'

'And that's all? Nothing else?'

Of course I told him everything – an extra threepence for washing the shop window, another threepence for taking the rubbish to the midden, another for getting the early-morning shopping and another for sweeping the landing and stairway.

'So it's really *six* shillings?' He raised his eyebrows. 'Six shillings – is that it?'

I looked at my father and said it was.

The man wrote something on the paper.

After he had gone my parents looked even more worried and sad. I said, 'Did I tell him what he wanted?'

My father sighed. 'Aye, ye told him.'

I learned a long time later that our unemployment dole money had been cut by a few shillings each week.

FATHERS AND FATHER-FIGURES

❧

taken from

1. *Autobiography of a Murderer* by Hugh Collins
2. 'The Good Fairy' by J.J. Bell
3. *The Year of the Stranger* by Allan Campbell McLean
4. *The House with the Green Shutters* by George Douglas Brown
5. *The Autobiography of a Working Man* by Alexander Somerville
6. *Two Worlds* by David Daiches
7. *Finding Peggy* by Meg Henderson
8. *The Corncrake and the Lysander* by Finlay J. Macdonald

1.   Glasgow 1950s/1960s

I'm five and a half years old, attending St Roch Primary School in Glasgow. The teacher, Miss O'Donnell, has asked us each to stand, walk to the front of the class, and tell the others what our fathers do.

'My da's a railway worker,' says one, and sits down.

'My da's a postman. He delivers the mail.'

It's my turn, and I walk to the front with some pride. 'My da,' I say, 'is Wullie Collins. He's like Robin Hood. He takes from the rich and gives to the poor. My da's a bank robber.'

The class erupts, shrieking with laughter. I'm immediately embarrassed. Miss O'Donnell is taken by surprise. That's the end of the exercise, and my grannie is summoned.

'He's not a bank robber, Hughie. You mustn't say that. You mustn't ever say that.'

So who had told me?

Did I get the idea from Ginger McBride? Once we get past the confusing stage in which it was maintained that my father was in the RAF, there are regular visits from men who have been with him in Peterhead Prison. They tell us how Wullie runs the prison; how all the screws are scared of him; that he won't speak to them, even to give them the time of day, that he's the boss. They always bring me something, a wee present for Wullie Collins's only son. Tony Smith, the skinny man with a nose hooked like a claw hammer, brings me a woven Celtic scarf. He is younger than my da, but one of his best pals (Skinny's brother, Granny tells me, was hanged for murder). Gypsy Winning is another. Gypsy is tall – six foot two – he tells us stories too, towering over my granny and me. When he comes, he brings me a toy gun. And then there is Ginger McBride.

I'm sure, in fact, it was Ginger who said that my da was the Robin Hood of Scotland, a bank robber who helped the poor. The last time he was here Ginger McBride brought me a knife. The knife is very heavy and has a tartan handle and a long, thick blade like a dagger. It is my first knife.

My first memory is not of my da – I know him only by the pictures

159

my granny shows me: it's of my ma on a cold, wet night. I can't be more than two years old and am wrapped in a blanket and held in her arms. We're walking fast, looking into deserted buildings. I remember the gaslights and the dark shadows. I'm crying for some reason, maybe because of the dark and empty streets. She's crying, unable to find the address she's looking for and needing a place for us to sleep. We spent the night in a room in a deserted tenement, huddling together on the floorboards, her coat around us.

[That] was the night my father was sent to prison. It wasn't for bank robbery; it was for razor slashing. The judge, one Lord Charmont, was determined to make an example of my father, a deterrent to other slashers. Until then, no sentence had been longer than two years: usually no one did time at all for slashing. But it had become a Glasgow epidemic and my father, having slashed the manager of the Locarno dance hall, was given ten years. The dance-hall manager got nine stitches. Ten years for nine stitches: that's thirteen months and ten days for each stitch. Everyone tells me it isn't right; everyone who comes with stories and presents says it isn't right. Much later, in prison myself for a slashing, I will hunt out the newspaper clippings and trace my father's fame, taping them to the wall, staring at them. His name and his picture were in all the papers.

I don't know this man, the father I've never lived with, but I feel a powerful loyalty to him. Where do they come from, feelings like these – so strong, yet based on so little? I have no experience of being his son, yet I want to look after him, defend him, protect him from justice. And I want him to look after me, to teach me things, everything: how to be like him. I want to be a son he could be proud of. When my mother takes up with another man while my father is still in jail, I explode with rage at the terrible unfairness of it all. Years later, unforgiving, I call her a whore (and then hate myself afterwards for saying it).

It's when we arrive at the funeral that I see my da. He's been let out of prison to see his father buried. I've seen him before, behind a plate-glass window, dressed in blue and smiling at me. He's different now. He doesn't acknowledge me, his only son. He doesn't acknowledge anyone. Wullie Collins is dressed in black: a long, immaculate black overcoat, a black suit, shiny black shoes, and black tie and steel handcuffs. He is surrounded by four screws and stands by the grave, silent. Everyone around him – the family, friends – is weeping. My father is still. His face, covered with scars, doesn't reveal a thing. I study the face and will remember it for ever: it is hard, like a stone. Wullie, the hard man, people say. Yes, my da, the hard man.

2. West of Scotland *c.* 1880

It was evening in the cottage. The meal was over. Everything was tidied up. On the right of the hearth sat Mr Brown, his uneasy countenance concealed by a weekly paper; on the left sat Mrs Brown, cold and stern, knitting steadily. On a stool, set apart from his relatives [his uncle and aunt], squatted John. *The Pilgrim's Progress* was on his knees, and his eyes were glued to it, but he had not turned a page for half an hour.

There had been a long silence, broken only by the wail of the wind in the chimney, when Mrs Brown spoke.

'Peter, the time has come.'

Her husband started. Behind the paper he muttered: 'I canna dae it.'

'It's yer duty.'

'Weel, I'll see aboot it in the mornin'.'

'It's got to be done the nicht, an' the suner the better.'

'Oh, woman,' said Peter, in a lowered voice, 'let it pass this time.'

'Spare the rod an' spile the child!' she retorted.

'Fudge!' Peter let fall the paper, possibly in astonishment at his own temerity.

'What?' exclaimed Mrs Brown, as one who refuses to believe her ears.

'There was plenty o' the rod afore he cam' to us,' said Peter, 'an' what guid has it done?'

'Peter,' said his wife, 'if ye dinna dae yer duty, ye'll be sorry.'

Peter knew he would be sorry either way, but habit reasserted itself and obedience followed. He cleared his throat.

'John,' he said ponderously, 'I was vexed to hear ye had been – a – tamperin' wi' yer aunt's eggs. What for did ye dae it?'

John, looking wretched, answered nothing.

'Tamperin'!' exclaimed Mrs Brown. '*Stole* is the word for't! An' eggs that few an' valuable!'

'Maybe he didna ken he was stealin',' said Peter. 'Did ye John?'

'I – I thocht the hens wud lay plenty mair, Uncle Peter.'

'Ye had nae business to think what the hens wud dae,' his aunt said bitterly. 'Peter, he's confessed to stealin' hauf a dizzen in the last twa weeks, but he wudna confess what he did wi' them. Ask him!'

'John, what did ye dae wi' the eggs?'

No answer . . .

'There ye see!' cried Mrs Brown at last. 'If he had confessed, I micht hae overlooked it. Dae yer duty, Peter, as ye promised me ye wud. It's for his ain guid,' she paused. 'I'll gang oot to the hen-hoose till ye get it ower.' She nodded in the direction of a cane, commonly used on carpets, that stood against the wall beside his chair, where she had placed it earlier. Then, taking up her shawl and a candle, she left the kitchen.

'The Lord help me!' sighed Peter, and added under his breath: 'I wish I had Solomon here!' Without looking at the boy he said: 'John, will ye tell me what ye did wi' the eggs'

'I canna.'

'Weel, I'm dam – I mean, I'm exceedin'ly sorry, but I'll hae to punish ye – gie ye a lickin', in fac'. Prepare yersel'!'

'Hoo am I to prepare masel'?' quavered John.

With a sudden inspiration the man pointed with the cane to the red cloth on the table. 'Tak' it an' wrap it roun' yer – a legs.'

A new form of torture, perhaps, but John obeyed.

Mr Brown advanced and took his victim carefully by the coat collar. 'Noo mind,' he said, 'I've got to try for to hurt ye. Ma duty, ye ken,' he added, rather apologetically. 'Are ye ready?' He flourished the cane and brought it down gingerly on the tablecloth. 'Did that hurt ye?'

'Ay – na, it didna, Uncle Peter.'

'Honest lad!' A slightly harder stroke. 'Did that?'

'Na.'

After several cuts the tormentor paused, looking helpless.

'Uncle Peter,' said John, 'ye'd best lick me proper, or she'll no' be pleased wi' ye.'

'Tits! Ye'll break ma heart! There!' (*whack*). 'Was that no sair?'

'A wee bittie.'

(Whack.) 'An' that?'

John winced.

'It wud be better if ye cried oot,' said Mr. Brown, and struck once more. 'Yell!'

John gave a squeak. Then suddenly, 'Oh, Uncle Peter, ye're awfu' kind,' he said, and fell to sobbing bitterly.

With a bad word Peter flung the cane across the kitchen. 'God forgi'e us a',' he muttered, and unwrapping the cloth, replaced it on the table.

'John,' he said, and patted his nephew's shoulder, 'dinna greet. This'll be a secret atween us. An' I'll tak' yer word if ye promise never to gang near the hens again, excep' by yer aunt's orders. I suppose ye sooked the eggs – a natural proceedin' for a hungry juvenile in cauld weather. An' ye'll tell yer aunt ye're sorry, an' try to mak' it up to her – eh?' Unable to speak, the boy nodded emphatically.

'Guid lad! Tell her the morn, an' gang to yer bed noo. Oh, wait a meenute! Here's anither secret. Tell naebody.'

John felt something put into his hand and himself guided from the kitchen. In the passage Peter took up a small safety lamp and carried it into the box of a room where the boy slept.

'Guid nicht, John, an' forget yer troubles,' he said and closed the door.

After a while John opened his hand expecting to find a ha' penny – and lo and behold – a shilling! It was long – for a little boy, at any rate – before he slept, but when slumber arrived it found him perfectly happy, for everything had come right . . .

When Mrs Brown returned to the kitchen, her husband, from behind the trembling weekly paper, managed to say:

'His sufferin's was terrible, Elizabeth. I hope ye didna hear him.'

She sat down as though very tired and moistened her lips.

'I had ma fingers in ma ears,' she said.

3.   Skye late nineteenth century

. . . I looked down at the tidy earthen floor, not able to face [my uncle] out, knowing my gaze would be drawn to that wandering right eye of his, and I would be seized by a terrible urge to glance

163

around and discover the object of its blind stare. It was queer the way his squint seemed to split his face clean in two. I always got the foolish notion that the two halves did not belong, that the wrong pieces had been matched, and that was why they made so ill-favoured a whole. It was always the same when I got to thinking like that, I could feel a nervous bubble of laughter rising in my throat. I swallowed it down, and sat still on the stool, watching a black beetle cross the floor.

'You were gone a terrible time putting out the cattle,' he said, in that soft voice of his that never rose above the same quiet drone no matter how wild he was. 'What was keeping you?'

'I took a walk,' I said, not able to remain still any longer, scraping at the leg of the stool with my thumbnail.

'So you took a walk,' he said, fairly purring, 'and it the Sabbath. Who learned you that the Sabbath was the day for the taking o' idle jaunts? Not me, boy. Not your mother. Putting out cattle beasts to grass is a work o' necessity and mercy, sanctioned by the Most High. We have the word o' Holy Scriptures for that. Only the wicked would make mock o' the Sabbath by taking idle jaunts, and it is laid down in Holy Scriptures that the wicked shall be crowded like bricks in a fiery furnace. I am telling you, boy, you should be down on your knees quaking and trembling at the thought of the everlasting fire that awaits the wicked. What a bed is theirs to lie on; no straw to ease their bones, but fire; no friends, but furies; no sun to mark the passage o' time, but darkness – fire eternal, always burning, never dying away. Who can endure everlasting flame, boy? It shall not be quenched night or day, and the smoke from the burning will rise for ever and ever, though mountains crumble and seas go dry.' He had to stop for breath, but he was soon on the go again, thrusting his long nose forward, and saying, 'Where were you after walking, boy?'

I gave a shrug.

'Where were you walking, boy,' he repeated softly, 'and you gone so long.'

'Och, here and there,' I said.

'Here and there, was it? You hear him, Iseabal?' he said to my mother. 'He says he was walking here and there.'

My mother shot me a dagger of a look, but she did not speak. She was too well acquaint with the ways of her brother to venture a word out of turn.

'Here-and-There,' he said, running the words together, and making them sound like a strange name that had him puzzled. 'I never heard tell of a place called Here-and-There. Where is it, boy? Likely over the hill beyond the Maoladh Mor, seeing the time you were gone.'

'I was putting out the beasts,' I said sullenly.

'Watch your tongue, boy. I am asking you – where?'

'Where else but the moor?' I said, not coming out with a straight untruth, but getting as near as I dared.

'Lies!' my mother shrieked. 'Lies! That tongue o' yours will be your undoing; it is a stranger to the truth, as sure as I am here.'

'Well, if he knows where I was, what is he asking me for?' I said to her, desperate for an end to the questioning. Anything was better than having him keep on at me.

She glanced at her brother, her mouth working, the tears starting to her eyes. But she had no need to struggle for words; one look at him was enough. He always had words in plenty ready fashioned dripping smooth from his tongue. 'Why am I asking you, boy?' he said. 'For to find the truth, so that justice can be done, and it not easy wi' you that full of sin.' He paused, and drew a heavy breath, and I knew what was coming before the words fell. 'It was not the moor you were on, but the laird's plantation above the road by the river, amn't I right? Sleeping, sprawled by the river, *naked!*'

'*A Chruitheachd!*' my mother cried. 'Naked! And it the Sabbath!' She started to sob.

'Naked as the day he was born,' Tomas Caogach affirmed, 'and that on the solemn word o' Fearghus Mor, and himself not the man for to be telling lies.'

There was a silence. I squirmed on the stool, more naked than I had ever been in the sun on the riverbank. Then the two of them started in on me, like a pair of hungry gulls tearing at a dead thing, each of them that eager to strike they were at it again before the one was right done, spewing the words that fast I was not sure who was saying what.

'Are you wise, boy?'

'Have you no thought of the shame of it?'

'You know fine it is eviction for trespass. That has been the way of it since years.'

'And your own sister in service at the Lodge. You think the factor would keep Marsalis in her good job and her brother caught trespassing at the river? Never the day. She would be down the road in disgrace.'

'Not just trespass. You would ha' been charged wi' poaching, nothing surer, and the factor cannot abide poachers. Good grief, I believe that is why we were cleared from Glenuig; the factor was scunnered to death wi' the poaching that was going on, and no wonder. That father o' yours was never away from the river supposing he saw the least chance of lifting a salmon.'

'What if one o' the gentry had come on you lying naked?'

'And word got to the *Ceistar*, and me an elder o' the kirk.'

'You will be the death o' me yet, boy. I do not know what has got into you, and that is the truth of it.'

'The Devil himself, that is easy seen.'

4.   Ayrshire *c.* 1860

John turned to escape. In the doorway stood his father.

When Gourlay was in wrath he had a widening glower that enveloped the offender – yet his eye seemed to stab – a flash shot from its centre to transfix and pierce. Gaze at a tiger through the bars of his cage, and you will see the look. It widens and concentrates at once.

'What are you doing here?' he asked, with the wild-beast glower on his son.

'I–I–I,' John stammered and choked.

'What are you doing here?' said his father.

John's fingers worked before him; his eyes were large and aghast on his father; though his mouth hung open no words would come.

'How lang has he been here, baker?'

There was a curious regard between Gourlay and the baker. Gourlay spoke with a firm civility.

'Oh, just a wee whilie,' said the baker.

'I see! You want to shield him. – You have been playing the truant, have 'ee? Am I to throw away gude money on *you* for this to be the end o't?'

'Dinna be hard on him, John,' pleaded the baker. 'A boy's but a boy. Dinna thrash him.'

'Me thrash him!' cried Gourlay. 'I pay the High School of Skeighan

166

to thrash him, and I'll take damned good care I get my money's worth. I don't mean to hire dowgs and bark for mysell!'

He grabbed his son by the coat-collar and swung him out the room. Down High Street he marched, carrying his cub by the scruff of the neck as you might carry a dirty puppy to an outhouse. John was black in the face; time and again in his wrath Gourlay swung him off the ground. Grocers coming to their doors, to scatter fresh yellow sawdust on the old, now trampled wet and black on the sills, stared sideways, chins up and mouths open, after the strange spectacle. But Gourlay splashed on amid the staring crowd, never looking to the right or left.

Opposite The Fiddler's Inn whom should they meet but Wilson! A snigger shot to his features at the sight. Gourlay swung the boy up – for a moment a wild impulse surged within him to club his rival with his own son.

He marched into the vestibule of the High School, the boy dangling from his great hand.

'Where's your gaffer?' he roared at the janitor.

'Gaffer?' blinked the janitor.

'Gaffer, dominie, whatever the damn you ca' him, the fellow that runs the business.'

'The Headmaster!' said the janitor.

'Heidmaister, aye!' said Gourlay in scorn, and went trampling after the janitor down a long wooden corridor. A door was flung open showing a class-room where the Headmaster was seated teaching Greek.

The sudden appearance of the great-chested figure in the door, with his fierce gleaming eyes, and the rain-beads shining on his frieze coat, brought into the close academic air the sharp strong gust of an outer world.

'I believe I pay *you* to look after that boy,' thundered Gourlay: 'is this the way you do your work?' And with the word he sent his son spinning along the floor like a curling-stone, till he rattled, a wet huddled lump, against a row of chairs. John slunk bleeding behind the master.

'Really!' said MacCandlish, rising in protest.

'Don't "really" me, sir! I pay *you* to teach that boy, and you allow him to run idle in the streets! What have you to seh?'

'But what can I do?' bleated MacCandlish, with a white spread of deprecating hands. The stronger man took the grit from his limbs.

'Do? Do? Dammit, sir, am *I* to be *your* dominie? Am *I* to teach *you* your duty? Do! Flog him, flog him, flog him – if you don't send him hame wi' the welts on him as thick as that forefinger, I'll have a word to say to you-ou, Misterr MacCandlish!'

He was gone – they heard him go clumping along the corridor.

Thereafter young Gourlay had to stick to his books. And, as we know, the forced union of opposites breeds the greater disgust between them. However, his schooldays would soon be over, and meanwhile it was fine to pose on his journeys to and fro as Young Hopeful . . .

5.   East Lothian 1823

I was in my fourteenth year when an occurrence fell in my way, or I fell in the way of the ocurrence, which may be related at length. It was harvest time, nearly the end of harvest.

[My father] came up to the stackyard, and commanded me to come down from the stack-head, where I was at work. I saw there was something of fearful importance to me in his face, and I would rather not have faced him; but I went down the ladder, and asked what he wanted with me, though truth to tell, it was no mystery, for he had in his hand a formidable cudgel, a fork shaft. He struck me a grievous number of blows with it. He at last left off, telling me I had disgraced myself and the family for ever: the only words he spoke. He burst into tears and went away. I was much nearer to the shedding of tears when I saw him in that condition than when he was giving me the blows, but I kept myself silent and gloomy, weeping not, speaking not . . .

It might have been an unworthy obstinacy that made me firm, but I took that as I have taken all other punishments, in silence. This feeling I can account for; but not quite so easily can I account for my standing as if willing to receive punishment. There was a kind of fascination, or if that is not the name, an influence without a name, that rooted me to the one spot of space whenever my father commanded me to stand there, or which made me move involuntarily towards him if he commanded me so to move. It was not easy to believe, when one's bones and skin were sore with punishment, that it was done in parental love; but my poor father was at all other times affectionate to me and to all his family, and showed it in so many ways of hard endurance on his part for our sakes, while I, on calm reflection, could always see within myself that I had done something reprehensible before he punished me. Still I do think that a milder course might have been more effective.

. . . On this evening I did not come home. I did not come home to sleep. I did not sleep at all. I lay down amongst the straw in the stable at Branxton, where the master's riding-horse stood, and planned during the night what I should do with myself. I was deeply affronted at having been so punished in the presence of so many people, and some of them strangers; and I resolved to go away and leave home for a long time, and not return until I had lived to be a man, and had done something that would entitle me to respect.

I then took a piece of chalk, and wrote on the top of the corn chest, 'Fare ye well, Branxton, I am away, never to come back'. My heart had been beating all night quick and strong, and my mouth was feverish and thirsty. I went to the pump to have a draught of cold water, and with all seriousness and sorrow, I bade the pump farewell. Coming away from it, my eyes caught sight of my old wheelbarrow on the dunghill, with which I wheeled the clearings from the stables; I turned it upon its feet, lifted it, and put it down again, and said, 'Poor old barrow, I shall never wheel you again'. Coming out of that close, I had to pass the cart in which I had taken the breakfasts and dinners, the porridge and bread and beer, so often to the fields to the shearers during that and other harvests. Taking my chalk, I wrote on the bottom of it, 'Parritch cart, I am done with you' . . .

All at once a thought struck me, that I would go up into the Fir Knowe, and see the cows, and my mother's cow in particular, and bid it farewell. I did not find them in the Fir Knowe, so I went down the steep hill side, amid the holly bushes, rabbit holes and high trees, to the meadow – a lovely green, framed, as it were, in rows of dark spruce trees . . . Here, as I expected, I found the cows. Some of them would have nothing to do with me, but others knew me well, and were kind and gentle, and allowed me to lay my hands upon them. My mother's was one of these. I put my hands on her head and neck, and said to her I was going away and would never see her again. The poor animal knew not what I said, but in her usual kindness she licked my hand with her tongue, and I felt as if it was a friend that sympathized with me . . .

. . . I tried to pray now, but could not. I felt myself to be a rebel against my father and against God, and the very prayers which I had once used now rebelled against me and would not be uttered . . . I could not pray. It was awful; yet I could not. Neither could I undo my resolve and remain at home. I made a sudden start and away I went.

My face and feet went towards England. Berwick-upon-Tweed was about twenty-five miles distant. I was over half of that distance while it was yet early.

I passed through that town [Belford, in Northumberland] and got to the fourth milestone on its south side. Near to this was a small bridge, and I sat down on the ledge of this bridge, and pondered over and over again what I was doing. The want of a change of clothes, not having even changed the shirt I had been working in, and the want of money, but above all the thoughts of my poor mother, how she would be distressed on my account; how I was grieving her who was no party to what I had suffered, who on the contrary would have willingly saved me from the suffering; all those things came into my thoughts, rushing one on the other; and for the first since I had left home I prayed to God to direct me what to do, and where to go. I had not so employed my thoughts many minutes, when I felt fully assured that it was best to go home. I started at once, my feet going faster than they had gone before, and my thoughts absolutely happy.

I reached Berwick without halting, and stood a few minutes looking over upon the Tweed, and then passed through the town. As soon as I got out of Berwick, I took off my shoes and stockings, and ran bare-footed. Soon after this the Union four-horsed coach came up. It was a fast coach; but so light-footed and light-hearted was I now, that I ran as fast as it. I kept up with it six miles, running about twenty yards behind. The guard once looked back to me, and asked if I had any money. I said 'No', whereupon he sat down on his seat and did not look at me again. It got away from me at Ayton. I was not able to run up hill with it; but I walked on as fast as I could, and got over the remaining eighteen miles between ten and eleven o'clock at night.

I did not feel enough of confidence to go to my father's door, but being outrageously hungry, having ate nothing but the crowdy at sunrise, and having walked or run over fifty-two miles of road since then, I was obliged to go to a neighbour's house to get something to eat . . . The distance I had travelled over that day surprised them, as it may do many, considering the want of food, but the number of fifty-two miles is correct . . .

. . . The master soon came to me and bade me get to work, but I had begun work in the stable before he came. He said that although I did not choose to go home to my father, that was no reason why I should run away from my service.

I did not feel confidence to go home that night; but was anxiously expected home when my day's work was done. My mother had come and entreated me to go home; but I had not seen my father, and could not go. I again slept in the stable among the straw. While I was yet in the straw, in the early morning, my father came to me. He said he had been lying awake all the night, and nearly the whole of every night I had been away, and so had my poor mother. With his eyes wet, and the tears running down his venerable face, he asked me to forgive him for the wrong he had done; for he had since found that the men sent me to take the whisky for their use, and that they drank it. For me to be begged of for forgiveness by my father! It was worse – aye, far more painful – than the hasty punishment was which he inflicted on me. I never again saw him raise his hand in punishment or rebuke; and, so far as I can remember, he never again spoke a severe word to me.

6.   Edinburgh 1920s

I suppose it is uncommon for a child of fifteen or so to feel in some respects paternal towards his parents, especially when one of the parents is at the same time a symbol of strength and dignity, but to me it was a characteristic feeling and coloured my childhood from early adolescence. Walking with my father to the synagogue on a Saturday morning I would search my mind for something to say which I felt would encourage him. I reported to him anything flattering that my schoolmasters had said, not by way of boasting but to make him feel happy about me, and on a few occasions I made up things to tell him which I thought would help him to remain convinced that the world was going as he believed and wanted it to go. Similarly, when I came into the kitchen and found my mother occupied with some domestic task there, I would try to find something to say that would please and cheer her. This was more difficult, for my mother was (or seemed to me) an emotionally more complicated person. To my father, I thought that anything I could say which indicated that a world of enlightened moral idealism was showing increased respect for the Jewish people and their religion, or that people I had met had read and approved something he had written, or that I myself was developing so as eventually to play my part with dignity and credit in the Anglo-Jewish or Scoto-Jewish world – anything of this sort would please and cheer him (as I am sure it did). But to find the properly cheering word for my mother was a more difficult business, and in talking with her I often ended by displaying my own problems, something I do not remember doing with my father.

7.   Glasgow 1950s/1960s

After the laughter and jollity of the funeral, something happened that was to scar my relationship with Skip [my father] forever. Coming back later that night with a long-lost cousin, Skip walked with him into the Crystal Bells pub, a favourite O'Brien haunt in the Gallowgate, leaving me outside. There was no warning, so I had no chance to protest. It wasn't the safest area to leave a thirteen-year-old girl to stand alone and it was getting dark. I was already feeling scared and humiliated, when a man suddenly came out of the pub and tried to talk to me. I ignored him, my heart thumping, and to my great relief he walked off, but then turned again to watch me from a short distance away. I was desperately watching the pub door, hoping Skip would come out, willing him to come out, but even when the man came nearer again I had absolute certainty in my mind that nothing would happen. He wasn't watching me, I was imagining the whole thing. Only, I wasn't.

He grabbed from behind, his forearm across my throat, and dragged me backwards through a close and into a derelict tene-ment. I have heard of women fighting bravely to protect their honour, but with me it was blind panic, not a thought-out response. As I fought against him, some mad desire to keep my dignity stopped me from screaming. Some Clark point of decorum told me I had to get out of this not just alive and as unharmed as possible, but without drawing attention to myself. The only reason I got away from the man was because he was drunk and that had made him less coordinated than a panic-stricken, teetotal girl.

I immediately ran into the pub, unheard of behaviour for a female of any age at that time. Everyone turned and stared in sudden silence as I entered. The cousin had gone and Skip was drinking alone. He looked up, calmly drained the remains of his whisky into his beer, drank it and walked out with me. As I told him what had happened he said impatiently, 'Ye know no' tae gae intae a pub, yur auld anuff tae know better than that!'

I tried again to explain what had happened, but I was wasting my time. He had no intention of listening or of going after the man. Instead he kept walking towards John Street, where the Drumchapel buses left from, all the time keeping up a perfectly normal, but one-sided conversation with me. He went over the events of the day, laughed at the jokes and insults, made comments of his own, and carefully edited out any reference to the minor fact that his daughter had been attacked and assaulted while in his care.

I couldn't think of anything to say. My mind whirled with the twin shocks of what had happened to me and Skip's surreal reaction to it. Then gradually I felt the physical things, like bruises and gashes. My clothes were ripped and torn and my hands were stiffening up because the skin across my knuckles had been scraped off; my knees were grazed and the hardened, dried blood stood out like shiny rivers down my legs. There was blood running down my throat from my nose, and over my chin from my split lips, and one eye was so swollen it was closed. As Skip ignored it all and fell asleep on the bus, I could see my reflection in the window and could well understand why the other passengers looked at me curiously. My obviously distressed appearance also explained the sudden silence when I ran into the pub earlier. As we got off the bus to walk the short distance to Halgreen Avenue, Skip made his only reference to the incident, then or ever. 'Ye'd better tidy yersel' up,' he said disapprovingly, with that characteristic frown expressing his distaste, 'An' we'll tell yer Ma that ye fell doon the stairs oan the bus. Nae point in upsettin' hur, is thur?' No; no point at all really . . .

Just as in the earlier incident with his old drinking pal, my uncle's father-in-law, I felt ashamed, but not this time of myself. I was ashamed that this man was my father. Curiously, all his life he liked to pretend that there was a special bond between us, but if there was, it was a bond of shame forged during those terrifying incidents. I found it impossible to meet his eyes after that time, because I had such contempt for him. For the rest of his life, whenever we talked about anything, I always thought of the assaults with a kind of furious wonder that he had managed to wipe them from his memory.

Adult perspective later brought some understanding, though I have to say no forgiveness. To have taken the incidents seriously he would have had to address the cause, which was his drinking, and to have done that would have threatened the man's very existence. He was an addict, he needed booze to live, and everything else came after that. This included the health and well-being of his wife, the care of his family and the protection of his child. Somewhere in his soul I think he knew this, and he didn't have to see the contempt in my eyes to know it was there, because I'm sure he held himself in the same contempt.

Like any child I had a right to better. The world may not have owed me a living, but Skip owed me care and protection, and I never got it. Though all my life I have tried to be logical and place the blame where it belongs, my self-esteem had remained dented by these assaults and the fact that Skip didn't care for me as much as he cared for the bottle. No matter what happened later, regardless of what I achieved or what others may have come to think of me, the shame and the guilt of being so debased and worthless in the eyes of the first man in my life, somehow linger on.

8.   Isle of Harris 1930s

. . . More and more the awkward loneliness of adolescence was beginning to haunt me; I was very tall for my age and what was referred to despairingly by teacher and parents alike as my 'slouch' was, I suspect in retrospect, a self-conscious effort to conceal the fact that I was a head taller than my contemporaries; each winter my boot size had jumped by two so that, by now, I was wearing a full size larger than my father. For lack of anything better to do I would still, occasionally, seek to join in the pastimes of my younger brothers and their contemporaries but I couldn't help but be contemptuous of their attempts at whatever imaginary edifices or citadels they were trying to create, nor could I avoid using crude logic to scorn their fantasies; the result was that they evolved ways of making it clear that they didn't want my company and I would be left to wander off on my own like a gawky pup rejected by frolicking kittens – hurt more by the snub than the scratches.

Because I had failed to win the bursary to High School at my first attempt my pride was hurt anyway, but what made things worse was that my immediate contemporaries, who had either left school or moved on to High School, had suddenly become denizens of another world – a world of adulthood in which they were either labourers in vineyards in which they earned their keep, or, what was more difficult to accept, knowledgeable snobs who came back to the village on holiday, wearing good shoes and using English swear-words even, occasionally, in front of their parents; and though their smoking was still secret they held their cigarettes elegantly between the tips of their first and second fingers and blew the smoke out slowly through their noses. I marvelled at how quickly higher education lifted people into a different social class and could only steel myself to wait for the day when I could join it.

At home things were little better. My father – who had been parent and friend and subtle mentor – had been delighted when I had won the scholarship, but, almost overnight, the relationship between us had changed; he became impatient with my attempts at adult conversation, sceptical of my arguments, and angry at my contra-dictions. Was I too much of a gentleman to wind bobbins for his loom? Would I deign to weave a couple of yards of tweed while he did some croftwork, and if I did would it be too much to expect that if I got a false 'cross-thread' I would spare time to correct it rather than ruin his reputation as a weaver? Would it ruin my golf-swing if I exercised my back to bring home a sack of peat from the hillside? Sometimes I felt the blood rush to my face and the tears swelling my eyelids as I bit them back and wished that he would just ask me to do things wheedlingly or sly-humouredly as he used to do: at other times I was angry with myself that I couldn't keep an edge of insolence out of the tone in which I spoke to him. My mother's attitude had altered less, except that, occasionally, she got tired of getting caught in the cross-fire and she would order me to get out from under her feet when she found me, after yet another brush with my father, crouched in a corner with a book.

Books were becoming an essential leaven of my being instead of just the indulgence of pleasure to which my father himself had led me; but because we had never got out of the small hut which had been supposed to be temporary when it had been built ten years before, and because the family had increased in number and in bulk, privacy was hard to find. On fine days I could occasionally escape down to the rocky shore of the Blue Skerries with the volume of the moment tucked under my ganzie, and I would lose track of time and place till the pangs of hunger or the prickles of conscience would urge me home. Books were an escape from everything, even though they were few and far between; Edgar Wallace, Algernon Blackwood, Annie S Swan, O Douglas, Leslie Charteris all plucked at different chords of the imagination as they became available in the wooden crates delivered to the school by the County Lending Library; those moulded and catered for the admissible curiosities: the ever gnawing pangs of sexuality which could find no physical outlet in the village, nor prurient gratification in the carefully vetted volumes of the library, had to be satisfied by the occasional dog-eared volume of *No Orchids for Miss Blandish* or *The Awful Confessions of Maria Monk*.

The abrasion of the special relationship with my father saddened me although I didn't understand it as sadness then; the only sadness now is that it never got a chance to heal because of time and inexorable circumstances – except for a brief spell, and through unusual circumstances, four years later. I learnt – as every man learns in time – that part of the tension was the inevitable father and son spasm of puberty; it took me longer to understand that there was an Oedipus strand in reverse, and that it was bitter for him to see his own son escaping from what he was beginning to accept as his own imprisonment. God knows what reactions to those years of war had deluded him into thinking that a new croft in a new land would ever provide the fulfilment for which he craved; whatever they were they were as illusory as the geographical change for the alcoholic. He was, heart and mind, a man of books and letters, and it was only natural that his joy would be tempered with envy, and his own frustration more sharply focused, by seeing the first of his family getting the chance to embark on the sort of life for which he himself craved, and in which he would have thrived.

ADOLESCENTS

taken from

One day I was standing on the ramparts of the castle on the south-western side [sic] which overhangs the green brae, where it slopes down into what was in those days the green swamp or morass, called by the natives of Auld Reekie the Nor Loch; it was a dark gloomy day, and a thin veil of mist was beginning to settle down upon the brae and the morass. I could perceive, however, that there was a skirmish taking place in the latter spot. I had an indistinct view of two parties – apparently of urchins – and I heard whoops and shrill cries: eager to know the cause of this disturbance, I left the castle, and descending the brae reached the borders of the morass, where was a runnel of water and the remains of an old wall, on the other side of which a narrow path led across the swamp: upon this path, at a little distance before me, there was 'a bicker'.

I pushed forward, but had scarcely crossed the ruined wall and runnel, when the party nearest to me gave way, and in great confusion came running in my direction. As they drew nigh, one of them shouted to me, 'Wha are ye, mon? are ye o' the Auld Toon?' I made no answer. 'Ha! ye are of the New Toon; De'il tak ye, we'll murder ye;' and the next moment a huge stone sung past my head. 'Let me be, ye fule bodies,' said I, 'I'm no of either of ye, I live yonder aboon in the castle.' 'Ah! ye live in the castle; then ye're an auld tooner; come and gie us your help, man, and dinna stand there staring like a dunnot, we want help sair eneugh. Here are stanes.'

For my own part I wished for nothing better, and, rushing forward, I placed myself at the head of my new associates, and commenced flinging stones fast and desperately. The other party now gave way in their turn, closely followed by ourselves; I was in the van, and about to stretch out my hand to seize the hindermost boy of the enemy, when, not being acquainted with the miry and difficult paths of the Nor Loch, and in eagerness taking no heed of my footing, I plunged into a quagmire, into which I sank as far as my shoulders.

Our adversaries no sooner perceived this disaster, than, setting up a shout, they wheeled round and attacked us most vehemently. Had my comrades now deserted me, my life had not been worth a straw's purchase, I should either have been smothered in the quag, or, what is more probable, had my brains beaten out with stones; but they behaved like true Scots, and fought stoutly around their comrade, until I was extricated, whereupon both parties retired, the night being near at hand.

'Ye are na a bad hand at flinging stanes,' said the lad who first addressed me, as we now returned up the brae; 'your aim is right dangerous, mon, I saw how ye skelpit them, ye maun help us agin thae New Toon blackguards at our next bicker.'

So to the next bicker I went, and to many more, which speedily followed as the summer advanced; the party to which I had given my help on the first occasion consisted merely of outlyers, posted about half-way up the hill, for the purpose of overlooking the movements of the enemy.

Did the latter draw nigh in any force, messengers were forthwith despatched to the 'auld Toon', especially to the filthy alleys and closes of the High Street, which forthwith would disgorge swarms of bare-headed and bare-footed 'callants', who, with gestures wild and 'eldrich screech and hollo', might frequently be seen pouring down the sides of the hill. I have seen upwards of a thousand engaged on either side in these frays, which I have no doubt were full as desperate as the fights described in the Iliad, and were certainly much more bloody than the combats of modern Greece in the war of independence: the callants not only employed their hands in hurling stones, but not infrequently slings; at the use of which they were very expert, and which occasionally dislodged teeth, shattered jaws, or knocked out an eye.

Our opponents certainly laboured under considerable disadvantage, being compelled not only to wade across a deceitful bog, but likewise to clamber up part of a steep hill before they could attack us; nevertheless, their determination was such, and such their impetuosity, that we had sometimes difficulty enough to maintain our own. I shall never forget one bicker, the last indeed which occurred at that time, as the authorities of the town, alarmed by the desperation of its character, stationed forthwith a body of police on the hill side, to prevent, in future, any such breaches of the peace.

It was a beautiful Sunday evening, the rays of the descending sun were reflected redly from the grey walls of the castle, and from the black rocks on which it was founded. The bicker had long since commenced, stones from sling and hand were flying; but the callants of the New Town were carrying everything before them.

A full-grown baker's apprentice was at their head; he was foaming with rage, and had taken to the field, I was told, in order to avenge his brother, whose eye had been knocked out in one of the late bickers. He was no slinger, or flinger, but brandished in his right hand the spoke of a cart-wheel, like my countryman Tom Hickathrift of old in his encounter with the giant of the Lincolnshire fen. Protected by a piece of wickerwork attached to his left arm, he rushed on to the fray, disregarding the stones which were showered against him, and was ably seconded by his followers. Our own party was chased half-way up the hill, where I was struck to the ground by the baker, after having been foiled in an attempt which I had made to fling a handful of earth into his eyes.

All now appeared lost, the Auld Toon was in full retreat. I myself lay at the baker's feet, who had just raised his spoke, probably to give me the *coup de grace*, – it was an awful moment.

Just then I heard a shout and a rushing sound; a wild-looking figure is descending the hill with terrible bounds; it is a lad of some fifteen years; he is bare-headed, and his red uncombed hair stands up on end like hedgehogs' bristles; his frame is lithy, like that of an antelope, but he has prodigious breadth of chest; he wears a military undress, that of the regiment, even of a drummer, for it is wild Davy, whom a month before I had seen enlisted on Leith Links to serve King George with drum and drumstick as long as his services might be required, and who, ere a week had elapsed, had smitten with his fist Drum-Major Elzigood who, incensed at his inaptitude, had threatened him with his cane; he has been in confinement for weeks, this is the first day of his liberation, and he is now descending the hill with horrid bounds and shoutings; he is now about five yards distant, and the baker, who apprehends that something dangerous is at hand, prepares himself for the encounter; but what avails the strength of a baker, even full-grown? – what avails the defence of a wicker shield? what avails the wheel-spoke, should there be an opportunity of using it, against the impetus of an avalanche or a cannon ball? – for to either of these might that wild figure be compared, which, at the distance of five yards, sprang at once with head, hands, feet and body, all together, upon the champion of the New Town, tumbling him to the earth amain. And now it was the turn of the Old Town to triumph. Our late discomfited host, returning on its steps, overwhelmed the fallen champion with blows of every kind, and then, led on by his vanquisher who had assumed his arms, namely, the wheelspoke and the wicker shield, fairly cleared the brae of their adversaries, whom they drove down headlong into the morass.

2.   Ayrshire 1914–1918

Cammy, Dougie McMillan's youngest boy, was the expert on poaching. He always had with him some fragment of the craft like an identity card – a white scut, a wire snare, the teeth-marks of a ferret on his hand. He knew how to cover one end of a burrow before releasing the ferret into the other so that it would chew the rabbit's backside till it broke. He knew that guddling was the technique of tickling a fish out of the water with your bare hands. He had seen a whippet catch a hare. He could recognise which birds's eggs were worth eating. His father had promised soon to sew a special pocket inside his jacket. For him the clearest image of the future was that pocket, out of which, like a magician, his manhood would draw endless game, excitement, amazing skill, numberless days among dark woods, bright rivers, fields whose principal crop was rabbit.

Rab Ritchie was waiting to be a soldier, probably a general, though he knew this wasn't a job you could just step into. It might take years. Meanwhile, he prepared himself. His memory was an arsenal of every known gun and explosive. He could recite the names of regiments like an epic poem. He throve on dares. Once when some older boys stole a posh boy's jacket, symbol of effeteness, and threw it with great difficulty over a hornet's nest in a tree, Rab had volunteered to retrieve it. He passed through the Kay Park like a motorised cloud, jumping fully clothed into the lake. Hanging over his life in the manner of a tragic destiny was the likelihood that the war would be over before he was of age.

Conn's province related mainly to fighting and girls. He had, in fact, fought but a few times, and wished they had been fewer. Nevertheless, he had so far always been successful. It wasn't so much that he had won as that he had stayed around until the other boy decided he had lost. Also, he was called Docherty, and in High Street that was enough. The authority Tam [Conn's father] imparted to the name, so that it had the force of a prohibitive notice, had been enlarged by recent stories of the strength shown by Angus [his older brother] in the pits. Conn's reputation for knowing about girls was only slightly less justified than that for knowing how to fight. It was founded primarily on the fact that the year before, when the writing of love-notes had become a seasonal preoccupation in his class, like collecting chestnuts, he had received four declarations of profound affection in one day. Since then he had done no more than conduct the usual tentative experiments with girls much in the same spirit as he had examined stationary motor-cars and, once, having been allowed into the mill with Mick's forgotten piece, the workings of a flat-machine. But it didn't matter. His name was made. When he let it be known that a girl could only have a baby every nine months, the others saw it had to be true.

The only non-specialist among them was Sammy Haggerty, whose chief contribution was a talent for awe. Almost everything astounded Sammy. Each dawn seemed to take him by surprise. 'Away ye go!' was his habitual response, breathed with the reverence of a prayer upon the myriad forms of an unfathomable universe. It was invoked in acknowledgment of the incredible truths the others were possessed of, that women's breasts were used for holding milk, rabbits could change the colour of their fur in winter, a gun could kill a man half-a-mile away. It also served as a measure of his astonishment when his own researches were declared erroneous, such as his contention that sleeping with your knees up gave you curly hair. It had caused waves, he had thought, in the bloodstream.

In relation to the others, each rather jealous of his area of expertise, Sammy's naivete was invaluable. It guaranteed at least one heartening response to any new discovery and gave to the others' knowledge a hint of vastness. With Sammy's help, their meetings remained essentially harmonious. Though each might secretly know that his own sphere was the most important forcing-ground for manhood, there was a loosely held agreement that the only complete man was a soldier who spent his leaves poaching, fighting and giving a girl a baby every nine months.

Other boys sometimes visited their smoking-room among the trees but the permanent membership remained at four. From there they made their sorties, armed in an identity that only themselves were aware of. They spat over bridges, noted pubs for future reference, appraised oblivious women, stood talking rough at corners, cased the entire town. They were a casual fifth-column. Everybody else thought they were just four boys. Nobody knew who they really were. At times they had only to look at each other to laugh, and the laughter was in code. Pacing out their property, they strolled. It seemed that they could feel their muscles grow.

Yet the surrender of the streets to them was illusory. They lounged in sights that they had never known were set. The town was a carefully organised trap. The first to fall was Cammy. His father having obtained him exemption from school, he went to work first, in a factory near the bottom of the town. It was a place the four of them had often walked past, tempted towards its cavernous entrance, unaware that it could close. Once the three of them thought they caught his face at a window, but he didn't wave. Later, meeting one of them, he would grudge hello, as if they had betrayed him, or he them. His silence left a root in each of the others.

3.   Glasgow 1930s

Groping for some sense, a clear view, trying to provoke Bernard out of his stonewalling, something made me say: 'All right, about this worker solidarity you talk about, if I go and fight in Spain, will the workers here make up my dole money to more than fifteen shillings a week when I get back? Better still, will the union fight to get me a decent job all the year round?'

I was ashamed the moment I had spoken. It was a silly way of expressing futility.

His forbearance snapped. Angrily he halted, tugged at my sleeve to stop me in my tracks, and pointed past me at something:

'Just you look at that!' He was hoarse with fury. 'For Christ's sake stop bellyaching and take first things first! Do you want to live like *that* all your life – you and everybody else round here? Do you? Look, man! Look!'

I turned to see what he was pointing at. We were at the mouth of a close, the narrow slit in a tenement facade entered directly from the street, giving on to a stone-paved corridor barely wide enough for two people abreast, about five yards long, leading to stone stairs up to flats on three storeys above. At the foot of the stairs the corridor angled itself sharply past them and continued, narrower still, in darkness untouched by the feeble yellow light of the gas-mantle projecting from a slender pipe on the wall above the stairfoot, to a little unpaved back yard with its ash-pits – rubbish dumps – and posts for clothes lines.

I took a few steps into the close and he followed. At first glance it could have been any one of hundreds in the Gorbals, sights and smells so familiar that I had long ago ceased to be aware of them. Looked at carefully as we stood between the nudging walls in the dim light, this one was worse than most, the one where I lived in Warwick Street for instance, but it required an effort to remember and compare. Nearly all the stone steps up to the half-landing were broken, with jagged edges where bits of tread had fallen away. Some had almost no tread left. Plaster had come away from the walls from ceiling to floor, and along the lower part the bared cement, originally grey, was stained yellow and smelt of urine. On a patch where the rough surface of the brickwork was exposed, someone had vomited, probably a passing drunk whose sense of propriety, demanding privacy, had deterred him from being sick in the street; or a returning resident who could not wait to climb the few steps to the communal toilet on the first half-landing. The detritus had stuck to the pitted surface in a wide streaky band as it slid lumpily from chest height to the floor. Judging by the strength of its smell, a mixture of beer and chips, the vomit was recent. Another powerful smell, of decaying rubbish, came mainly from the ash-pits at the end of the corridor, but also from a deposit scattered over the floor. Despite the cold wet wind blowing in hard from the street, the cloud of mephitic vapours lingered stupefyingly about our heads.

No one could afford to throw away food leavings that had any good left in them. They used up what they could in broths and soups and pies. But a final residue, potato peelings, fish heads or meat bones from which repeated boiling had extracted all nourishment, or food that had gone off – refrigerators were for the rich – was thrown on the ash-pits, whence it was scavenged by rats and stray cats. At dead of night, sometimes even in daytime, one heard their furious scrabblings there, resulting in a scatter of rubbish all over the close, so that one picked one's way among little heaps so far gone in putrefaction as to be rejected by even these ravening beasts. Here at our feet, great holes among the broken flagstones overflowed with such rotting material, foul bits of paper, excrement, mud, broken glass.

I realised I was looking at a close, really looking, for the first time.

Perhaps the sickly yellow gloom, all the light the tiny gas mantle produced, worsened the impact. A revulsion hit me like a heavy punch to the head. In the fleeting dizziness I had a nightmare vision. I stood among gigantic glistening boils that had burst and the pus scattered on me and oozed down, like the vomit on the wall, in a foul stream to the floor.

In most of the houses we knew every foot of space was taken up by beds, mattresses on the floor, a few bare wooden chairs, a battered kitchen table. One or even two of the younger children commonly shared the parental bed, usually a mattess on planks resting on trestles in a curtained alcove in the kitchen.

To enable a coupling to take place in a semblance of privacy behind the curtain, the woman would step out in her shift, snatch a blanket off the bed and wrap the child in it and lay him on the floor boards near enough to the cooking range for him to get some radiated warmth from its banked-up fire. Afterwards she parted the curtains and came out naked to lift the unsleeping, finely aware child back into bed, to lie between her and the man lying open mouthed in post-coital sleep. And then the mother and child might lie awake for a while, locked in unique perplexities. She, her body prompting her still, with no finality in her, turned her world over and over again in her mind's restless fingers. The child, possessed by wonder and nameless hauntings, tried to join together the heavings and creakings and groans and gasps and little cries he had heard as he lay on the floor, his mother's disturbed concentration now, his father's stillness as if felled, and the sticky warmth in which he lay between them, something more than the sweat that was there before, a substance he divined as elemental, mysterious, newly decanted, that touched his flesh and senses with profound unattainable meaning.

If there had been two children in the bed, the other, a toddler, also put out on the floor, might well have slept through it all. His turn for nocturnal wonderment would come.

4.   Nairn 1925–1928

Canon Ballard's sensitivity and kindness converted me to the faith he so sincerely held, but to the spiritual part of it only. It seems that a minister entrusted to prepare a boy for confirmation must also introduce his charge into knowledge of the physical transformation from boyhood to manhood. And he did this clumsily. At the last of our religious sessions I thought he had been struck by indigestion ten times as painful as that which usually caused the politely disguised belches which punctuated our lessons after his midday meal. To make our situation more awkward we sat not side by side at his writing table as we always had during lessons, but facing each other in armchairs – a position he had kindly chosen for its informality and to make me feel at ease.

He began by stammering. I had never heard him stammer and throughout our friendship which grew closer as I aged I never again heard him stammer. His pale, lined face turned red as he managed to utter the word 'seed'. There ensued a long silence so unbearable to me that I was forced to break it by telling him I had learned a bit about it at Sandwood croft; not wheat, I told him, because they grew none, but I had learned to judge seed oats and barley by sniffing for must and by testing the grain of dryness and hardness by biting it with my front teeth.

— The seed God gave you.

Now I knew what he meant, but said nothing, which led him to a gesture which shocked me. He raised his arm and pointed his forefinger, at a safe distance, to his flybuttons. It was I who blushed then because I had seen the gesture made by a strange man one evening to a shy girl whom I knew. This I had seen in the dusky Newton woods.

— Do you understand? said Canon Ballard.

I nodded.

— God gave you that seed to enable you, after marriage, blessed by our Church and subject to secular law, to produce children.

— I understand, Canon Ballard.

— Then consider it, my child. Let your mind dwell on the purpose of that seed.

— Yes, Canon Ballard.

— You must not waste it. I hope, in God's name, that you have never wasted it and never will.

I wished to say something but confused images, appearing in my mind, kept me silent. I thought first of 'wet dreams', which gave me delights I had never known till that year. They wasted it, but how could anybody stop a thing that happened while one was asleep? Then I thought of the Ayrshire bull. The silvery stream that fell from him to the ground was certainly a waste. I guessed that Canon Ballard was warning me to stay inside my wife until I was sure that the last drop had entered her.

Of course I know now that he was telling me not to commit the act of Onan. It took me four years to find that out, to solve the puzzle he so shyly set me. I had seen very little of other boys, and it was by chance, at the age of sixteen that I first experienced that private and harmless pleasure. Had I been less ignorant in the year of my confirmation, Canon Ballard's well meant warning would certainly have taught me to experiment. The only physical pleasure I learned at my confirmation was love of alcohol. It seems to me now that the Christian Church, and especially the Scottish Churches, which preach every word in the Old and New Testaments as literal truth, twisted the words of The Book to make them fit various modes of modern morality.

For when Onan spilt his seed on to the floor it was not for his own pleasure, which would have been enhanced by Tamar, the woman who lay on the bed beside which he stood, but to obtain for himself the rights of primogeniture. When Er, his brother, died, their father Judah said 'Go in unto thy brother's wife and marry her and raise up seed to thy brother', which would by law have given to the child, and not to Onan, the inheritance.

5.   Oban 1950s

I want both of my parents to be right so I have to divide myself up. Part of me is male: the strong-minded, energetic, spiritual, honourable, hard-working, thrifty, left-wing part that thrills to folk-music – Celtic, Negro, Slavonic – *Scottish*. Part of me female: the decadent, artistic, intuitive, romantic, self-indulgent, sentimental, bourgeois part that wallows in classical music – German, Italian, French – *English*. Ambivalent, I skip through Mozart, languish with Chopin, then have indigestion like an overdose of sweeties. You'd be better off practising your scales young lady, says my thick-skinned, one-track minded granny, whose technique is so good she never had to be nervous: just took off her glasses so's she couldn't see the audience and got on with it.

Female, I sit quietly in our kitchen, cramped with metal stands and tattered scores and leather cases, when my mother has her musical evenings, inwardly swooning or exulting; or turn pages, pulse racing, eyes devouring the notes, anticipating the next great swell, the heart-melting return of a beloved theme, the next stomach-turning key-change. Watch with satisfaction the science teacher's hands (deft for Bach, neat for Haydn, strong for Brahms) passing tea-cups and pouring milk like in a proper house.

Male, I revolt against the flashy selfishness of the violin, against the perjink science teacher pecking at a biscuit or genteelly milking breadcrumbs from his English beard. Am captivated when the silence between two movements of a piano trio is broken by divine comment from the ceiling above. A terrible rumbling, beginning *sotto voce*, crescendos to a roaring climax then fades in a long, teasing reprise. The science teacher sits bolt upright, alarmed. 'Whatever is that dreadful noise, Mrs G—? Should we go outside and check the roof?' Valiantly Granny attempts to distract attention. 'Haven't the daffodils been nice this year' and 'Anne did such a lovely drawing in school today, why don't you show Mr Kay your drawing Anne.' But no soft pedalling can damp the exquisite naughtiness of my daddy standing upstairs, straightlegged, po on the wooden bedroom floor, peeing from a great height, making his own chamber music for devilment. For sheer devilment Mary. Dear me I never knew such a man. Right in the middle of the Gypsy Rondo. What must poor Mr Kay think of us?

6.   Glasgow 1956

. . . It was in a cafe in Townhead in Glasgow that I first heard the King. On the jukebox, because you couldn't get to hear the Hillbilly Cat on the wireless. You could get things like *She Wears Red Feathers in a Hula-hula Hat* or some such rubbish, but in those days anything, well, rhythmic, was out for Auntie Beeb.

And then Elvis happened and I heard him first on the jukebox and I have never forgotten it. There were teenagers about, the sort you didn't get before when adolescents were simply cut down wee men just like their Dads. Emasculated by class and the womenfolk the boys were. The girls were sterilised by culture and morality. It was an awful time before Elvis.

I stood in the cafe and saw the youths in their long hair, with quiffs and duck-arse coiffures at the back, and drape jackets, and drainpipe trousers and then I knew what I was going to be. I was going to be a dandy, a macaroni, just like them. I was going to get a girl in a sticky-out dress and a pony tail and I was going to slur my speech and turn up my shirt collar and grow sideburns and move as though I was free and alive instead of the way the grown-ups did, as though their trousers had been starched and a steel bar running from their buttocks to their brains.

And when Elvis pronounced in an intro on an early Sun recording 'Let's get real real gone for a change' he had me and I was real real gone, all the way from the previous generation's notion of the sort of stability which really means stagnation. And the oldies and the boss class bloody hated it and reviled Elvis, who was in fact a polite and religious boy from the bongo-bongo land of the Southern States.

There are people who yet revile Elvis for it, and people who take the mickey out of him, especially of course for the later visions of the boy from East Tupelo, Tennessee. I still like the later Elvis too, or at least a lot of the records, and you have to understand the musical culture of the poor white trash to grasp why it ended up the way it did.

In 1956 I saw Elvis and that confidence and I looked at the shabby and quiet nihilism which was supposed to stretch for all my life ahead.

And have worn metaphorical blue suede shoes ever since. Thank you, Elvis.

RELIGION

taken from

1.

My mother was extremely pious. She inspired me with devotion. But unfortunately she taught me Calvinism. My catechism contained the gloomiest doctrines of that system. The eternity of punishment was the first great idea I ever formed. How it made me shudder! Since fire was a material substance, I had an idea of it. I thought but rarely about the bliss of heaven because I had no idea of it. I had heard that one passed one's time there in endless praise of God, and I imagined that that meant singing psalms as in church; and singing psalms did not appeal to me. I should not have wished to go to heaven if there had been any other way of not going to hell. I imagined that the saints passed the whole of eternity in the state of mind of people recently saved from a conflagration, who congratulate themselves on being in safety while they listen to the mournful shrieks of the damned.

My mother was of that sect which believes that to be saved, each individual must experience a strong conversion. She therefore entreated me often to yield to the operations of Divine Grace; and she put in my hands a little book in which I read of the conversions of very young children. I remember that one of these children was only three years old. The servants diverted me with an infinity of stories about robbers, murderers, witches, and ghosts, so that my imagination was continually in a state of terror. I became the most timid and contemptible of beings . . .

2.

SUNDAY 19 DECEMBER. (Writing on Monday the 20th.) It was a very wet day. So I stayed at home and made the children say divine lessons. In the afternoon I read one of Mr Carr's sermons, and my wife another. At night after we were in bed, Veronica [aged 6] spoke out from her little bed and said, 'I do not believe there is a GOD.' 'Preserve me,' said I, 'my dear, what do you mean?' She answered, 'I have *thinket* it many a time, but did not like to speak of it.' I was confounded and uneasy, and tried her with the simple argument that without GOD there would not be all the things we see. 'It is he who makes the sun shine.' Said she: 'It shines only on good days.' Said I: 'God made you.' Said she: 'My mother bore me.' It was a strange and alarming thing to her mother and me to hear our little angel talk thus. But I thought it better to let the subject drop insensibly tonight. I asked her if she had said her prayers tonight. She said yes, and asked me to put her in mind to say them in the morning. I prayed to GOD to prevent such thoughts from entering into her mind.

MONDAY 20 DECEMBER. (Writing Tuesday the 21.) By talking calmly with Veronica, I discovered what had made her think there was not a GOD. She told me she 'did not like to die.' I suppose as she has been told that GOD takes us to himself when we die, she had fancied that if there were no GOD, there would be no death; so 'her wish was father to the thought' – 'I wot through ignorance.' I impressed upon her that we must die at any rate; and how terrible would it be if we had not a Father in Heaven to take care of us. I looked into [Archbishop] Cambrai's *Education of a Daughter*, hoping to have found some simple argument for the being of GOD in that piece of instruction, but it is taken for granted. I was somewhat fretful today from finding myself without fixed occupation; and my toe not seeming to heal. But my mind had a firm bottom.

1780

SUNDAY 9 JANUARY. (Writing on Monday the 10th.) . . . I kept the house all day, and heard the children say divine lessons. I told them in the evening so much about *black angels* or *devils* seizing bad people when they die and dragging them down to hell, a *dark* place (for I had not yet said anything of *fire* to them, and perhaps never will), that they were all three [Veronica 6, Euphemia 5 and Sandy 4] suddenly seized with such terror that they cried and roared out and ran to me for protection (they and I being in the drawing-room), and alarmed their mother, who came upstairs in a fright, and she and Bell Bruce took them downstairs. This vexed me. Yet without mixing early some *fear* in the mind, I apprehend religion will not be lasting. Besides, however mildly we may interpret the divine law, there *is* reason for *some* fear.

SUNDAY 6 FEBRUARY. (Writing on Friday the 11.) . . . Grange dined with us, and in the afternoon I read to my wife and him and the children two of Mr Carr's sermons. The children said divine lessons well. In the evening Veronica and I sat a good while on the settee in the drawing-room by ourselves. I was dotingly fond of her, and talked with earnest, anxious, tender apprehension of her death; how it would distress me, but that I must submit to GOD's will and hope to meet her in heaven. She was quite enchanting. I prayed extempore while we knelt together.

3.   Edinburgh mid-nineteenth century

'It's all a dumb lie! – God's dead!'

The statement which contained so emphatic a denial of the eternity of the Trinity was made by Cleg Kelly, a bare-legged loon of twelve, who stood lone and unfriended on the floor before the superintendent's desk in the gloomy cellar known as Hunker Street Mission School. Cleg Kelly had at last been reported by his teacher for incorrigible persistence in misconduct. He had introduced pins point upwards through the cracks in the forms. He had been caught with an instrument of wire cunningly plaited about his fingers, by means of which he could nip unsuspecting boys sitting as many as three or four from him – which is a great advantage to a boy in a Sunday-school. Lastly, he had fallen backwards over a seat when asked a question. He had stood upon his hands and head when answering it, resuming his first position as if nothing had happened so soon as the examination passed on to the next boy. In fact, he had filled his cup of iniquities to the brim.

His teacher did not so much object to the pranks of Cleg Kelly himself. He objected mainly because, being ragged, bare-legged, with garments picturesquely ventilated, and a hat without a crown, he was as irresistible in charm and fascination to all the other members of the class as if he had been arrayed in silver armour starry clear . . .

So when Cleg's teacher, a respectable young journeyman plumber, could stand no more pranks and had grown tired of cuffing and pulling, he led Cleg up to the awful desk of the superintendent from which the rebukes and prizes were delivered.

Thereupon 'Pund o' Cannles', excellent but close-fisted tallow chandler and general dealer, proceeded to rebuke Cleg. Now the rebukes of 'Pund o' Cannles' smelt of the counter, and were delivered in the tone in which he addressed his apprentice boys when there were no customers in the shop – a tone which was entirely different from the bland suavity he used when he joined his hands and asked, 'And what is the next article, madam?'

'Do you know, boy,' said the superintendent, 'that by such sinful conduct you are wilfully going on the downward road? You are a wicked boy, and instead of becoming better under your kind teacher, and taking advantage of the many advantages of this institution devoted to religious instruction, you stick pins – brass pins – into better conducted boys than yourself. And so, if you do not repent, God will take you in your iniquity and cast you into hell. For, remember, God sees everything and punishes the bad people and rewards the good.'

The superintendent uttered, though he knew it not, the most ancient of heresies – that which Job refuted.

It was at this point in the oration of 'Pund o' Cannles' that Cleg Kelly's startling interruption occurred. The culprit suddenly stopped making O's on the dusty floor with his toe, amongst the moist paper pellets which were the favourite distraction of the inattentive at Hunker Court; and, in clear voice, which thrilled through the heart of every teacher and scholar within hearing, he uttered his denial of the eternity of the Trinity.

'It's all a dumb lie – God's dead!' he said.

4. Glasgow 1929

And so we come to the end of September 1929. Rosh Hashannah, the Jewish New Year, was upon us once more. And eight days after that came Kol Nidrei night, the eve of the Day of Atonement, the holiest day in the Jewish calendar.

My mother had warned me to be in good time for the meal that night as she had to go to the synagogue early. And my heart pounded madly as I raced along Apsley Place in the Gorbals of Glasgow. I glanced over my shoulder. Yes, they were still after me. Small finger-shaped shadows pointed their accusations at me. On this holy night my sins were almost upon me. I must atone for my sins.

There was a weird atmosphere in the darkness of the silent street. The feeble gleam of the little gas mantles failed to light up the distance between one lamp-post and the next. Not a soul could be seen walking the pavements or crossing the road. For this was Kol Nidrei night, the eve of Yom Kippur, the holiest day of our year.

A musty tomb-like air hung over the tenements. I ran into my close. No protecting safety swept down to enfold me that night. As I trod fearfully up the stairs, I could almost see through every Jewish door. There stood the sinners, one and all, laying out their best clothes to go to the synagogue and pray for forgiveness.

The next day they would fast all day, without so much as a drop of water through their lips, so that all their transgressions of the past year should be wiped out. Then they could begin a new year with a clear conscience.

'Oh, God!' my little eight-year-old brain throbbed, as I jumped the stairs two at a time, 'forgive Mr Vineberg for short-weighting the meat.' I had heard Ma accusing him of this. And I prayed that Miss Duncan's own God would forgive her for hating children.

Ma was already dressed and ready for the evening service. My sisters were hurrying on with the dish-washing. A cold meal awaited me in the kitchen. It was to be last food until breakfast the next morning. Children were supposed to fast for one evening. Adults fasted for twenty-four hours until the end of Yom Kippur was signalled by our Rabbi blowing the ancient Ram's Horn.

. . . 'I'm going to shul now,' said Ma, hurriedly serving the quick meal. She already had on her hat and her best black coat. Ma lifted my final plate from the table. 'Mind now! Not a drop of water do you take until tomorrow,' she threatened me as she prepared to leave. 'Tomorrow,' she said, 'I will fast all day and ask God's help for another year. Even a child like you can fast for a few hours. You got plenty to think about.'

My assenting eyes agreed with her. There was a scramble as the rest of the family grabbed their coats and followed her. The Kol Nidrei night service was so solemn that children were not usually taken. I was all alone in the house. Two tall white candles burned high on the kitchen table, which was covered by a white cloth. The candles were the only lighting in the whole flat. Ma had turned off all the gas so that she would not need to touch a light when she returned. The family had to undress in the darkness of their bedrooms and grope their way to bed.

I moved over and sat beside the dying fire. My small figure huddled down on the stool against the comforting warm black grate. Gazing upwards, I felt God was near to me. He appeared to be staring at me from the corner just where the glare of the fire ended at the ceiling. He looked kind. Ma had always said He was kind. God had been good to us, she would say, providing food the day that she was left a widow with eleven children. He had looked after us in our need.

I was not afraid of Him. I knew vaguely that there were other Gods that people believed in. I had listened to the forbidden Christian prayers every morning in school. 'Give us this day our daily bread. And forgive us our debts as we forgive our debtors.' I repeated snatches of the morning prayer.

Their father, Jesus Christ, did not seem much different from my own Jewish God, who was the only father figure I knew. But at the age of eight I was afraid to mention this to my mother. All over the kitchen wall my sins were written, in shadows, haunting me. I thought of the many lies I had told Ma during the year gone by. I would speak silently about this in the synagogue tomorrow, hoping for forgiveness. Then I shook my head in regret at the thought of the forged note to the teacher after I had stolen half a day from school.

Suddenly I remembered my greatest sin of all. I had eaten a forbidden slice of buttered bread, given to me by my gentile school-friend Jean, on a Passover day. Oh! that lovely moment of succulent abandon, like all such moments, soon to be paid for in a Hell of remorse! The clock ticked like a metronome in my head. There was creaking noise from the dark pit of the lobby. I feared man not God. Nothing on earth would have moved me from the protecting candle-light. I listened carefully. The hall became silent again.

I peered up at the clock. But in the dim light I could not make out the time. It seemed like days had passed since my last meal. But it could not have been more than three hours. What a long evening! I ran my tongue over my cracked hungry lips. My throat was dry and parched. 'Water?' I cried to myself. If only I could have a drink of water! Now I knew why the soldiers of the Foreign Legion staggered in agony across the desert.

Once more I heard a noise. Though it had been there all the time. It was the constant drip of the tap over the sink. Here was a way out of my painful thirst: I edged over towards the sound. Sharp, cutting pointers of candle-light flickered over me. I bent over the sink. What a relief it would be to catch just one drop of water on my tongue. In the full knowledge of my guilty desire I glanced round. It was now or never before the family returned.

I thought I heard voices on the stairs. In a matter of minutes they would all be home again. There could be no rescue from my fort of thirst until the next morning. As I leaned over the sink, my tongue hanging out for succour, the moon came out from behind a stack of chimneys on top of the flour mills. It lit up the window, catching my reflection on the pane. I really saw myself that night. I was a small fat female creature, soft in body and in mind. Only a few short hours ago I had acknowledged God's goodness. I had thanked him for his kindness to my mother and my family when they were poor and hungry.

Now this snivelling, perpetual sinner, this me, unwilling to endure an hour or even a moment of self-denial. I saw myself as the weak-willed female being that I would surely grow up to be. I drew my tongue back. Then my body slumped to the floor, sobbing. On her return my mother carried me, stirring in my sleep, from under the kitchen sink into the warmth of her bed.

5.   Edinburgh 1920s

We always had dinner about one o'clock on Saturdays, soon after we came home from *shul*. After dinner my parents would take a nap and we children would be left to read in the dining room (which was also the living room). On a winter's day when we had a maid, we would sit round a roaring fire and read, helping ourselves at regular intervals from a large bag of boiled sweets which Mother provided every weekend; they came from Cooper's, the large Edinburgh grocers with branches all over the city, and were technically known as 'Cooper's finest boilings', a description we considered expressive and appropriate. When there was no maid, we would huddle round a small electric radiator which would warm only those parts of the body immediately in front of it. I don't think I have ever been so cold as I have been sitting reading in our unheated house in Edinburgh on a winter Saturday afternoon. On one such afternoon I was reading an account of Scott's final and fatal expedition to the Antarctic, and the coldness of the scene described in the book mingled with coldness of the room to produce in me the impression that I was slowly freezing to death, and it was a long time before I felt really warm again. The South Pole, Cooper's finest boilings and the coldness of our dining room are still connected in my imagination.

The electric radiator – which did, I suppose, make some difference, though memory links it only with extreme cold – could be switched on and off on the Sabbath, as the electric light also could, in accordance with a decision of my father's which differentiated his position sharply from that of my grandfather, patriarchal rabbi of an orthodox Jewish congregation in Leeds, who would have been shocked if he had known how cavalierly we treated electricity. Gas light or heat, which required the striking of a match, was another matter: that was clearly prohibited. But electricity was a phenomenon unrecognised by the Talmud, and my father felt free to make his own interpretation of the nature of the act of switching on the electric light or heat. He decided that it was not technically 'lighting a fire', which a biblical injunction prohibits in the home on the Sabbath.

The coldness of maidless winter Saturdays I took to be part of the nature of things, and it never occurred to me to complain or rebel, or to feel in any degree sorry for myself. It seems to me now that I accepted a great deal of physical discomfort as a child with extra-ordinary equanimity: perhaps all children do and always have done. In the winter time the bottoms of my short trousers would rub against the inside of my leg, above the knee, causing a painful irritation that lasted for months, and which sometimes became so acute that walking was most uncomfortable. But I never mentioned this to anybody, and I am sure that my mother never knew anything about it. It was part of winter, like getting up at seven o'clock in an icy cold bedroom and proceeding to have a cold bath (which I had been told was good for the physique). Every winter morning began with that tremendous summoning of the will to enable me to leave the beatific warmth of my bed for the cold linoleum floor of the chill bedroom; time never made it any easier; it was always an act of tremendous resolution, worked up with enormous effort. Yet it never occurred to me that the situation was anything to complain of, and the notion that bedrooms might be heated (except in cases of illness) would have struck me as bizarre in the extreme if I had ever heard of it, which I hadn't. Exercising the will became almost an obsession with me during parts of my childhood. Nobody compelled me to have cold baths on winter mornings – my brother Lionel, though he started when I did, soon gave them up – but

I felt that I had to challenge myself to keep on having them without any interruption (except Sabbath mornings, when one never took a bath), and the more I was tempted to skip it for this one morning the more fiercely something inside me compelled me to go through with it.

6.   Orkney *c.* 1900

. . . I was now fourteen, and, except when I was reading, very unhappy. I paid no attention to the visit of Mr Macpherson [a revivalist]; the boys I went about with jeered at his converts whenever they met them; some of their acquaintances had already been saved. Then my sister Clara was converted, and my mother in her delight drew closer to her. I felt alone in the house; but I was reading *Les Miserables*, and consoled myself with the thought that I too was capable of loving noble things. Yet gradually, by a power independent of myself, I felt impelled towards the only act which would make me one with my family again; for my father and mother and sister were saved, and I was outside, separated from them by an invisible wall. A tremor of the fear which had cut me off in a world of my own at Helye returned, and I began to listen to Mr Macpherson's outdoor services at the head of the pier, standing well back in the crowd so as not to be seen by my friends. Then one dark cold night – how it happened I do not know – I found myself in the crowd which marched after the preacher, all the length of Kirkwall, to the mission hall. As we passed through the narrow streets groups standing there turned round and stared at us: the unredeemed, whom I still feared so much that I slipped for safety deeper into the heart of the crowd. The people round me marched on side by side, ignoring one another in a sort of embarrassment at still being lost sinners, their eyes fixed straight before them. At last we reached the hall; after the darkness outside the whitewashed walls and the yellow benches were so bright that they dazzled me; the worshippers entered, ordinary men and women and children now, smiling at one another as if in secret understanding; the doors were shut; the service began. I remember nothing of it; I probably did not listen, for I was filled with an impatience which did not have anything to do with the words the preacher was saying; all round me people were bursting into sobs and loud cries, as if they too felt the same agonized anticipation and could wait no longer for redemption; and when Mr Macpherson stopped at last and asked those who had accepted Christ to rise in their places the whole audience rose, lifting me with them, and I found myself on my feet with a wild sense of relief. But the great majority of the audience had accepted Christ already, and the difficult moment came now, for when we had all sat down again the new converts, a mere handful, were asked to walk up to the platform and kneel down at the penitent form, a long wooden bench set there in full view. I hesitated; I was appalled by this naked exposure before people whom I did not know; but when a small group – men, women, boys, and girls – had risen, I rose too and followed them and knelt down. The preacher went along the bench where we were kneeling and asked each of us in turn, 'Do you accept Jesus Christ as you personal Saviour?' and when my turn came and I replied, 'I do,' I felt that these words, which were the seal of my salvation, yet were uttered deliberately, not torn from me, must bring with them an overwhelming assurance; and I was deeply disappointed when they did not, for they seemed merely to be two words. The preacher asked me to offer up a prayer, but I could not think of one, and felt that it would be presumptuous of me, so newly converted, to address God out of my own invention . . . When I got up at last, dazzled, an involuntary smile of joy on my face, and returned to my seat with the others, all the faces of the congregation melted into one great maternal face filled with welcome and wonder, and I felt I was walking straight into a gigantic pair of loving arms.

I went home and told my mother, and returned with a sense of absolute security to *Les Miserables*, which now seemed a new and holy book, with meanings which I had never guessed at before. But a doubtful look came into my mother's face when she saw me returning so eagerly to a profane story; she stood and thought for a moment, then smiled whimsically, glancing at the book and then at me. I felt she doubted that my conversion was real, and was deeply offended.

. . . I made friends with the Kirkwall boys of my own age who had been saved, and avoided my old companions. Among the saved were some of the roughest boys in the school; they were now incapable of speaking a rude word, and their faces shone with grace. A sort of purification had taken place in us, and it washed away the poisonous stuff which had gathered in me during that year; but it was more a natural than a spiritual cleansing, and more a communal than a personal experience, for it is certain that if the whole audience had not risen that night I should not have risen. To pretend that it was genuine religious conversion would be ridiculous; I did not know what I was doing; I had no clear knowledge of sin or of the need for salvation; at most I wished to be rescued from the companions among whom I had fallen and to be with the good, with my father and my mother and my sister. Yet the change itself was so undeniable that it astonished me. I was not trying to be changed; I was changed quite beyond my expectation; but the change did not last long.

7.   Glasgow *c.* 1930

. . . The value for money was fantastic. For one penny you got a cup of tea, two Paris buns, a lantern-lecture with coloured slides, the Silver Band, six hymns and a bangup show from the stage on the evils of drink or a drama about betting on horses.

I would never go so far as to say that our Saturday nights at Grove Street Institute improved our spiritual awareness one whit. That would be an exaggeration.

What *was* true was that Alex Redpath, Johnny Ryan, his sister Jenny and I enjoyed ourselves thoroughly . . .

Of *course* Johnny Ryan made a waggling rabbit shape with his hands in front of the slide projector. Of *course* Jenny dropped her bag with one half-eaten bun in its bag over the balcony. Naturally. And Alex Redpath would have considered the evening a failure if he hadn't hummed 'Shall We Gather at the River?' through a paper and comb while the band played.

But, all in all, it was pretty harmless fun and – looking back now – did little to divert the attention of the two or three hundred people from their devotions.

It was no accident that Grove Street Institute was situated right in the middle of the greatest congregation of pubs and fish-and-chip shops and screaming, squalid tenements imaginable. Saturday night when the Institute emptied was for me a hullabaloo of the silver band playing and drunken men on the pavements and packed streets and shouting, fighting people and barrow-men selling roasted chestnuts or cheap wrist watches.

8.   Highlands 1930s

. . . This display of the lights was the most extraordinary and brilliant ever seen in the north of Scotland.

I stood at our front door with Herself [my grandmother] who was quite convinced that the display heralded the Lord's return. Although she had seen northern lights throughout her life none had been as startling as this, and she was sure that by morning the Lord would have come again. Usually, the auroral display lasted only a few minutes. But that night's went on continuously for hours with constantly changing colours and shapes. The splendour was terrifying and while the bright flashings continued outside we sat round the kitchen table while my father read the entire Book of the Revelation.

The towering New Testament language matched the towering castles in the sky. As St John's angels and beasts passed before us in my father's quiet, clear voice so all the colours of the rainbow flashed outside, changing from red to green and white to yellow, lighting up the whole earth with a false dawn. The heavens flamed with burning tongues and froze with icy fountains, but still the Lord did not emerge from his throne. We climbed the stairs to bed and Alec, not a little afraid, crossed the yard to the bothie, taking out his false teeth which had been put in ready to meet his Maker.

I went to sleep wondering if I should still be alive when morning came, if indeed another morning there was to be. But there was and after the disappointment over the Lord's return, I took a rather more detached view of northern lights.

9.   Dumfriesshire *c.* 1930

The sermon that morning had sparked off the eternal debate about predestination and freewill. I had heard it all before and I waited for my father to get to the bit where God, because he was God and could do anything, could offer a genuine option of freewill whilst knowing all the time which option would be taken, therefore remaining the master planner predetermining away like anything. 'What would happen if I did something God didn't expect?' I asked. It was explained that this was impossible. God was omniscient and therefore knew what was in my mind. I couldn't surprise him. 'I've got a surprise for God,' I said.

'I don't believe in him. Why do you think that God knows everything? Is it because you want to believe he does?' The conversation was taking an unusual turn. I could see that no one liked it at all . . . Sheila looked miserably at the carpet – she could see a family row looming and there was nothing in the world she hated more than a family row.

'Why should I believe in God anyway?' I went on. 'There are lots of gods just as good as yours. He's just a leftover from what the tribes in Palestine used to believe. He's their tribal god and has got nothing to do with us at all. Why not Shiva? Why not Thor?' The words that had been dammed up for four years came out in an avalanche and as the adrenalin began to flow I pounded on. Faint cries came from both parents but I was unstoppable and only when I ran out of steam did I sink back into the golden plush of the Craigielands dining room chair and wait for the counter-attack.

There was silence when I finished. I had expected an immediate onslaught from both parents but they were mentally winded, too shocked to respond. . . . Aggie Crosbie looked round the door and with her usual sense of occasion shut it with a bang. Sheila looked more miserable than ever.

Then the storm broke. My mother was white with anger. 'Denis,' she said, 'how can you say things like that? Jesus Christ is a divine God. We all know that. The other gods were not divine' – My father broke in, equally angry but more controlled. It was a matter of proven historical fact that Jesus had lived and his divinity was also a proven fact. He explained in his lifetime how it was that he was the same God as the God of Abraham. This was also a proven historical fact. Then they both started talking together.

The argument became uncouth. I was rude to my parents. They were superior and crushing. Their anger grew to the point when my father was shouting and my mother's visage had turned from white to red. When Aggie Crosbie looked in for the third time we moved, arguing all the way, into the echoing Palladian hall. We got no further. My mother stood on one side of the hall table, her hands pressed down on it. I faced her on the other, my father stood some yards away with his shoulders hunched. Sheila slipped into the library and stood listening. My mother leant forward over the hall table as she told me that all that was decent, true and loving was due to Christ and his divinity, that I was not only wrong but wicked to say that he was just an ordinary man. Christ's word was the salvation of mankind. 'What about Plato?' I asked. Plato was a very good chap, said my father and God had helped him to become one of the best of philosphers, but the Greeks, although clever, had no god that was divine and that was why their religion, such as it was, could not endure. Our religion could never have lasted so long if it had been based on untruth. It was the only true religion, many of the others were decent enough religions but they were simply not true. Christianity had been proved to be true and that was why people believed in it. 'More people believe in Buddha or Mohammed than in Christ,' I said and then we got lost in a furious argument about the numerical count of each major religion in which ignorance in no way inhibited wild assertions on both sides. In calmer times we would have resorted to *Chambers Encyclopedia*, but we were too angry for facts. The climax came over the virgin birth. On the matter of Christ's divinity my mother, who simply couldn't grasp the depth of my scepticism said 'But Denis don't you see – Christ was divine because he was THE SON OF GOD, God was his father and he used Mary to send his son to us.' 'There are virgin births in dozens of religions,' I shouted back. 'Jesus was the son of Joseph just like any other baby, or he might have been the son of some other man that Mary had been going with.' There was silence for a moment. I noticed that there was a tear running down my mother's left cheek and that she was panting. I had never seen her like this before. 'Denis,' she said. 'Go to your room.'

. . . I went upstairs and lay down on my back on the bed. I was trembling and realised that I was in a state of panic. I knew that some family crisis was taking place. . . . I lay in misery for a long time and then went to sleep. When I woke up it was getting dark and Sheila was in the room with a mug of tea.

'Mumsie,' – our intimate word for my mother, pronounced Mumzie – 'Mumsie's gone to bed with a headache,' she said. 'She wants you to go down.' So I was not to be excommunicated. . . . I now realised that it was the thought of losing her that had terrified me so. Now it was going to be all right I realised just how frightened I had been. She was the one person in the world who was close to me, we shared music, jokes, mimicking other people. I realised for the first time that I loved her, and loved her more than anything else in the world.

Sheila and I went downstairs together. She stood outside the North Room door. I opened it quietly and slipped in. My mother lay in bed in her headache position, her face looking very small and white. I went close to her and she took my arm and said 'It will all come right when you grow older.' Optimist, I thought and gave her the statutory kiss which was no more than a peck. 'Go and see Dad,' she said, 'he's in his office.' So maybe there were going to be reprisals, if not punishment. My father was pretending to read the *Moffat News* but he had heard me coming and had prepared his act. 'Sit down Denis,' he said. 'Mumsie's very upset.' 'I know,' I said. 'I have just seen her.' 'I don't want you to behave like that again,' said he. 'You were very rude.' 'So were you,' I said. He could see things were not going according to the script. He had planned a dignified reprimand, not a resumption of our shouting match. 'I don't think we should discuss these things for a week or so,' he said. 'That will give you time to think about it.' . . . The interview was over and I left the office and went straight out into the gloomy March evening and walked round the lodges.

It turned out that my father and mother did feel differently towards me after the great religious row. My father had always regarded me as something of a nuisance, showing off, talking too much and also – as I see it in retrospect – as his rival in gaining the attention of female visitors. Now he felt I was a bad lot, an unbeliever, not through conviction but to gain notoriety. I was defiling the name of Jesus to attract attention to myself and although he was liberal in allowing that the best of the heathen might be admitted to heaven (Plato, Montezuma, Mohammed), there is no doubt that he did tend to equate atheism with immorality. I had now become an immoral boy in his eyes . . .

My mother was just sad that a son she loved very much had lost his way. It was almost unbearable for her to think about it . . . She never talked to me on any subject approaching religion, philosophy or belief, even skirting round the matter of going to church or references to the deity. When the conversation bordered upon dangerous matters she looked down sideways with her head turned slightly away from me and she would go a little pink . . .

10.   1756 onwards

. . . My youthful desires became strong. I was horrified because of the fear that I would sin and be damned. It came into my troubled mind that I ought to follow the example of Origen. But that madness passed. Unluckily a terrible hypochondria seized me at the age of sixteen. I studied logic and metaphysics. But I became a Methodist. I went back to Moffat. There I met an old Pythagorean. I attached myself to him. I made an obstinate resolve never to eat any flesh, and I was resolved to suffer everything as a martyr to humanity. I looked upon the whole human race with horror. That passed, I know not how; I think by yielding to received opinions. For even now it does not seem clear to me.

At eighteen I became a Catholic. I struggled against paternal affection, ambition, interest. I overcame them and fled to London with the intention of hiding myself in some gloomy retreat to pass my life in sadness. My Lord —— made me a deist. I gave myself up to pleasure without limit. I was in a delirium of joy. I wished to enter the Guards. My father took me back to Scotland. I spent two years there studying Civil Law. But my mind, once put in ferment, could never apply itself again to solid learning. I had no inclination whatever for the Civil Law. I learned it very superficially. My principles became more and more confused. I ended a complete sceptic. I held all things in contempt, and I had no idea except to get through the passing day agreeably. I had intrigues with married actresses. My fine feelings were absolutely effaced . . .

. . . Sir, I have given you in haste an account of all the evil in my nature. I have told you of all the good. Tell me, is it possible for me yet to make myself a man? Tell me if I can be a worthy Scots laird . . . O charitable philosopher, I beg you to help me. My mind is weak but my soul is strong. Kindle that soul, and the sacred fire shall never be extinguished.

11.   Glasgow 1930s

It transpired that my father's father was a Spencerian, an evolutionist, a materialist, an ethical humanist, an avowed agnostic, and possibly an atheist.

My father turned out to be a very ambiguous believer. We would argue for hours a day for three or four years over God.

If God is good why does He allow all the awful things that go on? This is an unfathomable mystery. Many things are not revealed. We see through a glass very darkly.

God helps them who help themselves. I won a bet of half-a-crown with my father that this was not in the Bible. I read the Bible from cover to cover without coming across it.

Does God exist? Yes, said my father. And what is God? He is the idealized conception of Man's own image. Then you are an atheist. Not at all.

They had told me they were Santa Claus. Now my father was virtually telling me that he was God. I did not want to believe him.

The Scripture Union, Crusaders and Covenanters were all strong in our school. I was a member of all three, but I did not feel I was 'converted' till I was fifteen, at a school camp.

We listened every night to the Gospel story recounted in twelve dramatic instalments by a Church of Scotland minister called the 'Boss' for the express purpose of converting boys to Christ. On the twelfth night, I gave in.

I told the 'Boss' I had chosen the Lord Jesus Christ. You have not chosen Christ. Christ, he prayed, had chosen me. Christ alone knew.

As quickly as I had felt 'converted', I felt unconverted. I longed to feel converted but I couldn't. I went to Scripture Union Meetings and played the organ at Sunday School, prayed, kept my innocence, but did not know any more what I believed or what to believe. At that same time I believed that what I or anyone 'believed' was somehow vitally important, more important than what one thought or felt. What one believed our life and death to be was, in all senses, truly a matter of life and death.

I read the sceptics, Epictetus, Montaigne, Voltaire, Marx, Nietzsche; I became a sort of nihilist, atheistic, dialectical, historical, materialist, Freudian, communist anarchist.

The trouble with Jesus, I told the 'Boss' a year later in my farewell conversation with him, was they got him too young. He didn't have time to mature like the Buddha. He said I was a fool. He said he would pray for me and suggested I read Karl Barth.

I started off believing, I think, everything I was told. I believed it because I had been told it. But I did not want to go through life believing what I had been told because I had been told it.

Did masturbation produce acne, sap one's moral fibre and lead to softening of the brain? I did not believe it did, but it still took courage to find out for myself. Was sexual intercourse sinful outside marriage? This question cannot be put to the test in the same way. The fact that I could fornicate without feeling guilty might only go to show how depraved I had become.

I fell away rapidly. I swore once or twice. I listened to a dirty joke. I could see nothing against masturbation or sexual intercourse or dance music. I went to a music shop and exposed myself, trembling, to jazz for the first time, *ever*, aged sixteen. I looked at nudes in books in bookshops. I smoked a few cigarettes. Two years later I got drunk. I sang blasphemous words to hymn tunes. I knew prayers were being said for me.

When I was eighteen, as I learned from my mother when I was twenty-one, her mother, Grannie, had come round to our house – 'the first time she had set foot in the door for sixteen years' – to tell my mother she had had a dream that 'Ronald has gone evil'.

Grannie and Mummy had not shared the awful truth with anyone that I had 'gone evil'. When my mother revealed this fact to me I assumed she still believed it.

FIRST LOVE

taken from

1. *Poems Original and Translated*
by George Gordon, Lord Byron
2. *The Life of Mansie Wauch* by David Moir
3. *Ranald Bannerman's Childhood* by George MacDonald
4. *The Life of Robert Burns* by Catherine Carswell
5. 'Handsome Nell' by Robert Burns
6. *Cleg Kelly – Arab of the City* by S.R. Crockett
7. *Poems and Songs Chiefly in the Scottish Dialect*
by George McIndoe
8. 'Shy Geordie' by Helen B. Cruickshank
9. *Memoirs of a Highland Lady*
by Elizabeth Grant of Rothiemurchus

When I roved a young Highlander o'er the dark heath,
And climbed thy steep summit, oh Morven of snow!
To gaze on the torrent that thunder'd beneath,
Or the mist of the tempest that gather'd below,
Untutor'd by science, a stranger to fear,
And rude as the rocks where my infancy grew,
No feeling, save one, to my bosom was dear;
Need I say my sweet Mary, 'twas centred on you?

Yet it could not be love, for I knew not the name, –
What passion can dwell in the heart of a child?
But still I perceive an emotion the same
As I felt when a boy, on the crag-covered wild:
One image alone on my bosom impress'd,
I loved my bleak regions, nor panted for new;
And few were my wants, for my wishes were bless'd;
And pure were my thoughts, for my soul was with you.

I arose with the dawn; with my dog as my guide,
From mountain to mountain I bounded along;
I breasted the billows of Dee's rushing tide
And heard at a distance the Highlander's song:
At eve, on my heath-cover'd couch of repose,
No dreams, save of Mary, were spread to my view;
And warm to the skies my devotions arose,
For the first of my prayers was a blessing on you.

I left my bleak home, and my visions are gone;
The mountains are vanish'd, my youth is no more;
As the last of my race, I must wither alone,
And delight but in days I have witness'd before:
Ah! splendour has rais'd, but embitter'd my lot;
More dear were the scenes which my infancy knew:

Though my hopes may have fail'd, yet they are not forgot;
Though cold is my heart, still it lingers with you.

When I see some dark hill point its crest to the sky,
I think of the rocks that o'ershadow Colbleen;
When I see the soft blue of a love-speaking eye,
I think of those eyes that endear'd the rude scene;
When, haply, some light-waving locks I behold
That faintly resemble my Mary's in hue,
I think on the long flowing ringlets of gold,
The locks that were sacred to beauty, and you.

Yet the day may arrive when the mountains once more
Shall rise to my sight in their mantle of snow:
But while these soar above me, unchanged as before,
Will Mary be there to receive me? – ah, no!
Adieu, then, ye hills, where my childhood was bred!
Thou sweet-flowing Dee, to thy waters adieu!
No home in the forest shall shelter my head, –
Ah! Mary, what home could be mine but with you?

2.   Midlothian *c.* 1780

Just after I was put to my 'prenticeship, having made free choice of the
tailoring trade, I had a terrible stound of calf-love. Never shall I forget
it. I was growing up, long and lank as a willow-wand. Brawns to my
legs there were none, as my trowsers of other years too visibly effected
to show. The long yellow hair hung down, like a flax-wig, the length of
my lantern jaws, which looked, notwithstanding my yapness and stiff
appetite, as if eating and they had broken up acquaintanceship. My
blue jacket seemed in the sleeves to have picked a quarrel with the
wrists and had retreated to a tait below the elbows. The haunch-
buttons, on the contrary, seemed to have taken a strong liking to the
shoulders, a little below which they showed their tarnished brightness.
At the middle of the back the tails terminated, leaving the well-worn
rear of my corduroys, like a full moon seen through a dark haze. Oh!
but I must have been a bonny lad.

My first flame was the minister's lassie, Jess, a buxom and forward quean, two or three years older than myself. I used to sit looking at her in the kirk, and felt a droll confusion when our een met. It dirled through my heart like a dart, and I looked down at my psalm-book sheepish and blushing. Fain would I have spoken to her, but it would not do; my courage aye failed me at the pinch, though she whiles gave me a smile when she passed me. She used to go to the well every night with her twa stoups, to draw water after the manner of the Israelites at gloaming; so I thought of watching to give her the two apples which I had carried in my pouch for more than a week for that purpose. How she laughed when I stappit them into her hand, and brushed bye without speaking! I stood at the bottom of the close listening, and heard her laughing till she was like to split. My heart flap-flappit in my breast like a pair of fanners. It was a moment of heavenly hope; but I saw Jamie Coom, the blacksmith, who I aye jealoused was my rival, coming down to the well. I saw her give him one of the apples; and hearing him say, with a loud guffaw, 'Where is the tailor?' I took to my heels and never stopped till I found myself on the little stool by the fireside, and the hamely sound of my mother's wheel bum-bumming in my lug, like a gentle lullaby.

3.   North-East *c.* 1830

During all that winter I attended the evening school and assisted the master. I confess, however, it was not so much for the master as to be near Elsie Duff, of whom I now thought many times an hour. Her sweet face grew more and more dear to me. When I pointed out an error in her work, or suggested a better mode of working, it would flush like the heart of a white rose, and eagerly she would set herself to rectification or improvement, her whole manner a dumb apology for what could be a fault in no eyes but her own. It was this sweetness that gained upon me: at length her face was almost a part of my consciousness.

I suppose my condition was what people would call being in love with her; but I never thought of that; I only thought of her. Nor did I ever dream of saying a word to her on the subject. I wished nothing other than as it was. To think about her all day, so gently that it never disturbed Euclid or Livy; to see her at night, and get near her now and then, sitting on the same form with her as I explained something to her on the slate or in her book; to hear her voice, and look into her tender eyes, was all that I desired. It never occurred to me that things could not go on so; that a change must come; that as life cannot linger in the bud, but is compelled by the sunshine and the air into flower, so life would go on and on, and things would change, and the time blossom into something else, and my love find itself set out-of-doors in the midst of strange plants and a new order of things.

4.   Ayrshire 1773

. . . But through the confusion and novelty the old clear call of harvest sounded – and with it for [fourteen-year-old] Robert a call still older and clearer.

Immediately upon his return from Ayr he was forced to lay aside self-culture for the fields. The fields claimed every hour of the day, and every hand in the family – some extra hands as well. One pair of the latter – rather too soft and small for the thistle-rich garnering of the Burnes acres – belonged to Nelly Kilpatrick, the blacksmith's daughter from Dalrymple way. Fair-haired, neat, charming, in her fourteenth year already a complete little woman, Nelly was coupled with Robert for the gathering and binding. All day long the two worked together, and often they would stop at the end of their row of sheaves for Robert to pick out the nettle-stings and thistle-prickles from the girl's aching palms. As he did so, his own large hands trembled, and it seemed to him that a drum was beating furiously in his breast.

This would have been enough, but there was more. Nelly could sing. Her favourite air was called 'I am a man unmarried', a dance measure, of which all the words except the title had been lost; but she had many others with and without words, and she could not sing too many or repeat them too often for her partner. Nelly silent could make his heart behave like a drum, but Nelly singing transformed it into that more mysterious wind-and-string instrument, an Aeolian harp. He said nothing to her of this drumming or thrumming, and supposed, therefore, that she was unaware of it. Perhaps she was. But at the close of each day, when the sun had set and it was too dark to work longer, she would hang behind the others till Robert fell back too and joined her. Far ahead, across the dim stubble, William Burnes's forward-leaning figure led the bandsters and shearers home to supper. He had walked like an old man these ten years and more.

Everybody saw that Robert was in love. His eyes alone would have betrayed him, but there was in addition an agitation of his whole body which made his brothers laugh but gave his father serious concern. Robert was far past caring what any of them saw or thought. What they did not know, and he did, was that Nelly had revealed something besides love to him – that wrapt up in love there was a further revelation. These drums and harps, set throbbing by her knowing little hand, were not for her alone.

One of her songs had new words, or so she had told him. A young man she knew had fallen in love with one of the servant girls in his father's house, and to please his sweetheart had made fresh verses to an old tune. Here was a discovery eclipsing the discovery of Ramsay's *Tea-Table Miscellany*. A lad in his own neighbourhood, not much older than himself, nor much above him socially, the son of a small laird, who assuredly knew more of shearing sheep and cutting peats than of Latin and French, had caused his beloved to be envied and himself to be admired by making a song for her. Robert was nothing if not emulative. He was fresh from intellectual triumphs in Ayr. He knew himself to be a brighter lad than most. He had been reading the *Tea-Table Miscellany*. And he was in love. Again and again he made Nelly hum the wordless air that was her favourite, until he felt he had mastered its rhythm. A tune he must have. Who could make words without a tune? Then, leaving her, crooning it over and over in his tuneless voice till it pounded in his heart-beats, he walked about the fields. In response to the music and his love, lines seemed to come of themselves. Transported he welcomed each line, furiously fashioned and re-fashioned it – till in a very short time he had seven four-line verses with a chorus of *Fal-lal-de-ral*, the whole to be called 'Handsome Nell'.

It did not occur to him to write the song down. It was for singing, not for reading; besides he could trust his memory. He repeated it to Nelly till she could sing it to him, which she did, delighted with it and him and herself. One verse in particular pleased her as it would have pleased any woman. It ran:

> She dresses aye sae clean and neat,
>   Baith decent and genteel;
> And then there's something in her gait
>   Gars ony dress look weel.

But harvest was quickly over. Nelly departed. The dreary isolation of winter descended upon Mount Oliphant and its inhabitants. Now there were other things than love to think of – sheep in fold and cattle in byre to be fed with bog hay.

5.   Ayrshire 1773

HANDSOME NELL

O, once I lov'd a bonnie lass,
    Aye, and I love her still,
And whilst that virtue warms my breast
    I love my handsome Nell.

As bonnie lasses I hae seen,
    And many full as braw,
But for a modest graceful mien
    The like I never saw.

A bonnie lass, I will confess,
    Is pleasant to the ee,
But without some better qualities
    She's no a lass for me.

But Nelly's looks are blithe and sweet,
    And what is best of a',
Her reputation is complete,
    And fair without a flaw.

She dresses aye sae clean and neat,
    Both decent and genteel;
And then there's something in her gait
    Gars ony dress look weel.

A gaudy dress and gentle air
    May slightly touch the heart,
But it's innocence and modesty
    That polishes the dart.

'Tis this in Nelly pleases me,
'Tis this enchants my soul!
For absolutely in my breast
She reigns without control.

6.   Edinburgh mid-nineteenth century

It was the hour of the vesper writing lesson . . . Cleaver's boy had
his head close down to the paper. His elbows were spread-eagled
over the table. His shoulders were squared with determination, and
his whole pose gave token of the most complete absorption and
studious intentness. He was writing the line, 'Kindness to dumb
animals is a sign of nobility of character.' As his pen traced the
curves, his tongue was elaborating the capitals, so exactly that you
could almost tell by watching the tip whether Cleaver's boy was
writing a K or an N . . .

There came the sound of angry voices at the door.
'What are you doin' here? I tell ye he's my chap!' said a voice sharp
and shrill.
'It's a black lee. I tell ye he's naething o' the kind!' cried another yet
louder and rougher.
Sue Murphy and Sal Mackay were at it again. So said the Society of
the Knuckle Dusters [part gang, part club, part evening class] as it
winked amicably and collectively to itself. Celie Tennant [young lady
teacher] was at that moment looking over the copy-book of Cleaver's
boy. As she stood behind him, she could see the scarlet swiftly rising
to his neck and brow. Adonis was becoming distinctly annoyed. It was
going to be a rough night for Venuses.
'I tell ye it was only on Saturday night that he knocked my bonnet
off my head, an' kickit it alang the street – an' ye will hae the impidence
to say after *that* that he is your lad!'
It was the voice of Sue Murphy which made this proud declara-
tion.
'That nocht ava', ye Irish besom,' retorted Sal Mackay;
'yestreen nae farther gane, he pu'ed a handfu' of the hair oot
o' ma heid. Aye, and rubbit my face wi' a clabber o' glaur,
forbye!'

It was the last straw. Cleaver's boy rose to his feet with a look of stern and righteous determination on his face. The assembled Knuckle Dusters watched him eagerly. Celie stood aghast, fearing that murder might be done, in the obvious endeavour which Cleaver's boy was now about to make, to excel all his records in the art of love-making, as practised in the Sooth Back and the Tinkler's Lands.

He walked slowly to the corner of the store-room, where on a little bench stood two very large water-cans of tin, painted a dark blue. They were the property of the Club and contained the drinking water for the evening. They had just been filled.

Cleaver's boy took one in his hand and opened the door. Then he swung the heavy can, and, tilting it up with the other hand, he arched the contents solidly and impartially upon the waiting Juliets. Returning, he seized the other, and from the shrieking down the passage it was obvious to Celie that he had been equally successful in quelling the ardour of the rivals with that.

Cleaver's boy came back with the empty cans in his hand, panting a little with honest toil, but there was no shamefacedness in his eyes now. He looked straight at Celie like a man who had done his full duty, and perhaps a little over.

'I pit to yoursel', Miss Celie, can a man do mair than that?'

And with no further word, Cleaver's boy dusted the drops from the knees of his breeches, and sat down to write six more lines of 'Kindness to dumb animals is a sign of nobility of character.'

But the next night he came to Celie in the blackness of despair.

'I will hae to resign, after a', Miss Celie,' he said, 'I canna bide here to be a disgrace to ye.'

'Why, what's the matter, James?' said Miss Tennant, who did not know everything; 'are the girls going to prosecute you in the police court for throwing the water over them last night?'

Cleaver's boy opened his mouth in astonishment and kept it so for some time.

'Prosecute me? – I wish to peace the wad!' cried he, after he got his breath. 'Na, faith, Miss Celie; will ye believe me, they are fonder o' me than ever. They were baith waiting for me at the stairfit this mornin' when I cam doon to gang to the shop.'

7.   Glasgow *c.* 1800

O Jenny thou's my joy and care,
    A dainty lass and leal;
Come, gang wi' me to Glasgow fair,
    And le'e the spinning wheel?
O Johnnie lad, I darena gang,
    I'll no go wi' thee there:
My minny flytes baith loud and lang
    When I gae to the fair.

Hout, heed nae mair your minny's flyte
    On me lay a' the blame;
I'll pledge my aith, before it's late,
    To see thee safely hame:
My daddy sayd 'Gae count your threads,
    And think on that nae mair:
For lasses tyne their maidenheads,
    When coming frae the fair.'

The tyning o' your maidenhead,
    There's little fear o' that:
To get a wean, I never try'd,
    Nor do I ken the gait;
Your minny's flyte, and daddy's frown,
    Ye needna mickle care;
I'll buy to you a braw new gown
    When we get to the fair.

So Jenny's she's gane to the town
    For a' her parents said;
But weary fa' the braw new gown,
    She tint her maidenhead:
And ay sinsyne she gaunts and grues,
    And ruggs, and tears her hair,
And greets, and cries, and sarely rues
    That ere she saw the fair.

First Love

Ye simple maids, be tenty a',
    When in ayont the stack;
For maidenheads, when once awa,
    Can ne'er be gotten back;
What tho' ye're wi' a canny chiel,
    Sic like was Johnny Blair;
And yet he played the vera Deil
    When coming from the fair.

gaunt: stutter; *grue*: shudder; *rugg*: drag; *tenty*: careful

8.   Angus *c.* 1900

SHY GEORDIE

Up the Noran Water
In by Inglismaddy,
Annie's got a bairnie
That hasna got a daddy.
Some say it's Tammas's,
An' some say it's Chay's;
An' naebody expec'it it,
Wi' Annie's quiet ways.

Up the Noran Water
The bonny little mannie
Is dandled an' cuddled close
By Inglismaddy's Annie.
Wha the bairnie's faither is
The lassie never says;
But some think it's Tammas's,
An' some think it's Chay's.

Up the Noran Water,
The country folk are kind;
An' wha the bairnie's faither is
They dinna muckle mind.
But oh! the bairn at Annie's briest,

222

First Love

The love in Annie's e'e –
They mak' me wish wi' a' my micht
The lucky lad was me!

9.   Edinburgh 1814–1815

[At seventeen years of age] I was high on the list of beauties, no ball
could go on without me, ladies intending to open up their houses for
dancing, solicited introductions to the mother for the sake of
ensuring the daughter's presence. Crowds of beaux surrounded
us when we walked out, filled our drawing rooms when we staid
within. It was very intoxicating, but it did not intoxicate me, young
and unformed as I was, and unused to admiration, personal beauty
being little spoken of in the family. I owed my steadiness to neither
good sense nor wise counsel, for neither of these was watching over
me. A simple happy temper, a genuine love of dancing, a little
highland pride that took every attention as the due of one of Grant
blood, these were my safeguards, these and the one all-absorbing
feeling which early took possession of the young heart to the
exclusion of other ideas.

. . . Poor dear mother, while you were straining your eyes abroad,
it never struck you to use them at home. While you slept so quietly in
the mornings you were unaware that others were broad awake. While
you dreamed of Sheffield gold, and Perthshire acres, and Ross-shire
principalities, my father and Miss Elphick both away, the daughter
you intended disposing of for the benefit of the family had been left to
enter upon a series of sorrows she never during the whole of her after
life recovered from the effects of.

The first year my brother [William] was at College he made
acquaintance with a young man a few years older than himself, the
son of one of the Professors. His friend was tall, dark, handsome, very
engaging in his manners, very agreeable in his conversation, and
considered by all who had been employed in his education to possess
abilities quite worthy of the talented race he belonged to. The Bar was
to be his profession . . . He was an only son. His father was rich, his
mother had been an heiress, and he was the heir of an old, nearly

223

bedrid bachelour Uncle who possessed a very large landed property on the banks of the Tweed . . .

When we all removed to Edinburgh Willam lost no time in introducing his friend to us; all took to him amazingly; he was my constant partner, joining us in our walks, sat with us every morning, was invited frequently as company and was several times asked to stay and partake of the family dinner. It never entered my head that his serious attentions would be disagreeable, nor my Mother's, I really believe, that such would ever grow out of our brother and sister intimacy. I made acquaintance with the sisters at the houses of mutual friends. We visited and exchanged calls as young ladies did then in Edinburgh; and then I first thought it odd that the senior members of each family, so particularly obliging as they were to the junior members of each other's households, made no move towards an acquaintance on their own parts. The gentlemen, as much occupied with their affairs, were excusable, but the ladies, what could prevent the common forms of civility passing between them. I had by this time become shy of making any remarks on them, but Jane, who had marvelled too, one day asked my mother why she did not cultivate the society of such agreeable persons. My Mother's answer was quite satisfactory. She was the last comer, it was not her place to call first on old residents . . .

Then came Miss Baillie's *fete*, and the poem in which I figured so gracefully. It was in every mouth, for in itself it was a gem, and I was so completely the genius of it, none but a lover could have mingled so much tenderness with his admiration. On the poet's next visit my Mother received him very coldly. At our next meeting she declined his now regular attendance. At the next party she forbade me dancing with him: after the indelicate manner in which he had brought my name before the publick in connection with his own, it was necessary to meet such forwardness by a reserve that would keep such presumption at a proper distance. I listened in silence, utterly amazed, and might, in such perfectly submissive habits of obedience had we been brought up, have submitted sorrowfully and patiently, but she went too far. She added that she was not asking much of me, for this disagreeable young man had no attaching qualities; he was neither good-looking, nor well-bred, nor clever, not much considered by persons of judgment, and certainly by birth no way the equal of a Grant of Rothiemurchus.

I left the room, flew to my own little attick, what a comfort that corner all to myself was then and often afterwards to me. I laid my head upon my bed, and covering my face with my hands, vainly trying to keep back the tears. The words darted through my brain, 'All false, quite false – what can it be, what will become of us,' for I had reached that turning point, though till this bitter moment unconsciously.

Long I staid there, half thinking, half dreaming, till a new turn took me, the turn of unmitigated anger. Were we puppets, to be moved about with strings. Were we supposed to have neither sense nor feeling. Was I so poor in heart as to be able to like today, and loathe tomorrow, so deficient in understanding as to be incapable of seeing with my eyes, hearing with my ears, judging with my own perceptions. This long familiar intimacy permitted, then suddenly broken upon *false* pretences. They don't know me, thought I; alas I did not know myself. To my mother throughout that memorable day I never articulated one syllable. My father was in London.

My first determination was to see my poet and inquire of him whether he were aware of any private enmity between our houses. Fortunately he also had determined on seeking an interview with me in order to find out what it was my mother had so suddenly taken amiss in him.

Both so resolved, we made our Meeting out, and a pretty Romeo and Juliet business it ended in. There *was* an ancient feud, a College quarrel between our fathers which neither of them had ever made a movement to forgive. It was more guessed at from some words his mother had dropt than clearly ascertained, but so much he had too late discovered, that a more intimate connection would be as distasteful to the one side as the other.

We were very young, we were very much in love, we were very hopeful. Life looked so fair, it had been latterly so happy. We could conceive of no old resentments between parents that would not yield to the welfare of their children. He remembered that his father's own marriage was an elopement followed by forgiveness and a long lifetime of perfect conjugal felicity. I recollected my mother telling me of the Montague and Capulet feud between the Neshams and the Ironsides, how my grandfather had sped so ill for years in his wooing, and how my grandmother's constancy had carried the day, and how all parties had 'as usual' been reconciled . . . So, reassured by these arguments, we agreed to wait, to keep up our spirits, to give time to be true and faithful to each other, and to trust to the Chapter of accidents.

In all this there was nothing wrong, but a secret correspondence in which we indulged ourselves was a step in the wrong, certainly. We knew we should seldom meet, never without witnesses, and I had not the resolution to refuse the only method left us of softening our separation. One of these stray notes from him to me was intercepted by my mother, and some of the expressions employed were so startling to her that in a country like Scotland, where so little constitutes a marriage, she almost feared we had bound ourselves by ties sufficiently binding to cause considerable annoyance, to say the least of it. She therefore consulted Lord Gillies as her confidential adviser, and he had a conference with Lord Glenlee, the trusted lawyer on the other side, and then the young people were spoken to, to very little purpose.

What passed in the other house I could only guess at from after circumstances. In ours, Lord Gillies was left by my mother in the room with me; he was always gruff, cold, short in manner, the reverse of agreeable and no favourite with me, he was ill selected therefore for the task of inducing a young lady to give up her lover. . . . He restricted his arguments to the inexperience of youth, the unsurmountable aversion of the two fathers, the cruelty of separating family ties, dividing those hitherto living lovingly together, the indecorum of a woman entering a family which not only would not welcome her, but the head of which repudiated her . . .

To my mother I found courage to say that I had yet heard no reasons which would move me to break the word solemnly given, the troth plighted, and could only repeat what I had said at the beginning that we were resigned to wait.

Lord Glenlee had made as little progress; he had had more of a storm to encounter, indignation having produced a flow of eloquence. Affairs therefore remained at a standstill . . . I would promise nothing, sign nothing, change nothing, without an interview with my betrothed to hear from his own lips his wishes. As if my mind had flown to meet his, he made exactly the same reply to similar importunities. No interview would be granted, so there we stopt again . . .

At length his mother proposed to come and see me, and to bring with her a letter from him, which I was to burn in her presence after reading, and might answer, and she would carry the answer back on the same terms . . . The letter was very lover like, very tender to me, very indignant with every one else, very undutiful and very devoted, less patient than we had agreed on being, more audacious than I dared to be. I read it in much agitation – read it, and then laid it on the fire.

'And now before you answer it, my poor dear child,' said this most excellent amd most sensible woman, 'listen to the very words I must say to you,' and then in the gentlest manner, as a cautious surgeon might cautiously touch a wound, rationally and truthfully, she laid all the circumstances of our unhappy case before me, and bade me judge for myself on what was fitting for me to do . . . She knew there was a noble disposition beneath [my] little follies, but her husband she said would never think so, never ever endure an alliance with my father's child . . .

They had been friends, intimate friends, in their School and College days; they quarrelled . . . All communication was over between them, they met as strangers, and were never known to allude to each other . . . My father had written to my mother that he would rather see me in the grave than the wife of that man's son. Her husband had said to her that if that marriage took place he would never speak to his son again, never notice him, nor allow of his being noticed by the family . . .

. . . At their age she feared there was no cure. She plainly shewed she had no hope of shaking any of the resolve in her house. She came then she added, to confide in me, to tell me the whole truth, as it would be safe with me, to shew me that, with such feelings active against us, nothing but serious unhappiness lay before us, in which distress all connexions must expect to share . . . I must set free her son, he could not give me up honourably.

She said what she liked, for I seldom answered her; my doom was sealed; I was not going to bring misery in my train to any family, to divide it and humiliate myself, destroy perhaps the future of the man I loved, rather than give him or myself some present pain . . .

I told her I would write what she dictated, sign Lord Glenlee's 'renunciation', promise to hold no secret communication with her son. I kept my word; she took back a short note in which, for the reasons his mother would explain to him, I gave him back his troth. He wrote and I never opened his letter; he came and I would not speak, but as a cold acquaintance. What pain it was to me those who have gone through the same ordeal alone could comprehend. His angry disappointment was the worst to bear; I felt it was unjust, and yet it could not be explained away, and pacified. I caught a cold luckily, and kept my room awhile. I think I should have died if I had not been left to rest a bit.

My father on his return from London never once alluded to the heart breaking subject; I think he felt for me, for he was more considerate than usual, bought a nice little pony and took me rides, sent me twice a week to Seafield for warm baths, and used to beg me off the parties, saying I had been racketted to death, when she, my mother, would get angry and say such affectation was unendurable – girls in her day did as they were bid without fancying themselves heroines. She was very hard on me, and I am sure I provoked her not; I was utterly stricken down and to have lifted up my voice in any way was quite beyond me. What weary days dragged on till the month of July brought the change to the highlands.

1815–1816

Had I been left in quiet, to time – my own sense of duty, my conviction of having acted rightly, a natural spring of cheerfulness, with occupation, change, etc., all would have acted together to restore lost peace of mind, and the lesson, severe as it was, would have certainly worked for good, had it even done no more than to have sobered a too sanguine disposition. Had my father's judicious silence been observed by all, how much happier would it have been for everyone.

Miss Elphick returned to us in June, and I fancy received from my mother her version of my delinquencies, for what I had to endure in the shape of rubs, snubs, and sneers and other impertinences, no impulsive temper such as mine could possibly have put up with. My poor mother dealt too much in the hard hit line herself, and she worried me with another odious lover. Defenceless from being blameable, for I should have entered into no engagement unsanctioned, I had only to bear in silence this never ending series of irritations.

Between them, I do think they crazed me. My own faults slid into the shade comfortably shrouded behind the cruelties of which I was the victim, and all my corruption rising, I actually in sober earnest formed a deliberate plan to punish my principal oppressor – not Miss Elphick, she could get a slap or two very well by the way. My resolve was to wound my mother where she was most vulnerable, to tantalise her with the hope of what she most wished for, and then to disappoint her. I am ashamed now to think of the state of mind I was in; I was astray indeed, with none to guide me, and I suffered for it; but I caused suffering, and that satisfied me. It was many a year yet before my rebellious spirit learned to kiss the rod.

INDEX OF SOURCES

Early Days

1. From: *The Howdie: an Autobiography* (short story) by John Galt (1779–1839), printed in *Selected Short Stories of John Galt*. Scottish Academic Press 1978.
2. From: *The Field of Sighing* (autobiography) by Donald Cameron. Longman 1966.
3. From: *The Hills of Home* (autobiography) by Amy Stewart Fraser. Routledge and Kegan Paul 1973.
   Amy Stewart Fraser's father was a parish minister.
4. From: *The Field of Sighing* (autobiography) by Donald Cameron. Longman 1966.
5. From: *The Life and Death of St Kilda* (history) by Tom Steel. Fontana/Collins 1975.
6. From: 'Smeddum' by Lewis Grassic Gibbon (James Leslie Mitchell 1901–1935). Published in *A Scots Hairst*, Hutchinson, 1967.
7. From: *An Autobiography* by Edwin Muir (1887–1959). Hogarth 1954. Canongate Classic 1993. (Originally published as *The Story and the Fable* 1940.)
8. From: *A Twelvemonth and a Day* by Christopher Rush (1944–). Aberdeen University Press 1985. Canongate Classic 1994.
   'In writing A Twelvemonth and a Day I have drawn freely on autobiography, family tradition and social documentary . . .'
9. From: *My Schools and Schoolmasters* (autobiography) by Hugh Miller (1802–1856). Nimmo, Hay and Mitchell 1889.
10. From: *Prefatory Note* by Mrs R.L. Stevenson in *Poems Volume Two* by Robert Louis Stevenson (1850–1896). Tusitala Edition 1924.
11. From: *Lanark* (novel) by Alasdair Gray (1934–). Canongate 1981.
12. From: *Peevers in Parliament Square* by John W. Oliver. Privately printed by his brother J.M. Oliver in the 1950s.
13. From: *One Way of Living* (autobiography) by James Bridie (Osborne Henry Mavor 1888–1951). Constable 1939.
14. From: 'The Princess and the Stick Insect' (short story) in *Auld Zimmery* by Robbie Kydd (1918–). Mariscat Press 1987.
15. From: *Son of Adam* (autobiography) by Sir Denis Forman (1917–). André Deutsch 1990.
16. From: *A Grammatical Introduction to the Modern PRONUNCIATION and*

SPELLING of the ENGLISH TONGUE. For private Perusal and for public Schools. By JOHN DRUMMOND, Teacher of ENGLISH in Edinburgh. Edinburgh: Printed (for the AUTHOR) by A. DONALDSON, and sold at his Shops in London and Edinburgh, and by other Booksellers in Scotland. MDCCLXVII.

Drummond acknowledges that 'wherever I found any thing consistent with my plan, it has been adopted', so it is possible that these 'Exercises for Reading' (and for improving children's behaviour) were by another author, probably English. The other object of books such as this, and of Edinburgh's eighteenth century 'English Schools', was to teach both adults and children 'proper' English pronunciation and to get rid of Scottish accents and forms of speech.

17. From: 'The Big Sister Poems' in *One Atom to Another* by Brian McCabe (1951-). Polygon 1987.

18. From: *Ebauche de ma Vie* (Sketch of my Life) written in 1764 for Jean Jacques Rousseau by James Boswell (1740-1795), then aged 24. English translation from *James Boswell, Laird of Auchinleck 1778-1782* (diary) ed. Joseph W. Reed and Frederick A. Pottle. Heinemann 1977. Edinburgh University Press 1993.

Boswell was the author of the 'Life of Samuel Johnson', sometimes described as the greatest biography ever written.

19. From: *Wisdom, Madness and Folly* (autobiography) by R.D. Laing (1927-1989) Macmillan London Limited 1985.

R.D. Laing became world-famous as an exponent of 'alternative psychiatry' in the 1960s and 1970s. His most influential books were *Sanity, Madness and the Family* and *The Divided Self*.

20. From: *A Child's Garden of Verses*. Robert Louis Stevenson (1850-1896). 1885. See p. 11 for an account of Stevenson's night-time fears.

21. From: Chapter 12, 'The Bad Old Psychiatry', in *To Define True Madness, Common Sense Psychiatry for Lay People* by Henry Yellowlees. First published 1953. This extract taken from the revised edition, Penguin Books 1955.

Prodigies

1. From: *The Life of the most holy St Kentigern, [518?-603] Bishop and Confessor, who is also called Mungu*, by Jocelinus, a monk of Furness (lived c. 1200). Translated by W.M. Metcalfe D.D. 1895.

St Kentigern was a contemporary of, and personally met, both St Columba and St David. He was Bishop of Glasgow and is the city's patron saint.

2. The 'extraordinary genius' was Walter Scott, described thus in *a letter by Mrs Alison Cockburn*, a kinswoman of his mother.

3. From: 'A Memoir of Jane Welsh Carlyle' in *Reminiscences* by Thomas Carlyle (1795-1881). Written five weeks after his wife's death in 1866 and published 1881.

4. From: *In Memoriam Jane Welsh Carlyle* (1801-1866) by Geraldine Jewsbury, quoted in full in *Reminiscences* by Thomas Carlyle (1795-1881).

In his grief at his wife's death, Carlyle objected to much of Geraldine Dewsbury's obituary. In a letter to her, dated a month after Jane's death, and included in *Reminiscences*, he wrote: 'DEAR GERALDINE, - Few or none of these Narratives are correct in all the details; some of them, in almost all the details, are *incorrect* . . .'

Three days later he wrote (in journal form): '– in fact, there is a certain mythical truth, in all or most parts of the poor scribble . . .'

The day after this, he wrote: '(*Gone* five weeks, ah me!). The Geraldine accounts of her Childhood are substantially correct; but without the light melodious clearness, and charm of a Fairy Tale all true, which my lost One used to give them in talking to me . . .'

5. From: *My Schools and Schoolmasters* (autobiography) by Hugh Miller (1802–1856).
6. From: *Journal One* (1810) by Marjorie Fleming (1803–1811).
   Sir Walter Scott was a friend and admirer of 'Pet Marjorie'.
7. From: *The House of Elrig* (autobiography) by Gavin Maxwell (1914–1969). Longman 1965. © The Estate of Gavin Maxwell 1965.
   Gavin Maxwell is best known as the author of *Ring of Bright Water* (about living with otters).
8. From: *Ploughman of the Moon*, autobiography of Robert Service (1876–1958). Ernest Benn 1946. Quoted in James Mackay, *Vagabond of Verse*. Mainstream 1995.
   Service was not a reliable autobiographer so we may suspect that this grace was polished when he was older. However, he was a slick rhymer and versifier, later famous for his poems of the Yukon gold-rush, *Songs of a Sourdough*, and as an adult was said to be able to conduct a conversation entirely in rhyming couplets on his side.
9. From: *Letters Vol. I* by Robert Louis Stevenson (1850–1894). Tusitala Edition 1924.

Grannies

1. From: *The White Bird Passes* (part autobiography, part novel) by Jessie Kesson (1916–1994). Chatto & Windus 1958. Hogarth 1987. Virago Modern Classic 1992. B & W Publishing 1996.
2. From: *Farmer's Boy* by John R. Allan (b.1906). Methuen 1935.
   'This is not an autobiography. It is an imaginative reconstruction of the past . . . the more distant the past, the more imaginative the treatment . . .' From a note 'To the Reader'.
3. From: *Nairn in Darkness and Light* (autobiography) by David Thomson. Hutchinson 1987.
4. By Kathleen Jamie, in *Dream States - The New Scottish Poets*. Polygon 1994.
5. From: *Finding Peggy* (autobiography) by Meg Henderson. Corgi/Transworld 1994.
6. From: *Shoes were for Sunday* (autobiography) by Molly Weir (1920–). Hutchinson 1970. Pan Books 1973.
   Molly Weir's famous autobiography is continued in *Best Foot Forward* (1972) and *A Toe on the Ladder* (1973).

Play, Adventure and Discovery

1. From: *A Grammatical Introduction to the Modern PRONUNCIATION and SPELLING of the ENGLISH TONGUE*. John Drummond. 1767.
2. From: *Memorials of his Time* (autobiography) by Henry Cockburn (1779–1854). Adam and Charles Black 1856. Reprinted by James Thin 1977.

Cockburn was later Solicitor General for Scotland and, as Lord Cockburn, a famous judge.

3. From: *Virginibus Puerisque* (1881) by Robert Louis Stevenson (1850–1894). Tusitala Edition 1924.

4. From: *Complete Poetical Works* by Robert Garioch (1909–1981). Macdonald Publishers 1983.

5. From: *Ranald Bannerman's Childhood* (novel, part autobiography) by George MacDonald (1824–1905).
   George Macdonald is best known for his children's tales, especially *At the Back of the North Wind* and *The Princess and the Goblin*, which are still in print.

6. From: *Lying Awake* (autobiography) by Catherine Carswell (1879–1946). Secker & Warburg 1950. Canongate Classic 1997.

7. From: *Growing up in Langholm* by Hugh MacDiarmid (1892–1978), an autobiographical article first published in *The Listener* and reprinted in *Memoirs of a Modern Scotland*. Ed. Karl Miller. Faber and Faber 1970.

8. From: *The Green Hills Far Away* (autobiography) by James Barke (1905–1958). Collins 1940. Reprint Cedric Chivers 1969.

9. From: *Highland River* (novel) by Neil M. Gunn (1891–1973). Porpoise/Faber 1937. Arrow paperback 1960. Canongate Classic 1990.

10. From: *The Prime of Miss Jean Brodie* (novel) by Muriel Spark (1918–). Macmillan 1961, Penguin 1965.

Homes from Home

1. From: 'An Occasional Paper' by William Quarrier (1829–1903) quoted in *A Romance of Faith: The Story of the Orphan Homes of Scotland and the Founder William Quarrier* by Alexander Gammie. Pickering and Inglis.

2. From: *The White Bird Passes* (part autobiography/part novel) by Jessie Kesson (1916–1994). Chatto & Windus 1958. Hogarth 1987. Virago Modern Classic 1992. B & W Publishing 1996.

3. From: *Haste Ye Back* (autobiographical account of her childhood in Aberlour Orphanage) by Dorothy K. Haynes (1918–1987). Jarrold 1973.

4. From: *The Adoption Papers* by Jackie Kay. Bloodaxe Books 1991.

Food and Clothes

1. From: *Cleg Kelly – Arab of the City*. S.R. Crockett (1859–1914). Smith, Elder and Co. 1896.

2. From: *That Village on the Don* (autobiography) by Hunter Diack. Ray Palmer Limited 1965.

3. From: *The Green Hills Far Away* (autobiography) by James Barke (1905–1958).

4. From: *A Childhood in Scotland* (autobiography) by Christian Miller. Murray 1981. Canongate Classic 1989.

5. From: *A Grammatical Introduction to the Modern PRONUNCIATION and SPELLING of the ENGLISH TONGUE*. John Drummond. 1767.

6. From: *Song of Myself* (autobiography) by Anne Lorne Gillies (1944–). Mainstream 1991.

7. From: *The Life and Death of St Kilda* (history) by Tom Steel. Fontana/Collins 1975.

8. From: *Lying Awake* (autobiography) by Catherine Carswell (1879–1946). Secker & Warburg 1950. Canongate Classic 1997.

9. From: *Shoes were for Sunday* (autobiography) by Molly Weir (1920–). Hutchinson 1970. Pan Books 1973.

10. By Margaret Hamilton (1915–1972). From: *Mungo's Tongues – Glasgow Poems 1630–1990*. Ed. Hamish Whyte. Mainstream 1993. By permission of Nora Hunter.

    A Dinner Ticket is for a free school meal. We do not propose to deprive the reader of the pleasure of working out the meaning of this poem by offering a translation.

11. From: *Haste Ye Back* (autobiography) by Dorothy K. Haynes (1918–1987). Jarrold 1973.

12. From: *A Patchwork of Memories* – 'just a few of the memories of a few of the tenants of a few sheltered housing units in Aberdeen'. The product of a Community Programme Project sponsored by Voluntary Service Aberdeen. 1980s.

13. From: *The Yellow on the Broom* (autobiography) by Betsy Whyte. Chambers 1979.

14. From: *A Childhood in Scotland* (autobiography) by Christian Miller. Murray 1981. Canongate Classic 1989.

15. From: *Fergus Lamont* (novel) by Robin Jenkins (1912–). Canongate Classic 1979.

16. From: 'The Saubbath' in *Linmill: Short Stories in Scots* by Robert McLellan (1907–1985). Akros Publications 1977. Canongate Classic 1989.

17. From: *Memorials of his Time* (autobiography) by Henry Cockburn (1779–1854). James Thin 1977.

18. From: *St Leonards School: 1877–1927* (history) by Julia Mary Grant. Oxford University Press *c.* 1930.

    Miss Grant became Head Girl in 1881 and Headmistress in 1891.

Schooldays

1. From: *Memoirs of the the Life of Sir John Clerk of Penicuik, Baronet* (1676–1755) extracted by himself from his own journals. Edinburgh University Press for the Scottish History Society 1892.

    Sir John became a member of the Scottish Parliament, and was, unwillingly, one of the four Commissioners who negotiated the Treaty of Union of 1707 with four English Commissioners.

2. From: *Roderick Random* (partly autobiographical novel, published 1748) by Tobias Smollet (1721–1771).

3. From: *Ebauche de ma Vie* (Sketch of my Life) by James Boswell (1740–1795), then aged 24.

4. From: *The Life of Robert Burns* (1759–1796) by Catherine Carswell (1879–1946). Collins 1930. Canongate Classic 1990.

    Carswell's candid account of Burns's life, and especially of his affairs with women, caused an enormous scandal in 1930. Churchmen, Burns Federation officials and ordinary readers of the *Daily Record* united to condemn it as disgusting. Perhaps the book's dedication to D.H. Lawrence (as well as to Catherine's husband Donald) had something to do with this.

5. From: *A Grammatical Introduction to the Modern PRONUNCIATION and SPELLING of the ENGLISH TONGUE* by John Drummond. 1767.

6. From: *Memorials of his Time* (autobiography) by Henry Cockburn (1779–1854). James Thin 1977.

7. From: *Lavengro* by George Borrow (1803–1881). First published 1851.
   The book is partly autobiographical: 'In the following pages I have endeavoured to describe a dream, partly of study, partly of adventure, in which will be found copious notices of books, and many descriptions of life and manners, some in a very unusual form.'

8. From: *Regulations for the External Discipline of the High School of Edinburgh* drafted by Drs Boyd and Gunn, and approved by the Rector and Masters in 1846. Printed in *The Royal High School* (history) by William C.A. Ross. Oliver and Boyd 1934.
   It used to be the practice for the Rector to read the complete Regulations to the first Assembly of the school session and, in the personal experience of one of the present editors (High School pupil 1931–37), the assembled boys carefully watched the faces of the staff for signs of merriment while the stern eye of the Rector prevented any similar signs on the part of the boys. Nowadays, we learn from the present Rector, the Regulations still constitute the basis of the first Assembly of each session, some being read out verbatim but a précis being made of others, the object being to introduce First Form pupils to the history of the school.

9. From: *My Schools and Schoolmasters* by Hugh Miller (1802–56). Nimmo, Hay & Mitchell 1889.

10. From: *The Autobiography of a Working Man* by Alexander Somerville (1811–1885). First published 1848. Ed. John Carswell, Turnstile Press 1951. McGibbon and Kee 1967.
    Somerville joined the Royal North British Dragoons (the Scots Greys) as a private and during the Reform Bill crisis of 1832, was given one hundred lashes for a minor offence, his real offence being that he had written to the press to the effect that while he and his fellow-soldiers 'would defend property from the unprincipled and lawless . . . but against the liberties of our country we would have never, never, never raised an arm'.

11. From: *The Autobiography of Andrew Carnegie* (1835–1919) Constable & Co. 1920.
    This extract is not about 'Schooldays', and is placed here to give another slant on early nineteenth century radicalism. Andrew Carnegie became one of the wealthiest men in America, and endowed libraries, colleges and scholarships in Scotland. Much of this book was researched in a 'Carnegie' library, now the Edinburgh City Central Library.

12. From: *Ranald Bannerman's Childhood* (novel, part autobiography) by George MacDonald (1824–1905).

13. From: *Sketches and Speeches* by David R. Forgan (1862–1932). Chicago, privately printed 1925.
    Mr Forgan became Senior Vice-President of the First National Bank of Chicago and later President of the National City Bank of Chicago.

14. From: *Ploughman of the Moon* (autobiography) by Robert Service (1876–1958). Ernest Benn 1946. Quoted in James Mackay, *Vagabond of Verse*, Mainstream 1995.

15. From: *An Autobiography* by Edwin Muir (1887–1959). Hogarth 1954. Canongate Classic 1993.
16. From: *A Twelvemonth and a Day* by Christopher Rush (1944–). Aberdeen University Press 1985. Canongate Classic 1994.
17. From: 'Tools, Skills and Feeling Small' (short story) in *Auld Zimmery* by Robbie Kydd (1918–). Mariscat Press 1987.
18. From: *The Yellow on the Broom* (autobiography) by Betsy Whyte. Chambers 1979.
19. From: *Song of Myself* (autobiography) by Anne Lorne Gillies (1944–). Mainstream 1991.

Work

1. From: *Aberdeen: Its Traditions and History* by William Robbie. D. Wyllie and Son 1893.
2. From: *Memorials of his Time* (autobiography) by Henry Cockburn (1779–1854). James Thin 1977.

    Acts of Parliament in 1775 and 1799 set colliers and salters 'free from their servitude'.
3. From: *My Schools and Schoolmasters* (autobiography) by Hugh Miller (1802–1856). Nimmo, Hay and Mitchell 1889.
4. From: 'A Rich Man; Or, He has Great Merit', a short story by John Galt (1779–1839) printed in *Selected Short Stories of John Galt*.
5. From: *Chapters in the Life of a Dundee Factory Boy* (autobiography) by James Myles. 1850. Quoted in *Scottish Voices 1745–1960*. Ed. T.C. Smout and Sydney Wood. Collins 1990.
6. From: *The Autobiography of Samuel Smiles LL.D.* (1812–1904). John Murray 1905.

    Samuel Smiles qualified as a doctor at the age of twenty but did not practice for long. He went into railway management and later became world-famous for his books *Self-Help*, *Character* and *Thrift*, and for his biographies of famous engineers.
7. From: *The Christian Watt Papers* by Christian Watt (1833–1923). Ed. Sir David Fraser. Paul Harris 1983.
8. From: *The Life and Death of St Kilda* (history) by Tom Steel. Fontana/Collins 1975.
9. From: *A Patchwork of Memories*. Product of a Community Programme Project sponsored by Voluntary Service Aberdeen. 1980s.
10. From: *My Friends the Miss Boyds* (novel) by Jane Duncan (1910–1976). Macmillan 1959.
11. From: *Memories of Maryhill* (autobiography) by Roderick Wilkinson (1917–). Canongate Academic 1993.

Fathers and Father-Figures

1. From: *Autobiography of a Murderer* by Hugh Collins (1951–). Macmillan 1997.
2. From: 'The Good Fairy' (short story) in *Kiddies* by J.J. Bell (1871–1934). Mills and Boon.

    J.J. Bell was later famous for his *Wee Macgreegor* series.

3. From: *The Year of the Stranger* (novel) by Allan Campbell McLean (1922–1989). Collins 1971. Richard Drew 1987.
4. From: *The House with the Green Shutters* (novel) by George Douglas Brown (1869–1902). First published 1901. Penguin Twentieth Century Classic 1985.
5. From: *The Autobiography of a Working Man* by Alexander Somerville (1811–1885).
6. From: *Two Worlds* (autobiography) by David Daiches (1912–). Chatto Windus for Sussex University Press 1957. Second edition 1971. Canongate Classic 1997.
7. From: *Finding Peggy* (autobiography) by Meg Henderson. Corgi/Transworld 1994.
8. From: *The Corncrake and the Lysander* (autobiography) by Finlay J. Macdonald. Macdonald & Co (Publishers) Ltd 1985. Futura Paperback 1986.

Other books in Finlay Macdonald's 'Memoirs of a Hebridean Childhood' are *Crowdie and Cream* (1982) and *Crotal and White* (1983).

Adolescents

1. From: *Lavengro* by George Borrow (1803–1881).

'Bickers' of the kind described by Borrow seem to have been regarded as a normal form of boys' 'play' in Edinburgh. According to Walter Scott (Appendix to *Waverley*) a 'George Square' gang, presumably of middle-class boys, had a banner made by a gang-member's mother, and engaged in bickers with a gang, presumably working-class, from Causewayside led by a boy known as 'Green Breeks'.

2. From: *Docherty* (novel) by William McIlvanney (1936–). Allen & Unwin 1975. Mainstream 1983. Sceptre 1987.
3. From: *Growing up in the Gorbals* (autobiography) by Ralph Glasser. Chatto 1986.
4. From: *Nairn in Darkness and Light* (autobiography) by David Thomson. Hutchinson 1987.
5. From: *Song of Myself* (autobiography) by Anne Lorne Gillies (1944–). Mainstream 1991.
6. From: 'Real real gone', an article by Jack McLean in the Scotsman of 15th August 1997.

Religion

1. From: *Ebauche de ma Vie* (Sketch of my Life) by James Boswell (1740–1795).
2. From: James Boswell's diary, quoted in *James Boswell, Laird of Auchinleck 1778–1782*. Ed. Joseph W. Reed and Frederick A. Pottle. Heinemann 1977. Edinburgh University Press 1993.
3. From: *Cleg Kelly – Arab of the City* (novel) by S.R. Crockett (1859–1914).
4. From: *Spring Remembered* (autobiography) by Evelyn Cowan. Southside (Publishers) Ltd 1974. Corgi Books 1990.
5. From: *Two Worlds* (autobiography) by David Daiches (1912–). Chatto & Windus for Sussex University Press 1957. Canongate Classic 1997.

6. From: *An Autobiography* by Edwin Muir (1887–1959). Hogarth 1954. Canongate Classic 1993.
7. From: *Memories of Maryhill* (autobiography) by Roderick Wilkinson (1917–). Canongate Academic 1993.
8. From: *The Field of Sighing* (autobiography) by Donald Cameron. Longman 1966.
9. Considerably shortened from: *Son of Adam* (autobiography) by Sir Denis Forman (1917–). André Deutsch 1990.
10. From: *Ebauche de ma Vie* (Sketch of my Life) by James Boswell (1740–1795), then aged 24.
11. From: *Wisdom, Madness and Folly* (autobiography) by R.D. Laing (1927–1989).

First Love

1. From: *Poems Original and Translated* (1808) by George Gordon, Lord Byron (1788–1824).
   Byron left Scotland when he was ten and this is one of a number of nostalgic poems he wrote in his late teens. The 'Mary' of this poem may have been his cousin Mary Duff, whom he met in Aberdeen when he was eight and she was the same age. He wrote: 'my misery, my love for that girl were so violent, that I sometimes doubt if I have ever been really attached since.' There were, however, other possible Marys.
2. From: *The Life of Mansie Wauch* (a series of fictional episodes) by David Moir (1798–1851). Blackwood 1828.
3. From: *Ranald Bannerman's Childhood* (novel, part autobiographical?) by George MacDonald (1824–1905).
4. From: *The Life of Robert Burns* (1759–1796) by Catherine Carswell (1879–1946). Collins 1930. Canongate Classic 1990.
5. 'Handsome Nell' by Robert Burns (1759–1796).
   His first song, written when he was fourteen. See Catherine Carswell's account of its composition on preceding pages.
   'The Ayrshire of those days must have been almost as much a nest of singing birds as Elizabethan England is reputed to have been: not even the Kirk could stamp out the singing and making of songs . . .' – Thomas Crawford.
6. From: *Cleg Kelly – Arab of the City* (novel) by S.R. Crockett (1859–1914). Smith, Elder & Co. 1896.
7. From: *Poems and Songs Chiefly in the Scottish Dialect* by George McIndoe (1771–1848). Edinburgh 1805. Anthologised in *Mungo's Tongues*. Ed. Hamish Whyte. (Mainstream 1993).
8. From: *Up the Noran Water* by Helen B. Cruickshank (1886–1975). Methuen.
9. From: *Memoirs of a Highland Lady* by Elizabeth Grant of Rothiemurchus (1797–1885). John Murray 1898. Canongate Classic 1988.
   These memoirs are continued in *The Highland Lady in Ireland* (Canongate Classic 1991).

INDEX OF AUTHORS